From

MESA VERDE to

The Professor's House

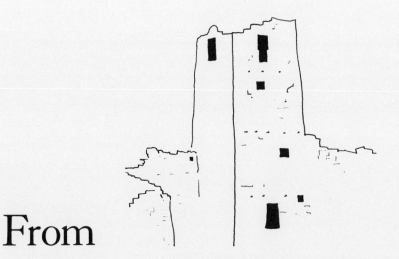

From

MESA VERDE to

The Professor's House

❋❋❋❋❋❋❋❋❋❋❋❋❋❋❋❋❋❋❋❋❋❋❋❋❋❋❋❋❋

DAVID HARRELL

University of New Mexico Press

Albuquerque

For my family

Library of Congress Cataloging-in-Publication Data
Harrell, David, 1948–
    From Mesa Verde to The professor's house / David Harrell. — 1st ed.
      p. cm.
    Revision of thesis (Ph. D.)—University of New Mexico.
    Includes bibliographical references and index.
    ISBN 0–8263–1386–8
     1. Cather, Willa, 1873–1947. Professor's house. 2. Cather, Willa,
  1873–1947—Knowledge—Colorado—Mesa Verde National Park.
  3. Mesa Verde National Park (Colo.) in literature. 4. Cliff dwellings—
  Colorado—Mesa Verde. 5. Archaeology in literature. I. Title.
  PS3505.A87P7   1992   92–16093
  813′.52—dc20   CIP

Selections from "Wild Grapes" from *The Poetry of Robert Frost,* edited
by Edward Connery Lathem. Copyright 1923, © 1969 by Hold Rinehart
and Winston. Copyright 1951 by Robert Frost. Reprinted by permission
of Henry Holt and Company, Inc.
Selections from *The Professor's House* by Willa Cather. Copyright 1925 by
Willa Cather and renewed 1953 by Edith Lewis and The City Bank
Farmers Trust Co. Reprinted by permission of Alfred A. Knopf, Inc.

Excerpt from *Willa Cather Living* by Edith Lewis. © 1953 by Edith
Lewis. Reprinted by permission of Alfred A. Knopf, Inc.
Excerpts from *Willa Cather on Writing* by Willia Cather. © 1949 by the
executors of the estate of Willa Cather. Reprinted by permission of
Alfred A. Knopf, Inc.

❋ *Contents*

❋ *Acknowledgments*

In its first version as my PhD dissertation for the English Department of the University of New Mexico, this volume owed much to many. I am happy to reacknowledge those debts here.

First and foremost, I wish to thank the members of my dissertation committee. In addition to the numerous specific suggestions about diction, organization, and emphasis, each member made a unique and valuable contribution: Bob Fleming encouraged and supported my work from its beginning over six years ago as a paper for his class in modern American literature; Louis Owens helped me to maintain the proper literary perspective on the subject; Paul Hutton showed me the value of on-site research and the usefulness of photographs; Pat Yongue shared with me ideas and information from her own work; and Jim Barbour, the chairman of the committee, helped me to see what it all means.

I received very generous assistance from others at the University of New Mexico as well. The Student Research Allocations Committee of the Graduate Student Association helped fund one of my research trips and my attendance at two conferences to present papers related to my dissertation. The Department of English presented me and another student of Willa Cather with the George Arms Award; R. Marcus Price, the Dean of the Graduate School, awarded me a grant-in-aid for the dissertation; Scott Sanders encouraged me to seek publication of my findings; and Jane Brill always had a concise answer to my questions and a kind word for my efforts.

Special thanks go to James R. Glenn, at the National Anthropological Archives in Washington, D. C., who found for me the long-lost correspondence between the Wetherill family and the Smithsonian Institution, a discovery that directed me toward this dissertation. Others from the Smithsonian who helped with my research are Susan W. Glenn, at the Smithsonian Archives; Richard S. Fiske, at the National Museum of Natural History; and Vyrtis Thomas, at the National Anthropological Archives.

The personnel at Mesa Verde National Park could not have been more helpful, whether in person, through the mail, or over the phone. My thanks to Superintendent Robert C. Heyder, Chief Archaeologist Jack E. Smith, Librarian Beverly Cunningham, and rangers Linda Martin, Art Hutchinson, and Mona Hutchinson. Others who supplied Mesa Verde material are historian Duane A. Smith, at Fort Lewis College in Durango—a steady and cheerful source of information; archaeologist Alden C. Hayes, at Portal, Arizona; James C. Work, at Colorado State University; and two members of the family that provided the accommodations at the tent camp where Willa Cather and Edith Lewis stayed, Fred T. Jeep and Jack A. Rickner. Thanks also to Boyd Richner, Nancy Rowe, and Rosemary Nusbaum for responding to queries.

The people in Mancos whom I contacted were always generous and helpful. I am particularly indebted to Jean Kelly Bader, C. B. Kelly's granddaughter; Fern Ellis, Mancos historian; and Walter Goff, life-long Mancos resident. Others I wish to thank for their help of various kinds are Horace Greer, Bill and Linda Hart, Ellen Holston, Lela Martinez, Murial Pope, Lottie Reddert, Jan Redwood, Sine Skaggs, and Joan Southcotte.

Through my research and my attendance at academic conferences, I have been fortunate to meet many members of the community of Cather scholars, all of whom have been gracious and helpful.

Particular thanks for information and encouragement go to Marilyn Arnold, the late Mildred R. Bennett, Mark Madigan, John March, Chapel Petty-Schmitt, Susan J. Rosowski, Helen Cather Southwick, David Stouck, and James Woodress. Others who kindly shared with me their unpublished work are Constance Mierendorf, Rhoda Orme-Johnson, Ann Moseley, and Jean Schwind.

Likewise, I have had the good fortune to meet many students and scholars of the Wetherill family, some of them descendants of the Mesa Verde Wetherills. Of these Harvey Leake, Gary Topping, Al Ward, Carol Ann Wetherill, Tom and Wren Wetherill, and Jerry Widdison were especially helpful and encouraging sources; but also helpful were Ruth Brentlinger, Jackson Clark, Marietta Davenport, Robert Delaney, Johnie Lou Duncan, Richard Ellis, Richard M. Wetherill, and Celeste Witherell.

Researchers are always indebted to librarians and archivists, and there are many from several institutions I wish to thank for answering questions or supplying material. At the American Museum of Natural History in New York: Belinda Kaye and Rose Wadsworth; at the Bailey/Howe Memorial Library, University of Vermont in Burlington: Connell Gallagher; at the Colorado State Historical Society in Denver: Katherine Engel and Carol Satersmoen; at the New Mexico State Records Center and Archives in Santa Fe: Pat Garcia, Arlene Padilla, Al Regensberg, and Richard Salazar; at the Pierpont Morgan Library in New York: Herbert Cahoon; at the Rocky Mountain Modern Language Association: Judith Hagan; at the University of California Research Library in Los Angeles: Anne Caiger; at the University of New Mexcio Zimmerman Library, Inter-Library Loan: Dorothy Wonsmos; at the University of Oklahoma Library: Patricia Webb; at the University of Pennsylvania Museum Archives in Philadelphia: Alessandro Pezzati; at the University of Virginia Library in Charlottesville: Robert A. Hull and Richard H. F. Lindemann; at the University of Wyoming Library: David A. Baldwin; at the Willa Cather Historical Center in Red Cloud: Ann E. Billesbach; at the Willa Cather Pioneer Memorial in

Red Cloud: Patricia K. Phillips; at the Wyoming State Archives: Jean Brainerd; and at the Yale University Library in New Haven: Judith Ann Schiff.

Finally, there are a number of other people whose assistance cannot be as neatly categorized as that of the ones already mentioned. My wife, Yolanda, helped with the proofreading and made all the arrangements for the reproduction of the photographs. Frank Carrasco read early drafts of two chapters, and he and Lucia Carrasco-Trujillo encouraged my initial efforts. And when I had questions about certain aspects of the historical and biographical parts of the dissertation, I received generous replies from George Arms, Pat Dietemann, Irv Diamond, Richard F. Fleck, Robert Lister, Anton V. Long, Tony Mares, Janet Robertson, and John S. Zeigel.

The first step toward book form was taken on my behalf by the members of the Popejoy Prize Committee at the University of New Mexico, who selected my dissertation as the recipient of the award for 1989–90, an honor that included automatic submission of the manuscript to the University of New Mexico Press. Then as I proceeded with revisions, I received generous assistance from a variety of other people: David Stouck read the manuscript with a kind and perceptive eye; Irv Diamond shared with me the typescript of his book *Letters of Gustaf Nordenskiold*; and Jean Brainerd, Jeffrey D. Marshall, Peggy S. McMahan, and Merrill Maguire Skaggs replied to queries.

Finally, I wish to thank my editor at the University of New Mexico Press, Barbara Guth. Throughout this process, which at times seemed interminable, she has been helpful, encouraging, and, most of all, patient.

From

MESA VERDE to

The Professor's House

✳ *Introduction*

In 1940 Willa Cather allowed the newly formed College English Association to publish in its newsletter four paragraphs from a letter that she had written to a friend. In the first three paragraphs, Cather explains the "two experiments in form" that she attempted in her novel *The Professor's House* (1925). Then in the last paragraph, Cather describes the connection between her fictional character Tom Outland and his real life prototype Richard Wetherill,[1] a cowboy from Mancos, Colorado, who has been credited with the discovery of several of the major ruins at Mesa Verde National Park. This brief comment was the first published notice of a southwestern background to the novel.

In 1953 the subject of a southwestern background came up again with the publication of three books that mention a trip to Mesa Verde made by Cather and her friend Edith Lewis in the summer of 1915. Of these, the only eye-witness account is the one in Lewis's memoir, *Willa Cather Living,* which comprises a scant nine pages that are hampered by errors and exaggerations. *Willa Cather: A Critical Biography,* by E. K. Brown and Leon Edel, merely repeats Lewis. The third source, Elizabeth Shepley Sergeant's *Willa Cather: A Memoir,* offers scarcely half a page of information, but it supplements Lewis because it is derived from cards and letters from Cather herself. One point of agreement among all three sources, though expressed only in general terms, is that the trip to Mesa Verde was important to the composition of *The Professor's House,* particularly to Book II, "Tom Outland's Story."

For the next thirty-one years people commenting upon this part of the historical background to *The Professor's House* did little more than repeat what was contained in that single paragraph and in those three books. Then in 1984 Susan Rosowski and Bernice Slote published a long-lost newspaper story that Cather had first published in January 1916, while her trip to Mesa Verde was still a fresh experience. As Rosowski and Slote explain, this newspaper story reaffirms the significance of Richard Wetherill as a source, but it also reveals the importance of Cather's own experiences with Mesa Verde.[2] Like many literary discoveries, however, this story and the accompanying essay by Rosowski and Slote raise many new questions in the process of answering some old ones. Therefore, even half a century after it was first acknowledged, the Mesa Verde background to *The Professor's House* merits the detailed study that is the purpose of this book.

The Mesa Verde material is central to both the composition and the interpretation of *The Professor's House.* Exact dates are elusive, but there is no question that Willa Cather began writing her novel in the middle. Apparently as early as 1916 she started working on a southwestern story called "The Blue Mesa," which she seems to have finished in 1922[3] and which at some point she renamed "Tom Outland's Story."[4] During the latter part of 1917, Cather wrote a short story called "Her Boss," which, as Bernice Slote and David Stouck have shown, bears striking similarities to the first and third books of *The Professor's House.*[5] Then in 1923 Cather seems to have conceived the idea of revising and combining the two stories by putting one within the other.[6]

As James Schroeter has remarked, "a fascinating chapter in the history of the creative process could be written if it were possible . . . [to determine] the influences on Willa Cather in the formative months when *The Professor's House* took shape in her mind."[7]

Schroeter's interest, however, is restricted to a minor part of the novel's biographical background, the destroyed correspondence between Isabelle McClung and Willa Cather, and to a brief period in its composition, May through October 1923. My thesis is that *The Professor's House* took shape over a period of years rather than months and that, of the many influences upon it, those related directly to Mesa Verde account for more of the novel's final form and meaning than any other.

The recycling of material previously used, exemplified by the joining of "The Blue Mesa" and "Her Boss," has long been recognized as one of Cather's compositional habits[8]; and a recent study demonstrates in considerable detail how Cather frequently reuses in later works themes and ideas that first appeared in earlier ones, sometimes modified quite extensively, other times hardly at all.[9] But even more than her other compositions, *The Professor's House* is the product of years of experience and thought and writing. It is also derived, more thoroughly than other works, from disparate origins whose separation in both time and place were no doubt a challenge to the creative power that finally brought them all together.

In the case of *The Professor's House,* the combination of stories required many more changes in the material derived from "Her Boss" than in "The Blue Mesa" because Cather chose to have Books I and III deal almost exclusively with problems and situations created by Tom Outland, the character whose story occupies Book II. As Patrick Sullivan has observed, the conflicts within "Tom Outland's Story" "are amplified within the design of *The Professor's House* as a whole."[10] Although Outland has been dead for several years when the novel begins, he is nonetheless the motivation behind almost all of the action, and his lingering presence colors the relationships among almost all of the other characters.

Another indication of Tom Outland's importance to the novel as a whole is the number of times he is mentioned. At the risk of sounding like Professor Sherman at the University of Nebraska, whom Cather ridiculed as a mere word-counter because of his quantitative approach to literature,[11] I find it both revealing and astonishing that in Book I alone, before his story is ever told, Tom Outland is mentioned by name 120 times. If one were to add the other nouns and personal pronouns that refer to him, the number of allusions would more than double, producing an average of well over one per page. In Book III, which is barely twenty-six pages long, Outland is mentioned by name twenty-two times. "Tom Outland's Story" may be confined to Book II, but the story of Tom Outland permeates the entire novel.

Therefore, I have approached this study with the supposition that "Tom Outland's Story" is the key to the novel,[12] and I hope to show that the history of Mesa Verde as Cather understood it is the key to "Tom Outland's Story." As many readers have noted, *The Professor's House* is a complex book, a product of diverse origins and a vehicle of several themes. In addition to the European backgrounds that some scholars have already identified[13] and in addition to the social and psychological themes that other scholars have already explained,[14] there is a line of descent through Mesa Verde (heretofore largely overlooked) that gives *The Professor's House* a distinctly American heritage.[15] As I hope to demonstrate, Cather uses this perspective to express a universal artistic theme.

I wish I could say that "one idle and rainy day" I found in an attic a barely legible manuscript entitled "The Blue Mesa," or a diary by a man named Wetherill that tells of a surprise visit by a persistent woman named Cather. Such treasures, however, are not forthcoming. In their absence I have had to rely to some extent upon the single paragraph and the three books noted above, along with the essay by Rosowski and Slote, of course. But I have also used a variety of material that, until now, has seldom or never been applied to this part of Cather studies: histories of southwestern Colorado in general and of Mesa Verde in particular; studies in archaeology and anthropology; correspondence of certain park officials; manuscripts, letters, and other archival material; newspapers; advertising circulars; reports and brochures; and correspondence and interviews with people whose relatives met Willa Cather either at Mesa Verde or at Mancos, Colorado. I have also drawn upon the wealth of critical and scholarly work done and being done on Cather.

The result of my research is an interpretive narrative that probably offers more suggestions than answers, but suggestions that I hope will contribute to the knowledge of the time and to the appreciation of Cather's work, both the process and the product. Chapter 1 discusses the possibility of Cather's early knowledge of Mesa Verde and of the archaeological work of the Wetherill family of Mancos. Chapters 2 and 3 present accounts of Cather's visits to Mancos and to Mesa Verde respectively and further illustrate how these visits are reflected in "Tom Outland's Story." Chapters 4 and 5 analyze the process of composition that produced the major parts of "Tom Outland's Story." Chapter 6 offers a new reading of the story in light of its historical background and Cather's theories of art. Chapter 7 focuses on Godfrey St. Peter, particularly in his relationship with Tom Outland. Chapter 8 proposes a reinterpretation of most of the characters, events, and symbols. Finally, Chapter 9 concludes the book with a discussion of the artistic theme developed by the preceding material.

James Woodress is certainly correct in saying that literary analysis cannot "unlock the ultimate secrets of an artist's act of creation,"[16] but it can at least reveal some parts of the process. I have not been able to look over Cather's shoulder as she wrote her book, but I have seen some of the places and learned about some of the people and events that inspired her; and I have followed as closely as I could the trail of the developing story, from Mesa Verde to *The Professor's House*.

1 ✳ *The Cliff Dweller Thrill*

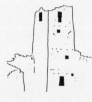*Even as a child,* Willa Cather was fascinated by the cliff dwellers. In a seldom noted interview from 1925, Cather says, "When I was a little girl nothing in the world gave me such a moment as the idea of the cliff dwellers, of whole civilizations before ours linking me to the soil."[1] Edith Lewis recalls this childhood fascination when she comments upon Cather's trip to Walnut Canyon in 1912:

> she had never seen any cliff-dwellings before; but she and her brothers had thought and speculated about them since they were children. The cliff-dwellers were one of the native myths of the American West; children knew about them before they were conscious of knowing about them.[2]

In the absence of other, more specific, information, one is hard pressed to account for the particular sources of this knowledge. Even if the Cather children did know about cliff dwellings "before they were conscious of knowing about them"—responding, perhaps, to the mystique of the Santa Fe and Oregon trails or other westward attractions—their knowledge had to come from somewhere. It seems unlikely that during the 1870s at Willow Shade, in Frederick County, Virginia, there would have been anything said about cliff dwellings in the far Southwest, virtually a world away. There were frequent visitors "from all over," including Washington, D. C.,[3] and in 1913 Cather told an interviewer that she had met "traveled people" in Virginia;[4] but at that time Mesa Verde and its Anasazi neighbors were known to few people outside the Southwest. This would not be the case for long, however.

When her family moved to Nebraska in 1883, young Willa Cather was in a better location to learn about the cliff dwellers. With rapt attention, probably, she listened to the stories told by the drivers of wagon trains between Nebraska and the mines in Colorado. Already the landscape was making an impression on her as these drivers told of losing count of the days of the week and month as their wagons passed over a long stretch of trackless grass.[5] Perhaps from these same drivers Cather heard stories of mysterious ancient villages built into inaccessible places in nearly inaccessible canyons.

Passengers on the railroad are another possible source. During the last third of the nineteenth century, there was a great deal of road building in the Rocky Mountain region to gain access to the mines that were extracting coal and precious metals; and in 1882 Red Cloud became a division point on the Burlington and Missouri Railroad connecting Chicago, Kansas City, and Denver.[6] Like other children in town, Cather gravitated toward the depot to watch passengers deboard to take their meals.[7] Perhaps some of them, fresh from Denver, had picked up rumors of cliff dwellings and were still chatting about them as they piled into the diner. Stories overheard there were probably repeated throughout the town so that Cather could have picked up news from farther west almost anywhere in or around Red Cloud.

Another, and more likely, means of early exposure was Cather's reading, an activity whose far-ranging importance Cather scholars have always recognized. Bernice Slote speaks for many others when she calls Cather's reading "the stream of experience most central to her own creativity."[8] This point notwithstanding, Slote also cautions that every account of backgrounds and books read—in general, the literary influences and sources of a writer's work—has its own seeds of disaster, for the bare alignment of book, time, and person says little of the interplay and transformation when the particular ingredients are combined.[9]

There is little danger of such disaster here, however: with rare exceptions, the most one can do in the case of Mesa Verde is to make broad suggestions about possible exposure to printed materials. In fact, one longs for more instances of "the bare alignment of book, time, and person" because when they can be examined they show that Cather's use of such material is almost always an expansion, at the very least a rearrangement, not a simple reproduction or a "rigid, unimaginative paraphrase."[10] Moreover, these alterations provide valuable insights into Cather's creative designs.

One who read "constantly and indiscriminately," Cather had the run of two libraries in Red Cloud, that of her family and that of her neighbors, Mr. and Mrs. Charles Wiener. She augmented these eclectic collections by starting one of her own, which consisted partly of paperbacks that Cather chose as the means of payment for her work in the local drugstore. The earliest accession date recorded in any of the volumes in this personal library is 1888,[11] the same year that Richard Wetherill and Charlie Mason discovered Cliff Palace at Mesa Verde.

In 1888 Cather also reached the age of fifteen, the year by which she said a writer had absorbed most of his basic materials. If she had wanted to read anything about the cliff dwellers during this formative period, she would have had a limited number of titles to choose from because by that time Mesa Verde, as well as other southwestern cliff dwellings, had appeared in print infrequently. There were a few articles in popular magazines such as *Scribner's Monthly* and *Popular Science Monthly,* but the most notable publications of this period were the reports of the Hayden expeditions.

Under the leadership of Ferdinand Vandiveer Hayden, these

surveys were the best publicized and the most widely known of those performed by the four major survey teams that, during the 1860s and 1870s, explored and mapped the territories west of the 100th meridian, which runs almost equidistant between Kearney and North Platte, Nebraska. Between 1874 and 1877, Hayden survey crews led by pioneer photographer William H. Jackson made excursions into the Four Corners region to find reputed cliff dwellings around Mesa Verde. Their first discovery was the ruin that became known as Two Story House, which was called to their attention by their guide, miner and Mancos resident John Moss. Although Jackson and his crew missed the major ruins later discovered by the Wetherills, their efforts produced the best early documentation of cliff dwellings, and, in the words of one commentator, made Hayden himself "world-famous."[12] Because the Wetherills obtained copies of these reports (and read them with great interest), one could assume that copies were available to other people as well—perhaps even to Willa Cather. In fact, there are some interesting similarities between "Tom Outland's Story" and parts of a Hayden article by William Henry Holmes, but without something more substantial to connect Cather with this report, there is little to be made of the parallels.[13]

Beyond the things that Cather might have read or heard during her childhood or adolescence, numerous possibilities emerge. By 1890, when Cather enrolled at the University of Nebraska in Lincoln, the number of Mesa Verde publications had begun to increase; and by 1895, the year she graduated, several major studies had been published, including articles by W. R. Birdsall and S. D. Peet and books by Frederick H. Chapin and Gustaf Nordenskiold. Then late in 1896 Cather's boss at *The Home Monthly,* James W. Axtell, left Cather to tend to the magazine while he toured the West.[14] Perhaps he returned with stories of the cliff dwellers.

Also during the 1890s the Denver & Rio Grande (D&RG) Railroad heavily and widely promoted its scenic tours through the Rocky Mountain region.[15] In fact, one of the railroad's turn-of-the-century brochures even highlights the family that would play a crucial role in the composition of "Tom Outland's Story":

> At Mancos headquarters should be made at the Alamo Ranch, owned and conducted by Wetherill & Sons, which is located in beautiful grounds about two miles from the railroad station in a lovely valley, fertile and well watered and in an advanced stage of cultivation. Conveyance to the ranch may be procured at Mancos, or the Messrs. Wetherill will meet parties who have corresponded with them.[16]

Even though Cather's brother Douglass worked for another line, the Southern Pacific, there is a good chance that he was familiar with the advertising matter of the D&RG. In those days of heavy railroad activity, competing and complementary lines alike often engaged in mutually beneficial arrangements; and one company bought stock in another with considerable frequency. Moreover, the D&RG sent its circulars all over the world.[17] Such publicity, together with the work of her own organization, allowed one early champion of Mesa Verde to boast in 1904, "To-day who does not know of the Cliff Dwellings?"[18]

By 1915, the year Cather and Edith Lewis visited Mesa Verde, the park bibliography comprised more than forty titles, many of them by Jesse Walter Fewkes, the Smithsonian archaeologist whom they met there. Evidently, Cather was reading something during this period because Sergeant says that by 1920 or so Cather had read "some archaeology," although she "had done very little reading in anthropology." That subject, Sergeant said, was one that she "had to work at" to stimulate Cather's interest.[19] Moreover, because Cather read several books in researching material for *Death Comes for the Archbishop,* it is reasonable to assume that by the early 1920s she was doing similar research for *The Professor's House.*

By 1924, the year that Cather was completing *The Professor's House,* the number of publications about Mesa Verde had increased so dramatically that one could spend years trying to locate and read all the works that Cather might have seen. Happily, however, the field can be narrowed, both logically and conveniently, to include at this point only the works of two authors, one of whom Cather mentions by name and the other whom she actually met.[20]

Popular belief to the contrary, Gustaf Nordenskiold was not a baron, but he was a descendant of a prominent family of Swedish Finns. He was also a scientist and an adventurer who, by the age of twenty-one, had already been on an expedition to Spitsbergen to collect fossils, to study the flora and fauna, and to measure and photograph glaciers. It was on this expedition that Nordenskiold developed tuberculosis, which he sought to relieve by traveling in warmer climates throughout the world. On 27 May 1891, he arrived in New York City, and a month later he was in Denver. There he visited museums and libraries and sought out local scientists. One of them was Alice Eastwood, a botanist who had recently come from southern Colorado and who told him about the work of the Wetherill family among some extraordinary cliff dwellings at Mesa Verde. With a letter of introduction from Miss Eastwood, Nordenskiold arrived at the Alamo Ranch in late June or early July.[21] He quickly became friends with the Wetherills and hired them to assist him in excavating a number of ruins and in making a collection of artifacts, which he took back to Sweden.[22] There he wrote and published *The Cliff Dwellers of the Mesa Verde,* the first extensive scientific study of those ruins and a book that remains useful even today.

That Cather knew something about Nordenskiold—and also about his book—is evident from the opening paragraph of her 1916 newspaper essay about Mesa Verde:

> Twenty-five years ago an adventurous young Swede, the Ba-
> ron Nordenskjold [sic], started on a trip around the world,
> sailing westward. When he got to Denver he heard rumors

about certain cliff dweller remains that had been found in the extreme southwest corner of Colorado. He went down to the Mesa Verde and got no farther on his trip around the world. He stayed on the mesa for some months and then went back to Stockholm and wrote and published the book which first made the Mesa Verde known to the world. Later the book was translated but the English edition also was published in Stockholm. There is no American edition.[23]

Cather probably read Nordenskiold's book before her trip to Mesa Verde. The newspaper story proves that she knew of it before January 1916, and there seems not to have been a copy of it at the park in 1915. Although the records of the park library do not include the dates, the accession numbers assigned to both the Swedish and English editions of Nordenskiold's book are high enough to suggest that they were acquired later.[24] Even as late as 1923 Superintendent Jesse Nusbaum had to borrow a copy from somewhere else.[25] As one of the Wetherills' friends observed, Nordenskiold's book "was not widely distributed."[26] One reason, surely, is that the twenty-dollar price was quite high for that time. Richard Wetherill was one of many who commented on the cost, but he hastened to add in a letter to his friend Gustaf that he and his family would do all they could to promote the sale of it among libraries and archaeological and historical societies.[27] The libraries in Pittsburgh, Washington, and New York would have been likely repositories where Cather might have found a copy.

It is with good reason, then, that Susan Rosowski and Bernice Slote suggest that Cather knew the book "at the time of her visit and that it is more important to *The Professor's House* than has been recognized":

The volume would have been well suited to ideas Cather associated with the Mesa Verde. By combining scientific objectivity with personal recollection, Nordenskiold provided a transition between an ancient and a modern world, his story a heroic adventure that has been brought into the twentieth century by being made scientifically credible.[28]

After noting some of the archaeological details found both in Nordenskiold and in "Tom Outland's Story," Rosowski and Slote further suggest that *The Cliff Dwellers* "is a source she [Cather] may have drawn upon . . . ," one that "anticipates the strongly personal mood Cather was to associate with the Mesa Verde."[29] Indeed, these scholars draw an interesting parallel between the feeling Tom Outland has for Cliff City and the poetic sentiments expressed in this passage from Nordenskiold, a description of Spring House:

> What a striking view these ruins present at a distance! The explorer pictures to himself a whole town in miniature under the lofty vault of rock in the cliff before him. But the town is a deserted one; not a sound breaks the silence, and not a movement meets the eye, among those gloomy, half-ruined walls whose contours stand off sharply from the darkness of the inner cave.[30]

With these similarities in mind, one would expect a more extensive comparison of the two texts to reveal even more parallels. And so it does. In almost all instances, Cather's treatment is more concise, more metaphorical, more imaginative—in a word, more artistic—but it was probably Nordenskiold who was responsible for the fact or the scientific concept, which Cather adapted into her art.

One of the first signs of ancient inhabitation noted by Tom Outland and Roddy Blake is "a number of straight mounds, like plough furrows, running from the river, inland." This they identify as "an old irrigation main."[31] Perhaps Cather saw for herself the prototype of this irrigation system near the mesa-top ruin of Far View House; or perhaps she read about it in Nordenskiold, who identifies certain low walls that cross shallow depressions as "the ruins of reservoirs" and who notes an apparent irrigation system of ditches and reservoirs on Chapin Mesa "above the great ruins,"[32] evidently referring to the location of Far View House.

Tom Outland's discovery of a second cliff dwelling may be a reflection of what Cather read in Nordenskiold.

> Not far from this place [Cliff Palace], but in a different cañon, they [Richard Wetherill and Charlie Mason] discovered on the same day another very large cliff-dwelling; to this they gave the name of Sprucetree House, from a great spruce that jutted forth from the ruins.[33]

Though in a better state of preservation, Spruce Tree House never received the attention lavished upon the larger and more spectacular Cliff Palace. For his part, Outland makes only a brief reference to his second discovery and then, after using it to draw a conclusion, never mentions it again:

> When I at last turned away [from viewing Cliff City], I saw still another canyon branching out of this one, and in its wall still another arch, with another group of buildings. The notion struck me like a rifle ball that this mesa had once been like a bee-hive; it was full of little cliff-hung villages, it had been the home of a powerful tribe, a particular civilization.[34] (*PH* 202)

To gain access to Cliff City, Outland and Blake use as a ladder "an old dried cedar trunk, with toe-notches cut in it," which they find lying beside one of the gaps in the ledge (*PH* 207). Interestingly, Nordenskiold mentions at least twice his surprise at finding no signs of ladders whatsoever; but he also notes that he and the Wetherills used a "long notched tree-trunk to serve as a ladder."[35]

Once they begin exploring Cliff City, Outland and Blake find a number of conditions and artifacts whose antecedents are probably in Nordenskiold's book, considering the similarities in both diction and detail. In addition to the similarities noted by Rosowski and Slote, Cather's two characters echo Nordenskiold's terms exactly when they mention cedar joists that had been "felled with stone axes" (*PH* 212); Outland and Blake find "what seemed like cotton cloth" (*PH* 213), and Nordenskiold notes "pieces of cotton cloth"; Outland and Blake discover "sheepskins tanned with the fleece on them" (*PH* 213), and Nordenskiold determines that the hides he found were "probably chiefly of deer and mountain-sheep"; when Outland and Blake discover Mother Eve, they notice that she still has "a great deal of coarse black hair" (*PH* 214), and Nordenskiold describes a mummy whose hair "was black and rather coarse, [and which] still hung to the head."[36] As for Mother Eve herself, "she had dried into a mummy in that water-drinking air" (*PH* 214), a circumstance also noted by Nordenskiold, though in somewhat less picturesque diction: "The entire absence of moisture had presumably been enough without further preparation to transform the corpse to a mummy."[37]

Still other similarities require a little more comment. Marveling at the construction skills displayed by the ancient home builders, Tom Outland says that the "little poles that lay across them [the cedar joists] and held up the clay floor of the chamber above, were smoothly polished" (*PH* 212). This description is probably a condensation and paraphrase of a similar passage from Nordenskiold:

> Thick beams of cedar or piñon and across them thin poles, laid close together, form the floors between the stories. In some cases long sticks were laid in pairs across the cedar beams at a distance of some decimetres between the pairs, a layer of twigs and cedar bast was placed over these sticks, and the whole was covered with clay, which was smoothed and dried.[38]

Another example of close borrowing is Outland's description of the doors in Cliff City: "The door lintels were carefully fitted (the doors were stone slabs held in place by wooden bars fitted into hasps)" (*PH* 213). Nordenskiold says almost the same thing although at greater length, and he includes additional detail:

> the door [is] a thin, flat, rectangular stone slab of suitable size. Through two loops on the outside of the wall, made of osiers inserted in the chinks between the stones, and placed one on each side of the doorway, a thin stick was passed, thus forming a kind of bolt.[39]

In one room of Cliff City, Outland observes "a painted border, little tents, like Indian tepees, in brilliant red" (*PH* 213). Minus the analogy to tepees, which southwestern cliff dwellers would probably not have seen, Nordenskiold finds the same thing in one of the rooms in a small ruin in Cliff Canyon and in a room in Spruce Tree House (the latter Cather may have seen for herself, of course). Describing a dark red border around the lower part of a wall, Nordenskiold says "this red paint projects upwards in triangular points [tent-like shapes, one might say], arranged in threes, and above them is a row of small round dots of red."[40] "It is difficult to conceive the idea which suggested this singular design," he adds later.[41]

Another detail perhaps taken from Nordenskiold is Tom Outland's camera. When he goes to Washington, Outland takes with him "some good pieces of pottery . . . and all the photographs Blake and I had taken. We had only a small kodak," he says, whose pictures "didn't make much show" (*PH* 226). Both Nordenskiold and the Wetherills used a Kodak too, at a time, incidentally, when cameras of this sort were new to the market.[42] For Nordenskiold, however, the Kodak was only a temporary substitute for his own more versatile view camera, which finally arrived, it seems, in late August.[43] But it was the more humble Kodak that inspired the name of one of the ruins, Kodak House, because "we kept one of these apparatuses hidden for some time in one of the rooms."[44]

"Probably these people burned their dead" (*PH* 215), Tom Outland surmises, echoing what Cather had already said in her 1916 essay in spite of extensive evidence to the contrary in just about anything she may have seen or heard. Yet, after three pages summarizing the various methods of burial that he and the Wetherills found, Nordenskiold does provide Cather with a scientific basis for Outland's hypothesis:

> That cremation, however, was sometimes practiced by the cliff-dwellers, seems probable from the fact that Richard Wetherill observed in the same ruin where the above-mentioned burial chamber was found [a small ruin in Pool Canyon, a branch of Navajo Canyon] bodies which had apparently been burnt together with the pottery belonging to the dead.[45]

Cather also seems to have derived some of Father Duchene's actions and theories from Nordenskiold. Like Nordenskiold, Father Duchene cuts down a tree to count the annual growth rings as a way of estimating the age of the dwelling. The underlying assumption in both cases is that the tree could not have grown where it did until after the inhabitants had abandoned the village. The tree Nordenskiold cut down was

> a huge spruce . . . projecting from the wall of an estufa. We counted the rings, which were very distinct, twice over, the results being respectively 167 and 169. I had supposed from the thickness of the tree that the number of the rings was much greater.[46]

In the case of Father Duchene's cedar tree, which had been growing "in the middle of the deep trail worn in the stone," the number of rings *is* much greater, 336 to be exact, some of them "so scant that [they] . . . were invisible except with a glass" (*PH* 218).

When Father Duchene "measured the heads of the mummies

and declared they had good skulls" (*PH* 217), he did so probably on the authority of Professor G. Retzius, a colleague of Gustaf Nordenskiold's whose illustrated thirty-page appendix to *The Cliff Dwellers* recounts in exacting detail the results of his measurements of the skulls brought back by Nordenskiold. Whatever was left of Wm. Cather, M.D., probably found this appendix, technical in the extreme, to be fascinating reading.

Finally, Cather may also owe to Gustaf Nordenskiold some of the amazement that Tom Outland feels when he first sees Cliff City, even beyond what Rosowski and Slote have already noted. With its point of view, its evocative language, and its imaginative use of detail, the following passage anticipates Tom Outland's awestruck effort to describe just what he saw there, *as* he saw it, when he happened upon that "little city of stone, asleep," "set in a great cavern in the face of the cliff" (*PH* 201):

> Strange and indescribable is the impression on the traveller, when, after a long and tiring ride through the boundless, monotonous piñon forest, he suddenly halts on the brink of the precipice, and in the opposite cliff beholds the ruins of the Cliff Palace, framed in the massive vault of rock above and in a bed of sunlit cedar and piñon trees below. This ruin well deserves its name, for with its round towers and high walls rising out of the heaps of stones deep in the mysterious twilight of the cavern, and defying in their sheltered site the ravages of time, it resembles at a distance an enchanted castle.[47]

Although Nordenskiold's book was probably unavailable at Mesa Verde in 1915, another helpful source was there: the park brochure for that season, titled *The Prehistoric Cliff Dwellings/Mesa Verde National Park*. In fact, copies of this succinct and informative publication must have been available in abundance because in February of that year park superintendent Thomas Rickner ordered twice as many copies as he had the season before,[48] and the increase in visitors fell far short of that projection.[49] The author of the brochure is not credited, but certain internal evidence points to Smithsonian archaeologist Jesse Walter Fewkes.[50] Cather does not acknowledge this document as a source—after all, it was neither as significant nor as picturesque as Nordenskiold's *Cliff Dwellers* or as the Howlett biography of Bishop Machebeuf that inspired *Death Comes for the Archbishop*—but it is unlikely that she could have missed it and quite improbable that, having seen it, she failed to use it.

The style of the brochure is not especially inviting, but the document contains a wealth of archaeological and anthropological detail. In addition, there are frequent quotations from Nordenskiold's book, including his account of the discovery of Cliff Palace by Richard Wetherill and Charlie Mason, which Cather must have found handy. Her use of this source in addition to Nordenskiold is suggested not just by the reappearance of some of the details in "Tom Outland's Story" but also by the reuse of similar terms to describe them.[51]

Nordenskiold's surprise at the absence of ladders notwithstanding, the brochure affirms that the cliff dwellers placed "notched logs . . . along the street to be used by visitors."[52] Cather turns such a ladder into an effective symbol by having her visitors use it to bridge not only a short gap in space but also an extensive gap in time.

Once they begin exploring the interior of Cliff City, Outland and Blake find "a row of grinding stones" arranged in the "back court" (*PH* 209); in one room of Cliff Palace, the brochure says, there was a row of four grinding stones, or *metates*.[53] The brochure also contains a detailed account of the doors used in the ruins. Although this description differs a little from Nordenskiold's, it might have further encouraged Cather to include this feature in her own description of Cliff City, especially since the brochure directed readers to a reconstruction of this type of door in Spruce Tree House.[54]

Some of Father Duchene's observations may have come from the park brochure, too. For instance, the priest concludes that the two "square towers on the mesa top . . . were unquestionably granaries"

(*PH* 218), while the brochure notes that each clan in a village had "inclosures, for granaries or storage of corn."[55] Likewise, Father Duchene's characterization of Cliff City as a "stronghold" (*PH* 218 and 221) might have been suggested by the numerous references throughout the brochure to the defensive advantages of a cliff dwelling, references somewhat more emphatic than those in Nordenskiold: the inhabitants were "protected from human enemies below"; "[i]n each of these villages is an elaborate system of fortification"; and "this room [in Spruce Tree House] was believed to be a bastion for defense. . . ."[56]

Finally, the comments about towers in each composition most strongly suggest a connection between the park brochure and Cather's story. Cather probably saw Nordenskiold's acknowledgment of the round tower in Cliff Palace, but she would have found nothing there to suggest that it was anything of particular significance, as Nordenskiold simply mentions it in passing.[57] In the brochure, however, references to towers run like a motif from beginning to end. In 1875 William Henry Holmes "drew attention to the remarkable stone towers so characteristic of the region"; four of the villages at Mesa Verde have "watch towers 30 feet high"; and one of the most striking features of Cliff Palace is its "tapering loopholed tower," a conspicuous landmark known as the "Round Tower":[58]

> The most prominent and picturesque building in Cliff Palace is the Round Tower, situated about midway in its length on a high angular rock, which raises it in full view above all the terraces. . . .
>
> The Round Tower, formerly two stories high . . . was little damaged during the centuries elapsing since Cliff Palace was abandoned and needed little repair. The walls show most beautiful examples of aboriginal masonry, perhaps the finest north of Mexico. Almost perfectly symmetrical in form, the stones that compose the walls are skillfully dressed, fitted to

one another, and carefully laid. This tower was evidently ceremonial in function, or it may have served as an observatory, for which purpose it is well situated. The presence of small peepholes through which one can look far down the canyon supports the theory that the tower was a lookout. . . .[59]

This is the tower that Cather distills into its poetic essence and transforms into a chief symbol, as Outland tries to describe the "round tower" that so struck him when he saw it "in the middle of the group" of "pale little houses of stone":

> It was beautifully proportioned, that tower, swelling out to a larger girth a little above the base, then growing slender again. There was something symmetrical and powerful about the swell of the masonry. The tower was the fine thing that held all the jumble of houses together and made them mean something. (*PH* 210)

To Tom Outland's hypothesis that the structure was used as a watch tower, Father Duchene adds his theory that, "from the curious placing of those narrow slits, like windows, I believe it was used for astronomical observations" (*PH* 219). If Cather had wanted scientific authority for this theory, she could have found it not only in the passage quoted above, but also in the brochure's description of the openings in a circular room of Spruce Tree House, "through which the sun priest watched the setting sun to determine the times for ceremonies."[60]

The park brochure may not have been the only one of Jesse Walter Fewkes's publications that Cather read. She could have come across his work in any number of popular and accessible periodicals, or she could have been led to him by the bibliography in the park brochure, by Fewkes himself when she met him, or by Nordenskiold, who cites Fewkes as one of his sources and even suggests that he was personally acquainted with him.[61] If Nordenskiold's spruce tree was not old enough, a stump that Fewkes found "on top of the highest wall of Sun Temple" would have been. In an article for *Scientific American,* Fewkes counted "360 annual rings of growth which germinated after the top of the walls that form the mound had fallen."[62] (Interestingly, Fewkes was working at Sun Temple in the summer of 1915.) In another article, cited by the *Literary Digest,* Fewkes reports finding "an astronomical observatory used by the cliff-dwellers in calculating time for their farming operations."[63] Even more directly than the park brochure, this piece could have suggested Father Duchene's assumption. Both of these articles appeared in time for Cather to have seen them and used them. Finally, an even earlier publication (1910) would have been especially helpful in bolstering Tom Outland's theory that the cliff dwellers practiced cremation. According to Fewkes's excavation of Cliff Palace, there is "no doubt that the inhabitants . . . cremated perhaps the greater number of their dead in special walled enclosures for that purpose," a practice that Fewkes claims to have verified in other cliff houses as well.[64] Of course, none of this establishes the alignment of book, time, and person; but considering Fewkes's fame, Cather's habit of omnivorous reading, her interest in cliff dwellings, and the textual similarities, one would be surprised if Cather did not use these sources.

In addition to what she read by Nordenskiold and Fewkes, Cather had several other kinds of opportunities to learn about the cliff dwellings at Mesa Verde. One such opportunity was news of a woman whose energy and devotion to her cause Cather would probably have admired, Virginia Donaghe McClurg. There is no record that Cather ever met McClurg,[65] but this irrepressible champion of Colorado's cliff dwellings was so much in the news that Cather could hardly have missed hearing about her. John March believes that Cather was familiar with McClurg's writings because some of Tom Outland's experiences "parallel those of Miss Mc-Clurg."[66] If nothing else, the name McClurg must have aroused

Cather's interest because of its similarity to the names of two people dear to her, S. S. McClure and Isabel McClung.

McClurg (then Virginia Donaghe) was one of the earliest tourists to visit Mesa Verde, first in 1882 and then in 1886.[67] During these early visits she was a guest of the Wetherills.[68] Al Wetherill remembered her as an "enthusiastic and tireless worker . . . [whose] persistence overcame all indifference . . . [and who] was able, through long and tireless effort, to interest the government, where we had failed in our attempts."[69]

McClurg was so enthralled by what she saw at Mesa Verde that during the 1890s

> she turned into a one-woman crusade, passionately devoted to saving the ruins and creating a park. She launched an emotional campaign in Colorado to awaken the public, and her message was soon transmitted to the rest of the American public.[70]

Quite tireless in her efforts, McClurg attended meetings, gave speeches, wrote articles, and lobbied congressmen and presidents. She also instigated the founding of the Colorado Cliff Dwellings Association, an off-shoot of the Colorado Federation of Women's Clubs, perhaps the organization most responsible for the preservation of the ruins at Mesa Verde. McClurg was assisted by many people, of course, among them Lucy Peabody, who eventually succeeded in having Mesa Verde established as a national park rather than a state one, as McClurg had wanted, but only after a nasty public airing of factionalism within the association that occupied the press for most of February and March 1906.[71] As one who kept up with current events, Cather probably read some of the coverage of this dispute and may, therefore, have learned of both women.

Evidently, McClurg took advantage of every opportunity to spread the word about Mesa Verde. In 1893 she lectured at the

International Folk Lore Congress of the Chicago World's Fair and presented a series of lectures in the Anthropological Building at the fair, "being the only woman so honored." The next year she gave a similar lecture series in Denver.[72] In 1900 she served as a delegate from the United States to the ethnological congresses at the Paris exposition, where she was decorated by the French government. Then in 1904 Virginia McClurg and her husband embarked upon another lecture tour, which took them to Chicago, the University of Michigan, the University of Wisconsin, the Board of Public Instruction of New York City, and finally to St. Louis for the World's Fair.[73]

If Cather heard of McClurg nowhere else, she must have read about her when she was in Washington in 1900–01 helping her cousin Howard Gore with the hasty preparation of the report of the United States Commission to the Paris Exposition. Acting in two capacities, as Juror in Chief and as Director of the Organization of International Congresses, Gore was responsible for two of the six volumes of the report. McClurg's name appears three times in Volume Six, the Report of the Director of the Organization of International Congresses. She is listed in the official register of persons attending the twelfth session of the International Congress of Americanists and is included as one of the presenters under the heading "Archaeology": "Mme. McClurg, of Colorado, U.S.A., 'Prehistoric Pueblo Country' (with lantern [that is, slides])." Finally, she is included among twenty-one other people as one of the "Officiers de L'Instruction Publique,"[74] apparently not the most prestigious of the titles bestowed by the French officials but one of which she was nonetheless proud.

Incidentally, Volume Six also lists the papers presented at previous sessions of the International Congress of Americanists. At the seventh session in Berlin in 1888 there were two presentations about the Hemenway expeditions in other parts of the Southwest, both by men well known for their work in the American Southwest: Frank Hamilton Cushing (though his paper was read by someone else) and a Mr. Bandelier, certainly Adolph. At the eighth session in Paris in 1890, a paper called "The cliff dwellers of the Sierra Madre" notes "the discoveries of the subject of this paper by Messrs. Jackson and Holmes. . . ." Then at the tenth session in Stockholm in 1894 there were three papers that would surely have interested Cather: "A la memoire de Mme. Mary Hemenway," by one Madam Nuttal; "Sur la disparition des Cliff-dwellers," by a Mr. Charnay; and "Recherches nouvelles dans les ruines et les tombeaux de Mesa Verde," by M. Gustave Nordenskiold.[75] Once again Cather's path to Mesa Verde crossed those of others who had been there before.

Although Virginia McClurg did attend the World's Columbian Exposition of 1893, Willa Cather, according to James Woodress, did not. "So far as any documentary evidence goes, Cather's first visit to Chicago was in the spring of 1895 when she went there to attend the opera."[76] There is no question, however, that Cather knew about the fair. She could have learned of it from Howard Gore, who served as a juror in the Department of Liberal Arts, or she could have read about it in the newspapers. This "grandest exhibition of modern times"[77] was good copy in the press nationwide, with writers by the dozen exuding hyperbolic praise; therefore, it could scarcely have escaped the notice of an insatiable reader heading toward her own career in journalism. In fact, Cather mentions the fair in one of her 1895 reviews when she writes disparagingly of Eddie Foy, the "highest salaried man on the American stage," for making an exhibition of himself one night "during the World's Fair."[78] And in three of her early stories Cather shows not only her own awareness of the fair but depends upon the reader's knowledge as well when she uses the event as a reliable means of establishing time or place.[79]

More than just a handy literary device, however, the World's Fair could have afforded Cather a preview of the major cliff dwellings at Mesa Verde. Near the Anthropological Building (where Virginia McClurg was lecturing), in the southeast corner of the grounds, workmen had constructed out of "timbers, iron and staff" an enormous replica of Battle Rock in Colorado's McElmo Canyon. Upon entering the structure,

> through a cavern made to produce the effect of a canyon, it was difficult for the visitor to comprehend that he was not in the country of the people who, ages ago, peopled the mesas and tablelands of the Southwest. The houses, perched far up the cliffs in places apparently inaccessible, were reproduced on a scale of one-sixth their real size. . . .[80]

The cliff houses themselves were replicas of Square Tower House, Balcony House, and Cliff Palace.[81] Had Cather toured this amazing structure and examined the display of artifacts, she would have come face to face with the prototype of Mother Eve, the mummy of a woman found by the Wetherills and named "She."[82]

Another attraction at the fair was the exhibit of cliff dweller artifacts by the state of Colorado. Because most of the items on display had been collected by Richard Wetherill and his brothers, Richard was sent there in September to answer questions from visitors. He was exhilarated and encouraged by the interest expressed, which contrasted sharply with the indifference he had encountered from people in Colorado the first few times he and his brothers showed a collection of artifacts.[83]

After the fair closed, Cather had other chances to see the artifacts that had been displayed in the man-made canyon because the collection was transferred to the museum of the University of Pennsylvania in Philadelphia, where it was first exhibited in 1895. This time, apparently, there was greater attention to scientific presentation. Critics received the exhibit quite favorably while condemning "the meaningless display . . . at the Exposition." Even if she did not see the museum exhibit, Cather probably read about it in the Pittsburgh papers because there was considerable publicity surrounding the arrival of the collection in Philadelphia.[84] In February 1896 the museum bought the collection for $14,500, with money provided by Phebe A. Hearst.[85]

Because Cather seems only to have heard of it and not to have visited it, the Chicago World's Fair and the cliff dweller exhibits it housed can be presented only as part of the collective culture from which Cather was already extracting facts and impressions, even if, as Lewis suggests, she was doing it unknowingly. Be that as it may, Cather knew precisely what she was doing in 1912 when she boarded a train for Winslow, Arizona, to visit her brother Douglass.

This trip to Arizona has long been recognized for its importance to Willa Cather's discovery of herself as an artist and to the composition of another of her novels, *The Song of the Lark* (1915). With her brother as guide, Cather spent several unforgettable hours touring Walnut Canyon, about ten miles east of Flagstaff, where she got her first look at ancient cliff dwellings. The result, of course, is Thea Kronborg's sojourn of self-discovery among "The Ancient People" in Panther Canyon. This literary benefit aside, simply because it afforded Cather her first impression of ancient cliff dwellings, the Walnut Canyon experience helped shape "Tom Outland's Story," too: crystallizing images, defining themes, and suggesting symbols. In addition, the trip to Arizona seems to have introduced Cather to an important source for this later story.

In a brief remark often overlooked, Elizabeth Sergeant says that Cather once told her that the "cliff-dweller part [of "Tom Outland's Story"] was based . . . on a true story that Willa had heard on the Navajo Reservation from a famous family of Indian traders, the Wetherills."[86] Quite explicitly, this statement points to a Wetherill source other than the one in Mancos in 1915: Mesa Verde, after all, is in Ute country, whereas Walnut Canyon is in Navajo country. Furthermore, the rest of the details in Sergeant's statement coincide with the history of one branch of the Wetherill family. In 1911, after learning the ways and gaining the trust of the Navajo in several other parts of Arizona, John and Louisa Wetherill moved their trading post and their family to Kayenta, about 160 miles north of Flagstaff. Therefore, they must be the "famous family of Indian traders" to whom Sergeant refers.

This connection raises the possibility that it might have been John Wetherill in Arizona whom Cather had in mind in 1938 when she wrote the letter explaining the Wetherill origin of "Tom Outland's Story." Cather mentions neither the name of the man nor of the place; and it is only from Lewis, thirteen years after the first publication of Cather's letter, that readers have learned of a Wetherill source in Mancos in 1915 and therefore assumed that he was Cather's only one.

Because the Kayenta guest register from this period disappeared many years ago,[87] it is impossible to say whether Cather met this famous family at their trading post; but she need not have gone to Kayenta to hear about John and Louisa or even to meet them. Never one to stay put for long, John Wetherill was often traveling about the country, frequently as a guide for one expedition or another, although he seems to have been close to home in 1912.[88] The list of people whom he helped to "discover" and to excavate various ruins is a Who's Who of southwestern archaeology. Also, he traveled frequently to Flagstaff for supplies,[89] over a road that he and his partner Clyde Colville had helped build.[90] Like John, Louisa too was often away from the post, usually to offer some form of aid to the Navajo—as interpreter, as peacemaker, as healer. In fact, she was so immersed in the Navajo culture that a widely believed legend made her a descendant of a particular Navajo family.[91]

It is little wonder, then, that the Wetherill trading post at Kayenta soon became one of the most famous in the Southwest.[92] Not only were the proprietors friendly and honest, their trading post "was the only patch of lawn in seventy miles of desert, and with the cottonwoods which grew near-by, and the trees which they themselves [John and Louisa] set out, it soon was an oasis of shade and coolness."[93] Surely Cather's brother Douglass was familiar with it and with the people who ran it, if for no other reason than that the parties that John Wetherill guided would have passed through Winslow on their way to Flagstaff.[94] And just as surely, Cather heard of the Wetherill name and reputation at this time, even if she had somehow managed to miss it in one of her earlier opportunities.

The other Wetherill brother in Mancos should still be regarded as Cather's principal family source, largely because Cather's contact with him is more extensively documented. But here is additional evidence of Cather's early knowledge of Mesa Verde history and the part played by the Wetherills, and yet another inducement, as if one were needed, for her to visit the place herself.

In 1914 Cather came a little closer to Mesa Verde by visiting a museum in the East, anticipating Claude Wheeler's visit to the Capitol in Denver to see "the collection of Cliff Dweller remains."[95] Accompanied by Sergeant "on a fine afternoon in May," Cather attended an exhibit of cliff dweller artifacts at the American Museum of Natural History in New York. There she saw "tan pots with ridged designs in relief, and great black and red pots with complex geometrical patterns," prototypes, no doubt, of the pots that Tom Outland would find.[96]

Evidently, Cather went to the museum for the same reason that "she had been going to singing lessons, hearing voices tested, [and] getting into a behind-the-scenes opera row": to replenish her energy for the book she was working on at the time, *The Song of the Lark*. "When a book did not write itself, she knew enough to leave her manuscript and do something that was germane to the story, in another way . . . ," Sergeant says.[97] At this museum, Cather found even more than she had hoped for. Although there is no extant catalog of the exhibit she saw, it is "safe to say . . . that the Hall [that housed the exhibit] included some or all of two collections acquired from the Wetherills. . . ."[98]

Three months later, Cather was back in the Southwest again, having escaped the heat in Red Cloud. Little is known about this trip, other than Cather's gloomy observation that not even among the Sangre de Cristo Mountains, east of Santa Fe, could one escape the looming menace of the war in Europe, which endangered "everything one most cared about. . . ."[99] It was not until 1922, or thereabouts, that Cather's world broke in two, but already the crack was forming.

Perhaps it was such discouraging signs in the modern world to the East that sent Cather on a personal quest to an ancient one in the West, toward a time when people followed their "natural yearning for order and security" and "built themselves into . . . [a] mesa and humanized it" (*PH* 221). According to Sergeant, Cather was never very interested in or even sympathetic toward living Indians,[100] so she probably would not have been flattered to have any of them claim her as a descendant. But these ancient ones appealed to her across the centuries, grabbed her imagination (and perhaps also her hope), and never let go. In 1925 Cather described this feeling as "the cliff dweller thrill," one of the sensations she had wanted to get into the book she had just finished, *The Professor's House*.[101]

As many readers have observed, the ancient cliff dwellers represented for Cather an ideal society more stable and harmonious than her own. *The Song of the Lark* (1915) introduces this dichotomy, and *The Professor's House* (1925) formalizes it and emphasizes it. In between came *One of Ours* (1922) and *A Lost Lady* (1923), each in its own way an examination of how the present often abandons the ideals of the past. To the extent that the past reminds people of these ideals it can beneficially affect the course of present events. Writing in 1926, Stuart Sherman was perhaps the first in a long line of commentators to affirm that Cather "has been clarifying for us our sense of what we have in common with the generation[s] before

1900, and our sense of the points at which we have departed from the old paths."[102] With each reminder that Cather encountered—from the stories heard in childhood to the visit to a museum as an adult—the grip of the ancient ones tightened until finally all the disparate times, places, and events coalesced in Cather's own discovery of Mesa Verde in the summer of 1915. The same fingers whose imprints could still be seen on potsherds hundreds of years old had already left their mark on Willa Cather's soul.

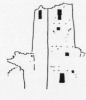*Like other forms of literature,* park brochures reflect their times. Today visitors to Mesa Verde National Park are informed not only of the attractions awaiting them but also of certain personal precautions:

> Visits to cliff dwellings are strenuous. Altitudes in the park vary from 6,000 to 8,500 feet. Steps and ladders must frequently be climbed. Hiking is not recommended for persons with heart or respiratory ailments. . . . Parents should be alert for their children's safety when near the canyon rims. . . . Park visitors can be the target of professional thieves who rob locked vehicles and campsites. . . . Locked cars and trunks are not completely safe. . . .[1]

In Cather's day, the official attitude was more carefree:

> For the benefit of those who have never make [sic] the trip to Mesa Verde National Park, this suggestion is made: Wear rough-and-ready outing garb—khaki suits and stout-soled, comfortable shoes will prove excellent. Ladies should wear divided skirts, as there are many ladders and steep trails to climb in getting in and out of the cliff ruins. The climate is mild, but the nights are cool, so sweaters or extra wraps of some sort

will come in handy. . . . From [a] picturesquely located camp, facing Spruce Tree House, . . . many excursions in the National Park can be taken in perfect safety and comfort.[2]

However it may be described, the Mesa Verde experience is enhanced through preparation. Judging from her comment to Sergeant about her newly-purchased khakis—just like Kurt's in *Fidelio,* she said—one could assume that Willa Cather was ready.[3] In fact, the extent of her preparation can be seen in that familiar photograph of her standing in Cliff Palace,[4] sporting a broad-brimmed hat, heavy leather jacket, and thick gloves and grasping a hefty stick. Cather's enthusiasm for the trip, evident in her appearance, never diminished. Even after hiking for many hours through the canyons and waiting a few hours more to be rescued, only to have to hike some more, Cather reported also to Sergeant that she had had a glorious time and that she was ready to return and be mauled again by the big brutality of the canyon.[5]

For Cather, this trip to Mancos and Mesa Verde in August 1915 was not just a stimulating excursion but also the major step along the way toward the composition of one of her finest narratives. It may well be, as Sergeant suggests, that Tom Outland "was not definitely born in her mind at that date,"[6] but there is little question that Cather herself had already begun playing the role that Outland would later fulfill: exploring, experiencing, describing, and, at least for herself, discovering the wonders of an ancient civilization built high into a cliff.

The trip began in Chicago, where Cather and Edith Lewis boarded the Burlington for Denver, riding "all one day across Nebraska and the Colorado desert."[7] At Denver they switched to the D&RG for the trip south toward Alamosa and then west toward Mancos. It is significant that Cather and Lewis took a more direct route to Mancos than the one the D&RG recommended to tourists. Evidently, Cather was more interested in reaching her destination than with sight-seeing along the way, suggesting a purposeful attitude that seems, in fact, to characterize most of the trip. Edith Lewis would have readers believe that Cather did not go to the Southwest "with any express purpose of writing about it—of 'gathering material,' as they say, for a story . . . [and that she] never spoke of its literary possibilities."[8] Certain aspects of this trip suggest otherwise, however. As Philip Gerber has observed, this time Cather visited the Southwest "with greater calculation aforehand" than in 1912. "Her *target* [emphasis added] was the Mesa Verde and its . . . cliff palace [sic]."[9]

If the D&RG had had its way, it would have taken Cather and Lewis on the famous "Around the Circle" tour, "a marvel in scenic grandeur, unsurpassed in the world, crossing mountain ranges, penetrating deep canons [sic], scaling stupendous cliffs, and, in a word, familiarizing the tourist with the grand and beautiful in nature."[10] Without the hyperbole, this tour went south from Denver through Colorado Springs and Pueblo, but then west to Cañon City and the Royal Gorge, then farther west through Gunnison and on to Montrose, where the line finally turned south through Lizard Head Pass on its way to Mancos.[11] Depending upon the route map that Cather saw, she might have noticed that the road between Gunnison and Montrose passed just north of a large land mass called Blue Mesa.[12] Instead of taking this "widely advertised five-day trip,"[13] however, Cather and Lewis boarded a train that pulled out of Denver one evening and headed due south so that by 4:00 the next morning it was crawling out of La Veta pass, some two hundred miles to the south and about a day and a half from Mancos.

It was probably around midday when they reached Antonito, Colorado, where the narrow gauge began.[14] "What a change from the grand commodious Sleeper, to the dirty, cramped little narrow gauge coaches," an earlier traveler had grumbled.[15] If the difference was still this striking in 1915, it had no effect upon Cather's spirits: "All day," Cather wrote, exaggerating only slightly the meandering route after Antonito, you are among high mountains, swinging back and forth between Colorado and New Mexico, with the Sangre de Cristo and the Culebra ranges always in sight until you cross the continental divide at Cumbres and begin the wild scurry down the westward slope. ("MV")

Perhaps at this point the train did proceed at a "wild scurry," but at others the progress was not so rapid. One old-timer from the Durango area recalled the narrow gauge as

> next to nothing as railroads go. The roadbed was uneven and poor. The trains had to move so slowly that a man could get off and walk alongside the moving train for exercise and not worry about being left behind.[16]

For Cather, apparently, it was enough to sit in the rear car and "signal to the engineer" when the route took a sharp turn ("MV").[17]

Their next stop was Durango, where they spent the night. Cather's exuberance over the final leg of the trip is evident in the words that follow, written several months after the fact:

> In the morning you take another train [the Rio Grande Southern, part of the D&RG line] for Mancos; a friendly train with invariably friendly passengers and a conductor who has been on that run for fourteen years and who can give you all sorts of helpful information. ("MV")

As her train approached the depot at the northwest corner of town, Cather had a virtually unobstructed view of Mesa Verde. (The tracks, no longer there, ran parallel to the current highway bypass.) Several days later as she headed east away from Mancos, Cather probably saw and felt what Tom Outland sees and feels as his train begins its eastward trek for Washington: "For a long while after my train pulled out, I could see our mesa bulking up blue on the skyline. I hated to leave it . . ." (*PH* 224).

"When you reach Mancos," Cather's travelog continues,

you find the station agent, the hotel people and the camp outfitters quite as cordial as the train crew. Your business transactions become of minor importance, and before you know it you are staying on in Mancos because you like the people. ("MV")

Cather liked not only the people of Mancos but also the town itself. She wrote glowingly of the tree-lined streets, the colorful vegetation, and the aroma of sweet clover, which was everywhere, "indoors or out." She had expected to find only a railway station where she would spend another single night on her way to Mesa Verde but found instead a thoroughly delightful community, where she stayed "in all six days" ("MV").[18] For "Tom Outland's Story," this would be time well spent.

Part of the attraction that Mancos held for Cather may have stemmed from its similarity to Red Cloud. Both were small but thriving towns first homesteaded in the early 1870s and established within a few years of each other (1872 for Red Cloud, 1881 for Mancos) by hardy people intent upon establishing themselves in their respective parts of the frontier. Before completing its second decade, each town could boast a school, an opera house, one or two banks, several stores, and two or three hotels. Moreover, Silas Garber, the founder and chief citizen of Red Cloud, had a worthy counterpart in George Bauer of Mancos.[19]

Mancos did not see as much railroad traffic as Red Cloud—eight passenger trains passed through the Nebraska town daily,[20] compared to two trains daily through Mancos[21]—and it was only about one-third as populous; but it was on the route of the tent shows, vaudeville acts, and circuses that Willa Cather had enjoyed as a child; and both communities seem to have taken special pride in their Fourth of July celebrations. Cather would also have been gratified to know that William Jennings Bryan, one of the few politicians who interested her and the only one "she ever profiled,"[22] caused a great commotion and a whole day of celebration in

Mancos when he made a whistle-stop speech there in October 1902.[23]

Granted, most of these features could be found in dozens of other small frontier communities, perhaps even in the "hundreds of ugly little American towns" that Cather says stand between New York and the Montezuma Valley ("MV"); but for Cather Mancos seems to have struck a chord in ways that these other towns did not. At that time her permanent residence was in New York City, a place that sometimes made her so homesick that she became physically ill,[24] and she had lived recently in two other large eastern cities, Pittsburgh and Washington, D.C. The surprising discovery of a small, friendly western town reminiscent of her own Red Cloud was probably a refreshing change, perhaps even a sort of homecoming.

At any rate, when Cather saw Mancos, it was still holding its own against Durango, its larger neighbor to the east, in the vigorous and sometimes virulent competition for tourist business[25] and still showing some promise as a growing community.[26] But it would not be long before Mancos, like Red Cloud, would recede from municipal prominence and endure largely because of its association with the history of something, or someone, else.

For Cather, the town played an important role beyond affording her a few days enjoyment in what two scholars have called "an idyllic world."[27] Just as she transformed Red Cloud into numerous fictional towns and settings,[28] she created Tarpin, New Mexico, out of Mancos, Colorado. To be sure, Tarpin does not figure as prominently in "Tom Outland's Story" as, say, Moonstone does in *The Song of the Lark;* but, like Moonstone, it is nonetheless derived from a real place that Cather knew and liked. "[T]he nearest railroad" to the Blue Mesa (*PH* 205), Tarpin is about thirty miles to the northeast (*PH* 196); "the nearest railroad point to the park,"[29] Mancos was said to be thirty-two miles northeast of the Mesa Verde "over the Government's new . . . automobile road."[30] Furthermore, Tarpin is home to a livery service used by Tom Outland and Roddy Blake, just as Mancos was the headquarters of a livery that brought some of the first tourists into Mesa Verde, the same livery that, years later, brought Cather and Lewis there as well.

There is more at work here than mere location, however. The liveryman whom Cather and Lewis employed was C. B. Kelly, by that time a prominent figure in the region whose career afforded Cather a convenient prototype for one of her minor characters.

"Charles Kelly," Cather says, "who now takes travelers out to the mesa by wagon or motor, is the same guide who formerly provided mounts and provisions and pack horses for people who came to see ruins on the mesa" ("MV"). As her comment suggests, Cather found in Kelly an able and experienced guide. He had come to Mancos in 1886, and in the early 1890s he had started a guide and packing business that by 1900 rivaled the one operated by the Wetherills.[31] In August 1898 Kelly acquired a new buggy, prompting the local paper to proclaim that Kelly was "determined to have as good livery as can be found in any town in the San Juan."[32] Then in 1907, at the age of fifty, he was hired as the first permanent ranger at the park.[33]

For a while Kelly continued to operate his guide business along with his new duties as park ranger, but in April 1911, after park superintendent Hans M. Randolph was suspended for "general neglect of duty," Kelly was advised that if he wanted to keep his position as ranger he would have to give up his other business. "The choice was not difficult," says Mesa Verde historian Duane A. Smith. "Kelly's stable and guide service promised a more profitable future than did a career as park ranger (seventy-five dollars per month salary that summer)."[34] Therefore, he resigned effective 31 May. The separation was far from absolute, however. Kelly maintained a relationship with the park by selling horses and gear and by carrying water, all at bid; and he was even rehired as Temporary Park Ranger for June on the grounds that "his long service and experience" would help ease the way for his successor.[35]

Meanwhile, Kelly's guide business had continued to prosper. A report by one of the agents for the D&RG in 1906 mentions him as the "proprietor of a stable [who] furnishes guide, team, food and lodging for the trip," as well as "divided skirts" for the women who "do not have their own."[36] Kelly's own advertising circular for 1909 describes this enticing trip in more detail. It began in Mancos at 7:30 A.M. and promised to deliver tourists to the Spruce Tree Camp "the same day." On the second day tourists would see the ruins, and on the third day they would return to Mancos. "Everything is provided for the three day trip, including conveyances, meals, sleeping accommodations and guide, at a cost of $15.00 for one person, $12.50 each for two or more," the same fee reported in 1906. An added attraction in 1909 was Smithsonian archaeologist Jesse Walter Fewkes, whom tourists could watch as he excavated Cliff Palace.[37] Tom Outland was correct: "the Smithsonian people . . . would come out here all right" (*PH* 243).

By the time Cather went out there, Kelly was using automobiles—two five-passenger Studebakers[38]—instead of horses and wagons and charging $25.00 for two passengers, with $5.00 more per each additional person, for a one-day trip that encompassed all that the three-day trip had offered.[39] Thus, for Cather and Lewis the cost would have been the same. However, Kelly also had an arrangement with the D&RG so that if Cather and Lewis had bought the package deal from Chicago, which included transportation to the park via the Kelly & French Auto Livery, they could have saved $9.00.[40]

Considering the nature of his work and Cather's evident knowledge of it, C. B. Kelly can easily be seen reappearing in "Tom Outland's Story" as Bill Hook, the liveryman from Tarpin, who "got our workmen back and forth for us, brought our supplies up on to the mesa on his pack-mules, and when one of us had to stay in town overnight he let us sleep in his hay barn to save a hotel bill" (*PH* 211). It is also Bill Hook who, upon Tom's return from Washington, relays the disturbing news about Roddy's "damnedest luck!" with the German buyer of Indian artifacts, Fechtig. In doing so, he reflects some of C. B. Kelly's commercial interests:

The transaction made quite a stir here in Tarpin. I'm not kicking. I made a good thing out of it. My mules were busy three weeks packing the stuff out of there on their backs, and I held the Dutchman up for a fancy price. He had packing cases made at the wagon shop and took 'em up to the mesa full of straw and sawdust, and packed the curios out there. I lost one of my mules, too . . . but Fechtig paid for her like a gentleman. (*PH* 238)

Incidentally, C. B. Kelly may have been one of the first people Cather met in Mancos because he was usually the one waiting at the depot to take tourists to their hotels.[41] To which hotel Cather and Lewis were taken is impossible to say because neither Cather nor Lewis identifies it and because the hotel registers from 1915 are not extant. The most likely candidate is the Hotel Ausburn, the one that Kelly seems to have patronized more than the others;[42] but the Wrightsman, a converted residence and hospital that had once belonged to a physician, might have attracted the ladies' notice as the most elegant hotel in town.[43] If they were interested in economy, however, as Cather was when she visited the Grand Canyon three years earlier,[44] then they may have chosen the Lemmon Hotel. Wherever they stayed, they seem to have maintained their privacy as the local paper, *The Mancos Times-Tribune,* makes no mention of these two guests.[45]

In one of her excursions from the hotel, Cather called upon a member of another prominent Mancos family:

Willa Cather had heard that one of the Wetherill family, a brother of the Dick Wetherill who first "discovered" the Mesa Verde, was still living in Mancos [Richard was killed in 1910], and on the evening before we started for the Mesa she went to call on him; and from him she heard the whole story of how Dick Wetherill swam the Mancos river on his horse and rode into the Mesa after lost cattle, and how he came upon the cliff dwellings that had been hidden there for centuries.[46]

Scholars have assumed that Cather alludes to this visit herself in her letter about the composition of *The Professor's House* first published in the *CEA Critic:* ". . . I myself had the good fortune to hear the story of it [the discovery of Cliff Palace] from a very old man, brother of Dick Wetherell [sic]" (*WCOW* 32). Of course, one would like to know more about this interview than Lewis and Cather divulge; however, until a diary or other record comes to light (if ever), the best one can do is to recreate some of the circumstances from what information is available.

To begin with, the visit that Cather paid to Richard's brother was probably a deliberate research venture, another instance of her purposeful approach toward the whole trip. The wording in Lewis's account, especially the parenthetical phrase "a brother of the Dick Wetherill who first 'discovered' the Mesa Verde," suggests that Cather knew something of Richard's story even before she met his brother. As chapter 1 shows, she had certainly had ample opportunities to learn about him.

In addition, Cather's account of the train ride to Mancos suggests the possibility of yet another pre-visit source, the "conductor who has been on that run for fourteen years and who can give you all sorts of helpful information." This conductor should have been a good source because of the way the D&RG had associated itself with the Wetherills in its promotion of Mesa Verde.[47]

Granted that Cather purposefully sought out this Wetherill brother, which one of the four still living did she find? In one sense, the question is of little significance. Except for the youngest, Win, who during the early days was in school, all of the brothers, including their brother-in-law Charlie Mason, worked together in the ruins and shared more or less equally in the rewards. Therefore, whether she met Al, John, Clayton, or even Win or Charlie Mason, Cather would probably have been told essentially the same things. In another sense, however, the question leads to an interesting insight into Cather's creative rationale, the subject of chapter 4. And, if nothing else, it contributes to the biographical record.

Judging from the number of times that he told his own story, Al would have been a freer talker; however, in a reply to a query from John March, Al's daughter Martha stated flatly, "it wasn't my father Willa Cather talked to." Nor did she believe that Cather had spoken to John.[48] John can be further discounted as the Mancos source because he seems to have been in town for only a few days early in July.[49] Instead, all the evidence points to Clayton, the next to youngest brother, as Cather's Wetherill source.

Richard's biographer Frank McNitt was probably the first to suggest Clayton, apparently after a process of elimination that accounted for the presence elsewhere of the other brothers.[50] More recently, Carol Ann Wetherill, Clayton's granddaughter, has reached the same conclusion through much the same means.[51] Moreover, according to an item in the *Mancos Times-Tribune* for 27 August 1915, Clayton and party "arrived Tuesday [24 August] from their exploring trip out in Northern Arizona and Southern Utah." It was a short visit. In its "Local and Personal" column the following Friday (3 September), the paper announced that Clayton Wetherill and family had left last Friday (27 August) for their home in Creede, Colorado. Therefore, Clayton, unlike the other three brothers, can be placed in Mancos for at least four days in late August, the time when Cather and Lewis were there. Given all this information, it would seem likely that Clayton was Willa Cather's Wetherill contact.[52]

If he was, the interview probably occurred at the home of one of Clayton's in-laws. Contrary to what Edith Lewis says, none of the Wetherills were still living in Mancos in 1915. Their Alamo Ranch was sold at auction in 1902,[53] nearly four years after the death of B. K. Wetherill; and shortly afterward the family members who had still been at the ranch established permanent residences elsewhere.[54] Clayton, however, like his younger brother Win, established new family ties to Mancos when he married "hometown girl"—virtually the girl next door—Eugenia Faunce, whose family, including her mother's family (Wattles), were still living in

Mancos in 1915.[55] During his frequent stopovers in town, Clayton probably stayed with one or the other of these in-laws, so it must have been to one of their houses that Cather came calling. Both families lived in the Mancos Valley southwest of town, not far from the Alamo Ranch.[56]

Assuming that Clayton was Willa Cather's Wetherill contact in Mancos, one also wonders what he told her. Again, some speculation is required, but certain aspects of "Tom Outland's Story" can be traced to him more readily than to any other source. In fact, this Wetherill brother seems to be an even more significant source than has previously been recognized.

The most obvious, and probably the most important, instance of this Wetherill influence is Tom Outland's demoralizing trip to Washington, D.C., which was surely suggested by the relationship between the Wetherills and the Smithsonian Institution. It must have been from this brother that Cather learned of the family's fruitless efforts to interest the Smithsonian in excavating the ruins they had discovered because none of the story had appeared in print by 1915—or by 1925, for that matter. In later years, this earnest but ineffectual correspondence between the family and the institution became a staple of Wetherill literature, although only recently has it been documented.[57]

During the ten weeks of this correspondence, there were at least seven letters back and forth: four from B. K. Wetherill (not Richard, as most accounts had stated, but his father), two from Secretary Samuel Pierpont Langley, and one from William Henry Holmes, staff archaeologist. Interestingly, this correspondence puts the Smithsonian in a less culpable light than Cather does. Holmes especially was interested in the discoveries, knowledgeable about Indian ruins, and experienced in exploring them, even though he remained noncommittal. Nonetheless, the letters still tell the story of an opportunity lost, or at least delayed. Moreover, because the Smithsonian officials failed to respond as the Wetherills had wanted, their letters may also account for some ill feelings between the family and the institution.[58]

It would not be surprising if Clayton Wetherill conveyed these ill feelings to Cather, who eventually turned them into a major conflict of values. It should also be noted, though, that Cather could have picked up some anti-Smithsonian sentiment from other people in Mancos if an attitude reflected in a newspaper story from 1898 was still current. The paper announces the departure of Al and Clayton Wetherill and T. Mitchell Prudden on an archaeological expedition and calls them "a trio that will gain more knowledge of sections visited than would all the Smithsonian 'legendary lore' sharps be able to glean in a quarter of a century."[59]

Another part of "Tom Outland's Story" that can be traced directly to the Wetherills, and to Clayton as the most likely conveyor, is Outland's reverence for the ruins—and perhaps also the possessiveness he comes to feel for them:

> Something had happened in me that made it possible for me to co-ordinate and simplify, and that process, going on in my mind, brought with it great happiness. It was possession. The excitement of my first discovery was a very pale feeling compared to this one. For me the mesa was no longer an adventure, but a religious emotion. I had read of filial piety in the Latin poets, and I knew that was what I felt for this place. It had formerly been mixed up with other motives; but now that they were gone, I had my happiness unalloyed. (*PH* 250–51)

Although they might not have felt filial piety for the place, the Wetherills did express a reverential attitude toward the ruins in Mesa Verde: "It was so much like treading 'holy ground' to go into those peaceful-looking homes of a vanished people."[60] They also took seriously their self-assumed responsibility for the ruins. At one point Al Wetherill said that they had considered themselves "custodians of a priceless heritage . . . [who] would allow no damage nor wanton pilfering. . . ."[61] At another time he said, "we could not shake off the feeling that we were possibly predestined to take over the job [of excavating the ruins], knowing what depredations had been committed by transients who neither revered nor cared for the ruins as symbols of the past."[62] Richard's widow Marietta made a similar point:

> I think that Mr. Wetherill [which is what she usually called her husband] was rather selfish about his ruins. He loved those ruins so that he hated to see them excavated. He really did. He hated to see them torn up. If he coulda found out all about the people that lived in them without taking out all that dirt and stone and stuff that had to be taken out, it would have made him very happy indeed.[63]

Tom Outland's diary is probably another feature of Cather's story that originated during this interview, suggested by what Cather must have learned about the records kept by the Wetherills. "We numbered each specimen," Tom says,

> and in my day-book I wrote down just where and in what condition we had found it, and what we thought it had been used for. I'd got a merchant's ledger in Tarpin, and every night after supper, while Roddy read the newspapers, I sat down at the kitchen table and wrote up an account of the day's work. (*PH* 212)

Although they have been faulted at times for not keeping better records, it does seem that the Wetherills were more scrupulous with record keeping than most early explorers, even to the point of numbering specimens as they dug them out.[64] In fact, park ranger and historian Don Watson concluded that they were probably the only early excavators who kept careful records and that, as a result, their collections have "real scientific value."[65]

Moreover, in his correspondence with Holmes, B. K. Wetherill asserts that his sons "keep a strict record of all our discoveries, where found etc. and all other items of interest." Wetherill even includes in his second letter to Holmes some proof of their efforts, "one days [sic] description of work done" at Sandal House, principally by John and Clayton. This diary entry lists a number of things that reappear in "Tom Outland's Story," among them yucca strings, grains of corn, squash seeds, and signs of domesticated turkeys; it speculates upon "a bone needle, four inches long, having the apperance [sic] of a large darning needle"; it presents the dimensions of a grave as "five feet long, four feet wide and two feet high"; and it describes the nature of the woodwork:

> All the wood work, [sic] shows the work to have been done with the stone axes, which must have required a long time of very laborious work; the chopping resembling the work of beavers, with the advantage in favor of the beaver.[66]

Cather did not use this beaver image in "Tom Outland's Story," but she did in the 1916 essay, partly as a way of emphasizing the harmony between the cliff dweller and nature: "When they felled cedars with stone axes they were but accelerating a natural process; the ends of their roof rafters looked as if they had been gnawed thru by a beaver" ("MV"). Of course, Cather's own observation could have produced this analogy, but the parallels point more strongly to her Wetherill source.

The impression that the cliff dwellers had just stepped out with the intention of returning may also stem from this interview. Tom Outland is struck by the appearance of some beautiful water jars "standing there just as if they'd been left yesterday" (*PH* 209). Likewise, Al Wetherill once observed that objects "were arranged in the rooms as if the people might just have been out visiting somewhere and might return any minute."[67]

Cather may also have learned from Clayton Wetherill about the difficulties encountered by the young Swedish explorer Gustaf Nordenskiold when he tried to remove his collection of artifacts from the country, a problem that Nordenskiold mentions only briefly and vaguely. Cather's German buyer of artifacts, Fechtig, takes pains to avoid such a problem himself by exporting his collection through Mexico.[68]

Finally, this Wetherill brother must also have been Cather's source of information about the work of Charles Mason, the Wetherills' brother-in-law. He and Richard were together in the discovery of Cliff Palace (in fact, Mason has sometimes been credited with naming it); and Mason, very much a part of the family, worked alongside the Wetherill boys—exploring, excavating, and collecting. As a participant in the action, however, he receives unequal treatment in Cather's writings. In the 1916 essay he is relegated to the status of "one of his [Richard's] cow men" and never heard from again. Then in "Tom Outland's Story" he reappears as Rodney Blake; however, as Frank McNitt first noted, "even more than Tom Outland he is a character of her [Cather's] imagination."[69] For this reason, there is probably little to be gained from an examination of biographical parallels. Nonetheless, Charlie Mason is important to this study because it is from him, through Clayton Wetherill, that one can surmise the origins of other parts of Cather's story.

In 1914 Mason wrote a detailed account of his and the Wetherills' explorations and excavations throughout Mesa Verde.[70] Because the manuscript was signed by Mason and all four of the Wetherill brothers who were still living, one can safely assume that they were all familiar with the contents and that Clayton probably told Cather some of the facts and incidents that Mason had recently recorded and that were therefore still fresh in Clayton's mind.

Some details have been noted already, for instance the discovery of particular ruins and artifacts and the impression that the occupants either left in a hurry or with the intention of returning.[71] Yet another part of "Tom Outland's Story" that the Wetherills may have suggested is the final theory proposed by Father Duchene, that the cliff dwellers were destroyed by a less cultivated tribe:

They were probably wiped out, utterly exterminated, by some roving Indian tribe without culture or domestic virtues, some horde that fell upon them in their summer camp and destroyed them for their hides and clothing and weapons, or from mere love of slaughter. (*PH* 221)

At the end of his manuscript, Mason proposes a similar explanation in similar terms: "It seems to me that there can be no doubt that the cliff dwellers were exterminated by their more savage and warlike neighbors, the men being killed and the women perhaps adopted into the tribe of the conquerers. . . ."[72] Nordenskiold also acknowledges this possibility but in words unlike Cather's and with considerably less emphasis than Mason.[73] The park brochure does not mention it at all.

Even more intriguing for its suggestive qualities is this passage from earlier in Mason's manuscript:

In the left hand fork of Johnson Canon [sic] are several houses. The largest has about forty rooms. In a room in one of these houses were the skeletons of four people who had no doubt been killed where we found them. There were two grown people, a man and a woman, [sic] one was that of a child twelve or fourteen years old, and the other a child a few months old. [Later Mason calls them a "family murdered," and Frank McNitt adds that the Wetherills believed the family "had been murdered by their own people."[74]] The skull of each of the three older people had been crushed in, and between them on the floor was a large stone ax, the blade of which just fitted the dent in the skulls. The bones of the skull of the child were scattered all about the room, so we could not tell in what manner it had been killed. Beneath the floor of an open passage way, in a small pit formed by a small [?] circular wall, the arms of which were against the cliff which formed the other side of the pit, we found our second mummy, that of a woman. The face was not handsome, but we called her She.

We had been reading Rider Haggard's story She; the building we called She Room.[75]

The parallels between this passage and Cather's story of Mother Eve are quite striking:

> At last we came upon one of the original inhabitants—not a skeleton, but a dried human body, a woman. She was not in the Cliff City; we found her in a little group of houses stuck up in a high arch we called the Eagle's Nest. She was lying on a yucca mat, partly covered with rags, and she had dried into a mummy in that water-drinking air. We thought she had been murdered; there was a great wound in her side, the ribs stuck out through the dried flesh. Her mouth was open as if she were screaming, and her face, through all those years, had kept a look of terrible agony. Part of the nose was gone, but she had plenty of teeth, not one missing, and a great deal of coarse black hair. Her teeth were even and white, and so little worn that we thought she must have been a young woman. Henry named her Mother Eve, and we called her that. (*PH* 214)

Like Mason and the Wetherills, Cather was familiar with the novel *She,* as evidenced in her two reviews of an unfortunate dramatization of the book in Lincoln in 1894.[76] Part *Typee* and part *Indiana Jones, She* is a wild romantic adventure with definite Gothic trappings by British author Sir Henry Rider Haggard. It was first published in 1887, only a year or so before the Wetherills were reading it. Also known as "She-who-must-be-obeyed" and "Ayesha" (pronounced Assha), the title character is a "temptress . . . more than human" with "beauty . . . greater than the loveliness of the daughters of men." The plot develops around She's efforts to locate her former lover, whom she expects to accept her again "although I sinned against him," an act similar to the one that Father Duchene attributes to Mother Eve. Throughout the story She is associated with snakes, which rather vaguely suggest evil and temptation, and at one point she is likened specifically to Eve standing before Adam, "clad in nothing but her abundant hair."[77] From She to Eve to Mother Eve is the evident progression of Cather's mummy.

If Clayton Wetherill mentioned this novel in the context presented by Mason, Cather, who "forgot nothing,"[78] must have made some instant associations that she recalled later as she began writing "The Blue Mesa." Cather alters the details of Mason's story, augments the tragedy, and infuses the scene with more meaning; but it is reasonable to see her story of Mother Eve as an expansion of the principal ingredients in Mason's story of "She": a murder, a violently damaged body, and the mummy of a woman discovered in an isolated location and given a universal female name.[79] Even if Cather missed seeing She in the cliff-dweller exhibit at the Chicago World's Fair in 1893, she must have heard about her at this time.[80]

One more question surrounding this Wetherill interview concerns the date when it took place. In fact, dating the trip as a whole is equally problematic because of the fragmented information. An exact chronology is probably impossible to determine, but there are enough certain, or nearly certain, dates to allow an educated guess.

As usual, neither Cather nor Lewis is much help. All Lewis says is that they spent a week at Mesa Verde during "the summer of 1915,"[81] and Cather says even less, leaving one to deduce the time of the visit from certain internal evidence like the aroma of sweet clover and the appearance of the wheat—"a veritable cloth of gold" ("MV")—nearly ready for harvest. These conditions could suggest mid to late August or even early September.[82] Luckily, the story of their celebrated rescue, which, to Cather's annoyance, appeared in the *New York Times,* dates the visit a little more precisely. Page twenty of the issue for 26 August 1915 carries a brief account under the ominous heading "Lost in Colorado Canyon":

MANCOS, Col., Aug. 25.—Miss Willa Sibert Cather, a former editor of McClure's Magazine, and Miss Edith Lewis, assistant editor of Every Week, had a nerve-racking experience in the Mesa Verde wilds, according to word received here today.

Both the dateline and the final phrase, "according to word received here today," suggest that Cather and Lewis must have gotten lost on the evening of 24 August—or possibly the evening before—and been rescued early the following morning. Lewis says that after they were driven back to their own camp, the tent camp across from Spruce Tree House, their "team and driver" (C. B. Kelly or someone in his employ) arrived at 8:00 that same morning and took them back to Mancos.[83] The news reached Denver early enough on Wednesday, 25 August, for the story to appear in the evening edition of the *Denver Times*.[84]

Other evidence that helps to date the trip comes from two post cards that Cather sent to Elizabeth Sergeant. The first, which bears a photo of Spruce Tree House as seen from the camp across the canyon, was written on 20 August, the diction suggesting that Cather and Lewis had already spent some time on the mesa.[85] It must also have been written before their adventure of getting lost because Cather makes no mention of the incident, which Sergeant did learn about later.[86] Thus, the evening Cather and Lewis spent in the canyon was no sooner than 20 August and no later than 24 August, with 23 August the most likely date.

Then on 31 August Cather wrote to Sergeant from Lamy, New Mexico, saying that she and Lewis had just spent a glorious week in Taos, which is about ninety miles north of Lamy.[87] A stop at Taos on the way to Lamy would have added at least a day to their trip because the railroad went not through Taos itself but through Taos Junction, "a tiny station"[88] about twenty miles to the west. To go from there to Taos, Cather and Lewis hired a team and driver, whom Sergeant identifies as John Dunne.[89] The ride took three or four hours each way.[90] Thus, the trip from Mancos to Lamy could easily have taken two days, meaning that Cather and Lewis were probably in Taos for no more than five days. (Lewis says that they spent about a month there,[91] but that is impossible. From Lamy they doubtless headed northeast on the Atchison, Topeka, and Santa Fe for the trip home; and by 13 September Cather was already back in Red Cloud writing to Ferris Greenslet.[92])

With all this information at hand, one is inclined to mark the week Cather and Lewis spent on the mesa from perhaps 17 or 18 August through 24 or 25 August, with four or five days in Mancos before then and one or two more afterward. Cather's saying she stayed in Mancos "in all six days" does seem to suggest noncontinuous time, and a typical visit would have sandwiched time on the mesa between two separate stays in Mancos. It must have been on 25 or 26 August when Cather and Lewis left Mancos for Taos.

If this chronology is accurate, then Cather could not have seen Clayton Wetherill in Mancos "on the evening before we started for the Mesa," as Lewis says she did.[93] Therefore, she must have seen him afterward, perhaps on 24 or 25 August, immediately after his arrival in town on the twenty-fourth and two or three days before his departure for Creede on the twenty-seventh. Obviously, this interpretation requires accepting some things Lewis says and rejecting others, but it appears to make the best use of what information is available.[94]

Whatever the actual dates may be, it was the time itself that Cather and Lewis spent in Mancos that was so valuable; and even then their southwestern adventure was only beginning. Five or six days after their arrival, C. B. Kelly took them to Mesa Verde.

3 ❄ *A Very Comfortable Tent Camp on the Mesa*

On 28 May 1914, a caravan of six cars made the first automobile trip up the Mesa Verde. Then on the following Fourth of July, amid a good deal of celebration, the road they took was officially opened to the public, many of whom had been clamoring for just such a development.[1] By the season of 1915, well over half of the visitors were arriving in cars, either their own or vehicles rented from a local garage;[2] and the park brochure for that season is full of references to automobiles, including a rule that teams and wagons, which remained in use for a while, would still have the right of way and another rule that cars must never exceed fifteen miles per hour and must go even slower under certain well defined circumstances.[3] All this progress notwithstanding, when Edith Lewis described the access to Mesa Verde, she made the place sound nearly as remote as Tom Outland's Blue Mesa: "I do not remember seeing any automobiles in that country then—but in any case, there was no road up the Mesa Verde that an automobile could travel."[4] Thus, for Cather and herself, the means of ascent was decidedly nineteenth-century—"a team and driver"—because, Lewis implies, nothing more modern was available.[5] The team belonged to C. B. Kelly, and the driver was probably Kelly himself.

Cather's account of their conveyance is both shorter and more accurate. "The journey to the Mesa Verde, which was a hard one in [Gustaf] Nordenskjold's time [1891],⁶ is now a very easy one . . . Charles Kelly . . . now takes travelers out to the mesa by wagon or motor" ("MV"). In fact, according to his granddaughter, Kelly had quit using a team and wagon as soon as the automobile road was opened.⁷ Given Cather's well known aversion to travel by auto, however,⁸ it is entirely possible that Cather could have prevailed upon Kelly to use the older mode of transportation. Nonetheless, she and Lewis would surely have seen automobiles somewhere "in that country" as they were bouncing picturesquely up the mesa. Furthermore, had they been interested, Kelly could even have sold them a brand new Studebaker Four, with electric starter, electric lights, and extra size tires, for a mere $985.00, F. O. B. Detroit.⁹

Although he had blazed his own trail some years before (about four miles west of the current park entrance), Kelly probably took Cather and Lewis along the main wagon road, which, as Cather said, was "recent" ("MV"). Open to "both horse-drawn vehicles and automobiles," it left the Mancos-Cortez road about eight miles from Mancos and about twelve miles from Cortez, approximately where the park entrance is today, and then wound through "pin-yon-covered hills at the base of Point Lookout and ascend[ed] to the top of the mesa. . . ."¹⁰ Then it followed more or less the route of the modern park road to the tent camp just across Spruce Tree Canyon from Spruce Tree House. That particular locale had been the place for guest quarters ever since the turn of the century, when Kelly built a small cabin that was still standing when Cather and Lewis were there. Even today one can find the spot, just down the side of the canyon from the present park headquarters, by locating a gnarled tree that appears in old photographs of Kelly's cabin.¹¹

At the tent camp, Kelly left Cather and Lewis in the care of concessionaire Oddie Jeep, the daughter of park superintendent Thomas Rickner, who was in her second year of operating the camp.¹² Although Lewis probably thought the conditions there were "primitive" (this was one of her favorite words for the whole of the 1915 southwestern tour), Cather found them quite to her liking, calling the place a "very comfortable tent camp on the mesa" where anyone "can be very comfortable . . . for several weeks" ("MV"). In fact, given Cather's fondness for writing in tents in various places,[13] one would not be surprised if she found this camp congenial to composition, too.

If, like other tourists, Cather and Lewis had inquired beforehand about the accommodations, they would probably have been led to expect a comfortable place by the reply of Superintendent Rickner, quoted here answering the inquiry of a prospective tourist from Chicago in April 1915:

> The camp will consist of a dining room [also known as the "eating shack"] and a lounge with ample piazza room and new tent bed-rooms, all completely and comfortably furnished. The table is excellent, and the location of the camp, on the edge of Spruce Canyon just across from Spruce Tree House which [sic] you can see from the camp, is ideal. At this camp there is an abundance of pure water, something not found everywhere in the park.[14]

Rickner's personal connection with the camp and its operator notwithstanding, photographs from the day seem to support this favorable description. They show not simple tents staked directly to the ground but permanent wooden walls with tents as roofs and a glimpse of bedroom-type furnishings inside. Moreover, in 1917 a park inspector found these items as standard issue: a bed, a dresser, a straight chair, a wash bowl, and a pitcher; and he recommended that if Mrs. Jeep would supplement these furnishings with a rocking chair, a slop jar, a large rug, and a kerosene lamp, she could increase her fee to $4.00 per day.[15] Evidently, Oddie Jeep took his advice because her son recalls these items from about 1918: a double bed; a dresser; a wash basin, pitcher and stand; a throw rug; chairs; and a kerosene lamp.[16] In 1915 the more meager but adequate furnishings from the first list were probably in place, at a cost of "seventy-five cents per meal and the same for a bed."[17]

Not every tourist, incidentally, was pleased with the camp accommodations. Disgruntled at both the nepotistic situation and the service, a guest from 1917 registered the following complaint:

> This is a family affair. The camp concessionaire being the wife of Ranger Jeep and a daughter of Supervisor Rickner. The meals are poor and the camp is more of a boarding house for road gangs who are served at the same time and in the same room with the guests, than a tent hotel for tourists.[18]

Willa Cather, on the other hand, seems to have been entirely satisfied not only with the accommodations but also with the "excellent food" provided by "the wife of the forest ranger" ("MV"). She may have been impressed by another facet of Oddie Jeep as well.

According to an item in the *Mancos-Times Tribune* for 2 July 1915, Oddie Jeep was "getting to be almost as skilled and daring a mountain climber as is Mr. Jeep himself and goes without hesitation over many places where the men's nerve fails when they assay to follow." An accomplished rock climber herself,[19] Cather would have appreciated Oddie's abilities; and she may have remembered them years later when she was creating Henry Atkins, the camp cook for Tom Outland and Roddy Blake. Mildred Bennett has already identified the source of the fictional Henry as the real English cook of the same name employed by Cather's brother Douglass,[20] but in her dual gender roles Oddie Jeep would have been a handy prototype for the combined talents of housekeeper and explorer that made Henry so valuable: "He was a wonderful cook and a good housekeeper" (*PH* 197); and "besides doing the housekeeping, [Henry] was very eager to help us in the 'rew-ins,' as he called them" (*PH* 212).

Cather also met Oddie's husband, park ranger Fred Jeep. It is he, in fact, whom Lewis praises as "a splendid guide, familiar with

every foot of the Mesa. . . ."[21] That Jeep had been their guide may
suggest that Cather's stature as a celebrity was growing: according
to one park historian, Jeep tended to reserve his services for "important people, government officials in particular. . . ."[22]

Jeep was indeed an able guide; and like his wife, he would also
have been a convenient model. Two months before Cather and
Lewis arrived, he and another man, named Clint Scharf, discovered
a new ruin in Navajo Canyon about four miles southwest of Spruce
Tree Camp. Like Tom Outland and Roddy Blake, they spent
several days devising a way into the ruin, which had evidently not
been entered since the days of its inhabitation. In both cases, the real
and the fictional, the explorers made ladders to enter the ruin but
from different directions: Jeep and Scharf "built a ladder thirty-
eight-feet long which they swung over the cliff from above fastened
securely to a cedar tree";[23] Outland and Blake use a technique
employed by the Wetherills: they "felled some trees and threw them
up over the gaps in the path" that led to Cliff City (*PH* 207).
Interestingly, Cather's two characters later devise a suspended ladder similar to the one used by Jeep and Scharf (see *PH* 211).

Another similarity is the size of the two ruins: the one discovered
by Jeep and Scharf, named Daniels House, was said to contain
about twenty-five rooms; Cather's Cliff City contains about thirty,
far fewer than the roughly two hundred estimated for Cliff Palace
in the park brochure for 1915. This smaller size is more conducive
to the sense of intimate grandeur suggested by Tom Outland's
"little city of stone, asleep" and "pale little houses of stone nestling
close to one another" (*PH* 201) than the more expansive view
afforded by Cliff Palace. There is no gainsaying that Cliff Palace is
the major prototype of Cliff City, but the fresh discovery of Daniels
House by two men whom Cather actually met may well have
influenced the story, too.

The day before Cather and Lewis were to return to Mancos, Fred
Jeep had planned to take them to an unexcavated cliff dwelling
called the Tower House.[24] Because of the unexpected arrival of a

large party of tourists, however (probably the Prairie Walking Club from Chicago),[25] Jeep had to assign Cather and Lewis to someone else. In such circumstances he sometimes recruited Oddie as guide,[26] but this time he gave the job to another member of the family, his brother-in-law, the "young man named Richnor" whom Lewis mentions and who inspired some apprehension in his two new clients. However, as Lewis says, because Jeep made this arrangement "in Richnor's presence, we could hardly decline, and we started off with him."[27] The trek to this final ruin justified their apprehension but also led to one of Cather's most fruitful misadventures.

Thomas Rickner had three sons, James, Jack, and Charles.[28] Jack, the middle brother, who was twelve years old in 1915 and who at this writing is "the last of the Rickner family living," seldom guided tourists and has no recollection of either Cather or Lewis. However, he does remember one occasion when his older brother James, who did serve as a tour guide, kept a party in the canyons long after dark and had to be rescued.[29] Moreover, on 22 May 1915, James had returned to Mancos after three years in medical school in Providence, Rhode Island, to spend the summer at home.[30] For these reasons, it must have been James Rickner with whom Cather and Lewis departed.

There are some interesting biographical parallels between James Rickner and Tom Outland that bear noting here, especially considering that Cather would likely have learned something about her young guide during their several hours together. First is their ages. The only boy in his graduating class of 1908, James Rickner was in his mid-twenties in 1915, an age much closer to that imputed to Tom Outland than Richard Wetherill's thirty years at the time he discovered Cliff Palace. Like Tom Outland, James Rickner was a student of science—medicine rather than physics or aviation—and his studies were interrupted, never to be resumed.[31] Finally, there is this intriguing possibility. According to his nephew, in 1916 or 1917 James Rickner served in the Balloon Corps, the forerunner of the Air Corps.[32]

Perhaps it is not too far fetched to assume that Rickner had an interest in this aspect of aviation as early as 1915 and that he shared this interest with Cather during their trek through the canyon. If so, Tom Outland's famous invention may have originated here.[33]

On that late August day, however, Cather was also thinking, probably, of the inventiveness of ancient people—and no doubt watching her step, as young Rickner led them farther from camp and deeper into trouble. One can easily discern the impatience in Lewis's voice as she narrates the experience:

> To get to the Tower House, one had to walk through the woods to the rim of Soda Canyon, climb down to the bottom of this canyon, and follow along it for some distance. The Tower House was up the other wall of the canyon.
>
> Richnor got us to the Tower House all right, but by a very rough trail—in climbing down to the bottom of Soda Canyon, we had in many places to hang from a tree or rock and then drop several feet to the next rock; we could not have returned by this trail without ropes. Richnor said he would take us back by another trail, further down the canyon. But by five or six o'clock that evening, after we had done a good many miles of walking, he was still unable to find this trail, and had to admit that he did not know how we were to get back. . . .
>
> We had by then come to a place where another canyon, Cliff Canyon, opened at right angles from Soda Canyon. Richnor told us he thought, but was not sure, that about four miles up Cliff Canyon there was an archaeologist's camp (Dr. Fewkes's camp), and suggested that we try for it. But Willa Cather sensibly told him he had better go up Cliff Canyon and find out whether the camp was really there; we would wait, in the meantime, at the intersection of the two canyons.
>
> The four or five hours that we spent waiting there were, I think, for Willa Cather the most rewarding of our whole trip to the Mesa Verde. There was a large flat rock at the mouth of Cliff Canyon, and we settled ourselves comfortably on this

rock—with the idea, I believe, that we should be able to see any rattlesnakes if they came racing up. We were tired and rather thirsty, but not worried, for we knew we should eventually be found. We did not talk, but watched the long summer twilight come on, and the full moon rise up over the rim of the canyon. The place was very beautiful.[34]

One has no difficulty seeing in this experience a moment of genuine inspiration. Just how much of "Tom Outland's Story" was conceived at this time is, of course, impossible to know, but it is still pleasant to speculate upon the myriad impressions that entered Cather's creative consciousness during those few hours and remained stored there until needed. What Lewis says about another time when she and Cather got lost in the Southwest applies to this experience, too:

it was precisely accidents like these that always heightened the special character of a journey, and fixed the light, the colours, the whole mood of one's surroundings forever in the memory. By changing the key of an experience, they sometimes became one of its most valuable elements.[35]

The full moon that Lewis mentions may have been especially suggestive. According to Bernice Slote, the moon is one of the "most deeply affective and complex symbols in Willa Cather's writing." It is "generally seen as some high, illimitable beauty; the sign of yearning and desire; the radiant or mysterious illumination of darkness; and the sign also of the voyage perilous [Cather's metaphor for artistic creation]."[36] Add to these associations the moon as a symbol of feminine creativity and one has a passage rich in suggestive possibilities. "The moon was up" for Tom Outland, too, the night he returns to the mesa after his argument with Roddy Blake, "and it had that glittering silveriness the early stars have in high altitudes" (*PH* 250). One can easily imagine Cather in the same attitude that she attributes to Tom Outland: "I lay down on a solitary rock that was like an island in the bottom of the valley, and looked up" (*PH* 250).

In May 1986, James C. Work organized a small party to try to locate Cather's rock. Led by an energetic Ute guide nicknamed the "Kamikaze Anasazi," Work and his party made their way through Soda Canyon—traversing not the "wide, grassy bottom" that Lewis described[37] but encountering instead "a jumble of house-size boulders and eroded sand"[38]—until they reached the point where Soda Canyon intersects Cliff Canyon. There they found the rock, "round, and mounded, and smooth," shaped like a loaf of Indian bread and "slightly larger than a two-car garage." Clearly, Cather was writing with authority, even understatement, when she described the floor of the box canyon in "Tom Outland's Story" as "a mass of huge boulders," many of them "as big as haystacks" (*PH* 200). Centuries ago this particular rock had been split in two, producing a flat stage-like surface a few feet high backed by the remaining portion of the rock. "You must scramble a little to get up on it, but once there you would be safe from snakes, indeed," Work writes. "You would also be quite comfortable, with the boulder shielding you from the night breeze."[39] Cather and Lewis seem to have made a good choice.

Incidentally, the rock is not in the national park but in the Ute Mountain Indian Reservation, a quarter-mile or so south of the current park boundary. In 1915 the park boundary was even farther north,[40] so that Cather and Lewis were well into Indian land before they stopped to await rescue. Today, when tourists follow the loop after visiting Cliff Palace, they drive through part of the Ute Reservation. If they were to stop at a sharp curve just before heading north again and then peer down into the canyon, they could see the location of the rock, if not the rock itself.

As Lewis predicted, she and Cather were eventually rescued. "We were sitting there in the moonlight, when we heard shouts from up Cliff Canyon, and presently two men came in sight."[41] They were indeed workers from the camp of Smithsonian archaeologist Jesse Walter Fewkes, who was excavating Sun Temple at the time. Lewis gives their names as Clint Scarf (the Clint Scharf already mentioned) and Audrey Grey Pearl.[42]

The way back was just as arduous as the way there, but at least this time Cather and Lewis were better assisted:

> Each of them [Scharf and Pearl] took one of us by the hand and steadied us over the rocks. (At one place we had to lie down and be pulled through a sort of tunnel in the rocks.)[43] Occasionally we would stop for a short time to rest, and then the men would quickly build a little fire, for an icy wind swept down the canyon at night.[44]

The physical details in "Tom Outland's Story" are no doubt richer as a result of Cather's experience navigating the canyons.

More specifically, it may have been on this return trip to Fewkes's camp when Cather conceived the perspective from which Tom Outland first views Cliff City. On the way there they probably did not pass beneath Cliff Palace, which was farther up the canyon than Fewkes's camp and which is not fully visible from the canyon floor anyway, if at all;[45] but they did pass a smaller ruin called Swallows Nest in the east side of Cliff Canyon.[46] If, as William Howarth suggests, the full moon that Lewis mentions shone upon this "thin line of ruins," it would have presented Cather with a perspective somewhat like the one that Tom Outland describes,[47] minus the snow, of course:

> In stopping to take breath, I happened to glance up at the canyon wall. I wish I could tell you what I saw there, just *as* I saw it, on that first morning, through a veil of lightly falling snow. Far up above me, a thousand feet or so, set in a great cavern in the face of the cliff, I saw a little city of stone, asleep. It was as still as sculpture—and something like that. It all hung together, seemed to have a kind of composition: pale little houses of stone nestling close to one another, perched on

top of each other, with flat roofs, narrow windows, straight walls. . . . (*PH* 201)

Swallows Nest was about a third of the way between the rock where Cather and Lewis had waited and Fewkes's camp, which they reached about 2:00 A.M. "On the whole," Lewis says, "we had greatly enjoyed this adventure. We suffered no ill effects from it, beyond feeling rather tired and stiff for a day or two." There was, however, an external irritation: "much to Willa Cather's annoyance, an enterprising reporter heard of it, and telegraphed a New York paper that she had been 'rescued' on the Mesa Verde, and *McClure's Magazine* sent her a whole bunch of clippings with this notice."[48]

Perhaps what annoyed Cather so much was not the notice itself but the different impression it creates. Probably by design, Lewis's version portrays Cather and herself not so much as victims but as adventurers, with Cather in control and "sensibly" giving orders. The *Times* story, on the other hand, recounts in a rather gossipy tone the "nerve-racking experience in the Mesa Verde wilds" of two fatigued and helpless women:

> Miss Cather sustained severe sprains, and both [Cather and Lewis] were exhausted by wandering all night in a rocky cañon, where they had been conducted by an inexperienced guide.
>
> When the women became too exhausted for further travel the guide left them and went ahead for assistance. At 3 o'clock in the morning he found the camp of Dr. Walter Fewkes, a Smithsonian scientist, who is exploring cliff ruins in the park. Dr. Fewkes sent *four* men *with* the guide [emphasis added], and they brought the women into his camp an hour later.[49]

This is not the stuff from which Cather would be likely to derive literary inspiration. Not only are there no leisurely, confident musings upon a rock; but Lewis's pleasant, though strenuous, return trip in the company of two "chivalrous" men who enjoyed nothing "so much as spending the night in this way"[50] becomes in this version a major rescue operation. Hardly a flattering story. Whatever the actual details, however, the incident at least serves to introduce another Mesa Verde figure who seems to have influenced the composition of "Tom Outland's Story."

In Jesse Walter Fewkes, Cather had the opportunity for face-to-face exposure to the major archaeologist at Mesa Verde. Precisely what she gleaned from him is impossible to say now, but, according to contemporary southwestern archaeologist Alden C. Hayes, "Cather couldn't have avoided meeting him."[51]

It was during his work at Sun Temple that summer when Oddie Jeep persuaded Fewkes to begin the series of campfire talks that continues even to this day. Each evening "when any visitors [were] present,"[52] Fred Jeep dug a fire hole not far from the tent camp and Fewkes "regaled the tourists with stories."[53] "Somewhat of a romantic, he drove himself to make the 'mystical red man known to the literate public.'"[54] Some of these campfire talks were so dramatic, in fact, that they could hardly have been missed or forgotten. Jack Rickner recalls his role in the production:

> Dr. Fewkes gave talks at a camp fire on the ledge below the museum looking towards Spruce Tree House. . . . Across the canyon there was a ditch cut in the rock. We took black powder & fuse. . . . When he came to the point in his lecture where the ball of fire came out of the earth we set the powder off—and the Indians came out of the ground on to this earth. That was their belief.[55]

It seems likely that during her week on the mesa Cather would have sat in on one or more of these sessions and later incorporated into "Tom Outland's Story" some of the material she absorbed in that ancient setting around that primordial fire. It would have been a good time to feel the excitement of modern discovery and to indulge in a wistful projection into a time long past. As the ranking scientific authority and an engaging talker to boot—"no one performed better than Jesse Fewkes, when he told the story of the cliff dwellers"—Fewkes would have been a likely source to complement Cather's own powers of imagination.[56]

Finally, beyond their influence as individuals, the three Rickners at the tent camp may also have suggested the family unit that Tom Outland forms on the mesa with Roddy Blake and Henry Atkins. These two "families" are hardly mirror images of each other and they pose no direct counterparts, but they have enough traits in common to suggest an influence, especially considering that Cather, like other guests at the camp, was surely aware of the family connections. In each case there are two men in a brotherly relationship, one several years older than the other (Fred and James/Roddy and Tom); someone who has made a significant discovery (Fred Jeep/Tom Outland); and an excellent camp cook who doubles as an explorer (Oddie Jeep/Henry Atkins). In addition, each group comprises three members on a more or less equal footing, a sort of fraternal unit rather than a conventional family of parents and children—"parenting displaced into male friendship," Susan Rosowski says of Tom's family.[57] In this sense, both families are atypical, but their members are united by the common bond of interest in, if not reverence for, the ruins of an ancient civilization. And for a while, at least, they both have the run of an idyllic setting. Jack Rickner has "fond memories of the park,"[58] and Tom says, "the three of us made a happy family" (*PH* 198).

For Tom and his family, however, the happiness is short-lived, first through the tragic loss of Henry and then the heart-breaking disruption of the friendship between Tom and Roddy. This dissolution is in keeping with the tone of *The Professor's House* as a whole, a book in which happiness remembered as opposed to happiness currently enjoyed is the state of the family. St. Peter's nostalgic recollection, "Oh, there had been fine times in this old house then" (*PH* 125), would do nicely as a subtitle to the novel.

It was a rich week that Cather spent on the Mesa Verde. Whether she realized it or not, she was surrounded by the raw materials of one of her future stories. To what she already knew about the discovery of Cliff Palace, she was able to add not only her own experiences but also those of the people she met and the material she read. Perhaps Cather began to formulate the story during the ride back to Mancos as her former anticipation at seeing Mesa Verde doubtless gave way to her exhilaration over having seen it—indeed, of having lived it. But whatever her demeanor or occupation during the return trip, "Tom Outland's Story" was already well under way, not just in Cather's mind but also in print.

Gustaf Nordenskiold.
Courtesy Mesa Verde National Park.

*Jessee Walter Fewkes, standing before the museum
he established in 1917. Courtesy Mesa Verde National Park.*

Willa Cather at Cliff Palace.
Courtesy Helen Cather Southwick.

C. B. Kelly.
Courtesy Jean Kelly Bader.

C. B. Kelly at his livery in Mancos.
Courtesy Jean Kelly Bader.

73

Charles Mason and Anna Wetherill Mason.
Courtesy Carol Ann Wetherill.

Oddie Jeep's Tent Camp.
Courtesy Mesa Verde National Park.

Three of the group of six autos at Mesa Verde National Park,
18 May 1914.
Courtesy United States Department of the Interior,
National Park Service.

Kelly's Cabin.
Courtesy Jean Kelly Bader.

One of the tent cabins at Oddie Jeep's camp,
occupied by Jesse Walter Fewkes.
Courtesy Fred T. Jeep.

Fred and Oddie Jeep with their son Fred T. (Fritz).
Courtesy Fred T. Jeep.

The Wetherills' tree-trunk ladder.
Courtesy New Mexico State Records Center and Archives.

The five Wetherill brothers, about 1893.
From left to right: Al, Win, Richard, Clayton, and John.
Courtesy New Mexico State Records Center and Archives.

*The Wetherills' Alamo Ranch, with Mesa Verde in the
background. Photograph by Gustaf Nordenskiold, 1891.
Courtesy New Mexico State Records Center and Archives.*

Cliff Palace, from a point near Sun Temple,
the approximate view of Richard Wetherill and Charlie Mason
on the day of discovery.
Courtesy New Mexico State Records Center and Archives.

Nordenskiold's photograph of Balcony House before excavation.
Courtesy Mesa Verde National Park.

4 ✳ *I Followed the Real Story Very Closely*

 *Like The Professor's House* as a whole, "Tom Outland's Story" was begun in the middle, with the moment when Outland discovers Cliff City. In other words, as an idea for fiction the discovery episode predates the rest of "Tom Outland's Story" in the same way that the story predates the novel. The proof lies in the number of times Cather used the scene in other stories before working it out to her satisfaction—or nearly so, at least—in "Tom Outland's Story." The process is a good example of one of Cather's artistic principles, which she explains in her preface to *The Best Stories of Sarah Orne Jewett:*

> The artist spends a lifetime in loving the things that haunt him, in having his mind 'teased' by them, in trying to get these conceptions down on paper exactly as they are to him and not in conventional poses supposed to reveal their character; trying this method and that, as a painter tries different lightings and different attitudes with his subject to catch the one that presents it more suggestively than any other. (*WCOW* 51)

Cather applied these terms to herself in speaking to Elizabeth Sergeant about *The Professor's House,* which was in progress at the time. According to Sergeant's recollection, Cather's aim was "to create a work of art, out of subject matter, new or old, that had 'teased' her, and had left, as she said, a deep impression upon her."[1] The discovery episode in "Tom Outland's Story" is one of those subjects.

The discovery episode has its origins in Cather's childhood. In the river near Red Cloud, Mildred Bennett says, "near the mouth of Indian Creek, stood the island where the children fished, ran barefoot on the white sandbars and hunted treasure."[2] Bernice Slote has called that sandbar "the early center of Willa Cather's creative imagination and the symbol of first dreams."[3]

One of these dreams is the simple thrill of discovery that is an important ingredient in Cather's first literary use of the childhood memory.[4] In this adaptation, Douglass Burnham, the central character in "The Treasure of Far Island" (1902), returns to his hometown after an absence of twelve years. Now a celebrated playwright, he is also identified in terms of his past as "the original discoverer of the island" (*CSF* 266). When he sets foot upon the scene of his discovery once again, the effect upon him is quite pronounced: "Do you know, Margie, it makes me seem fifteen again to feel this sand crunching under my feet. I wonder if I ever again shall feel such a thrill of triumph as I felt when I first leaped upon this sand bar?" (*CSF* 278).

A corollary to the joy of discovery is the right to name. Although the island receives a new name every summer from the "new chief [who] claims it," "it seemed particularly to belong to the two children who christened it Far Island, partially because they were the original discoverers and claimants. . . ." (*CSF* 265).

Each of these elements reappears in subsequent treatments leading up to "Tom Outland's Story," but the thread that binds them all most closely is what Bernice Slote calls the "dreaming expectancy of youth."[5] In "The Treasure of Far Island," Margie Van Dyck says to Burnham, "You remember that night when we lay on the sand bar . . . and in the light of the driftwood fire we planned the conquest of the world?" (*CSF* 272–73). The same sentiment resurfaces a year later in the dedicatory poem of *April Twilights* (1903), when Cather alludes to the autobiographical incident behind the literary ones: "the three who lay and planned at moonrise, / On an island in a western river, / Of the conquest of the world together."[6]

As Bernice Slote explains, the allusions in these earliest dream scenes are to the old world to the east.[7] In 1909, however, retaining the mood and the setting, Cather changed the direction of her children's aspirations to the American Southwest, a part of the country that still seemed "distant and mysterious."[8] At that time Cather had not yet visited the region, but she knew enough about it (there are shades of Nordenskiold even here) to begin using some of its features, even though the story itself is still set in a very familiar locale.

In her short story "The Enchanted Bluff" (1909), a group of six boys "sworn to the spirit of the stream" (*CSF* 70) camp on a sandbar along a river in Nebraska and dream of being the first to ascend a legendary mesa where ancient Indians once lived. According to Bernice Slote, Arthur Quinn was the first to acknowledge the link between "The Enchanted Bluff" and "Tom Outland's Story" when, in 1936, he remarked that the earlier story "contains the first description of that city, high in the air, which was to become Outland's story in *The Professor's House.*"[9] Since then, others have commented in a general way upon the thematic connections. Philip Gerber, for instance, has observed that the use of a "much older civilization as a standard of measurement began in Cather's short works such as 'The Enchanted Bluff,' was promoted to the status of a major incident in *The Song of the Lark,* and became a sizable, separate section of *The Professor's House.*"[10] Beyond such broad points, however, there are a number of details in "The Enchanted Bluff" that make striking anticipations of "Tom Outland's Story."

Tip Smith tells the other boys that the place is called the Enchanted Bluff "because no white man has ever been on top of it" (*CSF* 74); likewise, the "old settlers" tell Tom Outland that "nobody had ever climbed" Blue Mesa (*PH* 186). The Indians whose ruins await discovery "were a peaceful tribe," Tip Smith continues, "that made cloth and pottery, and they went up there to get out of the wars. You see, they could pick off any war party that tried to get up their little steps" (*CSF* 74). Father Duchene's words reiterate these same points. After praising the ceramic and textile arts of the people who had isolated themselves in their Blue Mesa "stronghold," the priest surmises that "they possibly declined in the arts of war, in brute strength and ferocity" (*PH* 220). Both ancient groups met similar fates. When they descended to the plains to hunt, the Indians of Tip Smith's legend were massacred by "a war party from the north" (*CSF* 74), while the Blue Mesa Indians "were probably wiped out, utterly exterminated, by some roving Indian tribe without culture or domestic virtues" (*PH* 221). Even the geographical features are similar. No one has yet discovered the ruins atop the Enchanted Bluff because the top is "bigger than the base. The bluff is sort of worn away for several hundred feet up. That's one reason it's so hard to climb" (*CSF* 75). Likewise, the Blue Mesa is "inaccessible" because of its "unbroken top layer" that "projected out over the erosions like a granite shelf" (*PH* 195).

In "Tom Outland's Story" the diction changes toward words more precise and mature, but the content has changed hardly at all. It is as if the same scene were being described from two different perspectives, the first youthful and fairly brimming with exuberance, the second older and more deliberative. For Cather and her characters alike, this is precisely the case.

The major part of "Tom Outland's Story" not found in "The Enchanted Bluff" is fulfillment. None of the six boys in the story ever achieves his dream; nonetheless, the story ends with the dream still alive: "Bert [Tip Smith's son and, of course, another boy] has been let into the story, and thinks of nothing but the Enchanted Bluff" (*CSF* 77). To a lesser extent, this preoccupation with discovering Indian ruins applies to Cather as well. In the years following 1909, she certainly thought of other things, but clearly she never forgot the dream either. As Mildred Bennett has observed, "the climactic episode connected with these memories is reached in . . . *The Professor's House* (1925), when Tom Outland discovers the little city of stone in the side of his enchanted bluff, the Blue Mesa."[11] Before that can happen, however, Cather would work the story through three other forms.

The dream next appears, though only briefly, in the first of Cather's two first novels, *Alexander's Bridge* (1912). On his way from New York to Moorlock, where there are serious problems with his new bridge, Bartley Alexander happens to glance out the window of his day-coach to see "a group of boys . . . sitting around a little fire." The image recalls the perspective of Douglass Burnham in "The Treasure of Far Island," but there are some significant differences: Burnham eagerly changes seats so that he can see the island, which he knows is approaching, and which he beholds with joyous anticipation; Alexander's view is accidental—and remorseful:

> Alexander looked back wistfully at the boys, camped on the edge of a little marsh, crouching under their shelter and looking gravely at their fire. They took his mind back a long way, to a campfire on a sandbar in a Western river, and he wished he could go back and sit down with them. He could remember exactly how the world had looked then.[12]

Alexander's recollection serves Cather's purpose in this text by highlighting the sad discrepancy between youthful dreams and adult inadequacies and disillusionment: "And those boys back there, beginning it all just as he had begun it; he wished he could promise them luck" (*AB* 96). More than this, however, the scene contributes to the progression of Cather's own dream by conjuring up the aspirations toward discovery held by those six boys camped on the sandbar in "The Enchanted Bluff." Furthermore, in the urban, Jamesian world of *Alexander's Bridge,* this homely scene seems curiously out of place, almost as if, beyond its immediate purpose, Cather had inserted it partly as a reminder to herself that here was something she wanted to develop later, once she had found her vein.

A few months after the publication of *Alexander's Bridge,* Cather finally made her first trip to the Southwest, seeing first-hand the country that had already begun inspiring parts of her fiction.

> Soon after the book was published I went for six months to Arizona and New Mexico. The longer I stayed in a country I really did care about, and among people who were a part of the country, the more unnecessary and superficial a book like *Alexander's Bridge* seemed to me. I did no writing down there, but I recovered from the conventional editorial point of view. (*WCOW* 92)

Perhaps it was actually being in the region that prompted Cather to think of the cliff dwellers as material not just for a passage here and there in longer works about other things but as material for an entire novel. At any rate, in a letter from Winslow, Arizona, she proposed that very idea to her friend George Seibel as material that she was saving for him to develop.[13]

Maybe Cather was saving the material, but in the fall of 1913 she also began using it herself, in "The Ancient People," one of six parts of her longest novel, *The Song of the Lark,* which was published in October 1915, only two months after her return from Mesa Verde.[14] In this narrative, the theme of discovering an ancient civilization becomes more prominent, more fully realized, and more personal than in any of the earlier treatments. Thea Kronborg does not discover the ruins in "The Enchanted Bluff" sense of being the first person from the modern world to see them, however. Instead, she seeks them out as objects of intense and long-standing interest, and once among them she begins to discover herself. (It is not until Tom Outland's discovery that both senses of the word are invoked.) For

Thea, the process of self-discovery begins even before she enters Panther Canyon for her sojourn among the ruins:

> Thea seemed to be taking very little through the wood with her. The personality of which she was so tired seemed to let go of her. The high, sparkling air drank it up like blotting-paper. It was lost in the thrilling blue of the new sky and the song of the thin wind in the *piñons*. The old, fretted lines which marked one off, which defined her—made her Thea Kronborg, Bowers's accompanist, a soprano with a faulty middle voice—were all erased.[15]

This much accomplished, Thea begins to see the experience as one of rediscovery:

> She was getting back to the earliest sources of gladness that she could remember. She had loved the sun, and the brilliant solitudes of sand and sun, long before these other things had come along to fasten themselves upon her and torment her. (*SL* 369)

Perhaps it is for this reason that Thea, no doubt like Cather herself, had always been interested in "the Cliff-Dweller ruins" and had "always wanted to go down there" (*SL* 361).

Like "The Enchanted Bluff," "The Ancient People" anticipates many of the details in "Tom Outland's Story." In Panther Canyon, all the houses "were clean with the cleanness of sun-baked, wind-swept places. . . ." (*SL* 371); likewise, in Cliff City "there was little rubbish or disorder. As Blake remarked, wind and sun are good house-keepers" (*PH* 208). Panther Canyon was once inhabited by "timid, nest-building folk, like the swallows" (*SL* 375), people akin to those who, declining in the arts of war, occupied the town called Cliff City, which "hung like a bird's nest in the cliff" (*PH* 213). "Old Henry Biltmer . . . had gathered up a whole chestful of Cliff-Dweller relics which he meant to take back to Germany with him some day" (*SL* 377). In "Tom Outland's Story," another German collector, Fechtig, takes a freight car full of artifacts back home with him.

More than these details, however, it is the meaning of the discovery, the effect it has upon her, that matters most to Thea and to Cather. Thea remembers "Ray Kennedy's moralizing about the cliff cities," his gift of sympathy that identified with "the hardness of the human struggle" exemplified by those ruins and that "made one feel an obligation to do one's best" (*SL* 375). Against this backdrop, Thea begins to feel an obligation, too. "She found herself trying to walk as they [the Indian women] must have walked" (*SL* 376), and she finally realizes that the ancient people "had lengthened her past" and given her "older and higher obligations" (*SL* 383). These are the rewards, not just for Thea but also for Willa Cather, of "her old idea: a nest in a high cliff, full of sun" (*SL* 371).

Undoubtedly, Cather had in mind her old idea of a nest in a high cliff when she came at last to Mesa Verde in 1915. More than just ready for this trip, she was primed for an experience that would crystallize the story that had been forming for years. One can imagine her at Mancos and at Mesa Verde, not just casually visiting with C. B. Kelly, Clayton Wetherill, and the Rickner family; not just touring the town and the ruins as idle curiosities; but approaching them with the same enthusiasm as those boys on the sandbar, with the same expectations as Thea Kronborg. George Seibel once described the child Willa Cather as "a flesh and blood dictograph— eyes in every pore."[16] It must have been in this attitude that Cather began absorbing and storing a wealth of material for a new story that would come closer than any other to expressing the old idea. At Mesa Verde and at Mancos respectively, Cather had found not only the grandest cliff dwellings in the country but also the home of the people who had discovered them.

To see more effectively the context in which all this was happening and the direction toward the story Cather would tell, it will be helpful to backtrack to the beginning of the story that Cather was told when she called upon Clayton Wetherill in Mancos.

In 1888, while Willa Cather was helping her father fight his political battles in Red Cloud, Nebraska,[17] a family of Quaker cowboys in southwestern Colorado were trying to make a living on their Alamo Ranch. Because the father, B. K. Wetherill, was in poor health, most of the work was done by his sons: Richard, John, Al, Clayton, and Winslow. While tending to their ranching chores, the Wetherill brothers had also been hearing stories of ancient Indians having lived in the mesa and had been finding evidence of these early habitations. Then on or about 18 December, as they were "on a cruise of exploration,"[18] Richard Wetherill and his brother-in-law Charlie Mason happened to pass along the edge of a canyon. Then they stopped and stared in amazement at the opposite wall. What they saw was Cliff Palace, "the grandest view of all among the ancient ruins of the Southwest," as Mason himself described it. Although they were seeing it for the first time, they were not really surprised to find it because Richard's brother Al had said he had caught a glimpse of the same ruins the year before as he trudged toward camp through the canyon below. The two cowboys then "rode around the head of the canon [sic] and found a way down over the cliffs to the level of the buildings."[19] Then, quite literally, they stepped into history, both the ancient Indians' and their own.

Such, anyway, is the familiar and generally received version of the discovery, the one that Cather probably heard. Although there is no point in disputing it, it should be noted that for decades afterward—and in some quarters even today—the actual discoverer of Cliff Palace remained a point of considerable debate. No fewer than ten other people claimed to have seen the ruin years before Wetherill and Mason did, although only in one case, that of a prospector named S. E. Osborn, does the claim itself predate 1888.[20] As Frank

McNitt says, Cather never became involved in this controversy,[21] yet it seems unlikely that she was unaware of it, especially considering that both C. B. Kelly and Jesse Walter Fewkes knew about it. In fact, it is Fewkes whom McNitt blames for inciting the controversy with his 1910 report on Cliff Palace that gives credence to one of the counter-claimants, a local man named James Frink. And if Cather was familiar with Fewkes's writing, there is additional reason to believe that she must have heard something about the controversy. Therefore, one can safely conclude that Cather rejected these complications of Richard Wetherill's story because they did not fit into her artistic design.[22]

The interview between Cather and Clayton Wetherill is discussed at length in chapter 2. What is of additional interest here is Cather's recollection of this interview over twenty years later:

> ... the Blue Mesa (the Mesa Verde) actually was discovered by a young cowpuncher in just this way [that is, as told in "Tom Outland's Story"]. The great explorer Nordenskjold wrote a scientific book about this discovery, and I myself had the good fortune to hear the story of it from a very old man, brother of Dick Wetherell [sic]. Dick Wetherell as a young boy forded Mancos River and rode into the Mesa after lost cattle. I followed the real story very closely in Tom Outland's narrative.[23] (*WCOW* 32)

Three points in this account are especially intriguing. The first is Cather's description of the Wetherill brother as "a very old man." In 1915 Richard Wetherill, had he lived, would have been only 57; Clayton, the second to youngest of the five brothers, was only 47, just five years older than Cather herself and, as John Murphy has remarked, hardly an age that one would term "very old."[24] Secondly, at age 30 in 1888 Richard could hardly have been the "young boy" that Cather says he was. Finally, these two points tend to make the reader a little suspicious of Cather's concluding assertion: "I followed the real story very closely in Tom Outland's narrative."[25] Indeed, an examination of the available material shows that, rather than follow Richard Wetherill's story very closely, Cather departed from it in a number of significant ways to produce a story almost completely her own.

The first instance of this departure is the newspaper essay that Cather wrote a few months after her visit to Mancos and Mesa Verde. Rosowski and Slote identify the 1916 essay as " 'Tom Outland's Story' in embryo."[26] It is also the first example of the creative method by which "Tom Outland's Story" as a whole was composed. This small story, then, becomes an emblem of the larger one; and differences become even more illuminating than similarities as Cather tells her version of Richard Wetherill's discovery:

one must always think with envy of the entrada of Richard Wetherill, the first white man who discovered the ruins in its [Mesa Verde's] canons [sic] forty-odd years ago. Until that time the mesa was entirely unexplored, and was known only as a troublesome place into which cattle wandered off, and from which they never came back. All the country about it was open range. The Wetherills had a ranch west of Mancos. One December day a boy brought word to the ranch house that a bunch of cattle had got away and gone up into the mesa. The same thing had happened before, and young Richard Wetherill said that this time he was going after his beasts. He rode off with one of his cow men and they entered the mesa by a deep canon from the Mancos river, which flows at its base. They followed the canon toward the heart of the mesa until they could go no farther with horses. They tied their mounts and went on foot up a side canon, now called Cliff canon. After a long stretch of hard climbing young Wetherill happened to glance up at the great cliffs above him, and there, thru a veil of lightly falling snow, he saw practically as it stands today and as it had stood for 800 years before, the cliff palace. . . . ("MV")

Although this account may seem accurate in general, its details are quite different from those of the actual event. To begin with, Richard was not the first white man to discover ruins in Mesa Verde, a fact noted by the park brochure for 1915 in its discussion of the expeditions of Jackson and Holmes. In fact, Anglo excursions had begun as early as the mid-nineteenth century,[27] so that by 1888 Mesa Verde and its treasures, far from being "entirely unexplored," were already familiar to a great many people. Moreover, Richard's discovery was more recent than Cather says, having been made fewer than thirty years before, not the "forty-odd" of the essay. Furthermore, Mesa Verde could be "a troublesome place" for cows to graze, but it was also highly desirable. In fact, the Wetherills enjoyed the unique privilege of Ute permission to graze their cows there, and other ranchers used the mesa for grazing even without this permission. As a result, by the time Jesse Nusbaum became park superintendent in 1921, the mesa "had been overgrazed for years."[28] The boy who "brought word . . . that a bunch of cattle had got away" is apparently an invention, as none of the other accounts of Richard's discovery mention him at all. Finally, the most striking divergence, which several people have noted, is Cather's version of Richard's physical point of view: at the bottom of Cliff Canyon looking up rather than the actual point of view from the opposite rim of the canyon looking almost straight across. It may be, as Rosowski and Slote suggest, that Cather has simply confused Richrd's perspective with that of his brother Al about a year earlier;[29] or perhaps, as William Howarth has suggested, Cather is remembering her own view of Swallows Nest as she and Lewis were being led to Fewkes's camp.[30]

At any rate, not even in this essay—ostensibly more fact than fiction—does Cather follow the particulars of Richard's story "very closely." It would seem, then, that the romanticist in Willa Cather is already imbuing in Richard Wetherill some of the special traits and circumstances that would reach full growth in Tom Outland. As one recent critic has observed, Cather was like most Americans, "more concerned with myth than with history."[31] In Cather's case, this interest extends to the point of creating myth out of history: by putting the actual historical incident a little farther into the past, Cather makes it seem more like a legend; and by making her Wetherill hero much younger than the real one, she invokes the youthful romanticism—"the eternal boy in us" (*KA* 323)—of those boys on the sandbar in "The Enchanted Bluff" and *Alexander's Bridge.*

By the time she wrote *The Professor's House,* Cather had left her acknowledged Wetherill model so far behind that a juxtaposition of significant details from both history and fiction becomes a nearly consistent study of contrasts, suggesting not a derivative story but a new creation—its parts cleaner, simpler, and more ideal than those of the historical incident that inspired it. "Art," Cather said, "should simplify" (*WCOW* 102).

Like the "mythic heroes, Tom Outland is of obscure origins."[32] An orphan uncertain of his age, he arouses the reader's sympathy and assumes the role of a man who must make his way in the world alone.[33] Quite fittingly, Outland "reads the myth of the castaway in its various forms—Book II of the *Aeneid, Gulliver's Travels, Robinson Crusoe.*"[34] He also joins the ranks of other American literary orphans—Huckleberry Finn, Ishmael, and Billy Budd—as well as the other orphaned characters, some of them still with families, of Cather's own creation: Paul, Don Hedger, Jim Burden, Niel Herbert, Lucy Gayheart, and Jacques Gaux. Despite his uncertain age, however, Outland is clearly youthful enough to fulfill the "young boy" role that Cather had first assigned to Richard Wetherill. Richard, of course, was part of a large nuclear family, and he knew how old he was.

The Blue Mesa is virtually inaccessible and, like Mesa Verde in the essay and like the Enchanted Bluff, still unexplored. As those "old settlers" told Tom Outland, "nobody had ever climbed" Blue Mesa; thus it remains a remote and mysterious challenge, a stronghold still protecting a treasure yet to be claimed by someone worthy of it. Quite the opposite of this romantic myth, by 1888 Mesa Verde—or at least certain parts of it—had been explored by several parties and individuals; artifacts had been removed; and the canyons and ruins had been surveyed, mapped, sketched, photographed, and described.

Tom Outland is the sole, undisputed discoverer of Cliff City. Unlike Richard Wetherill, he is unaccompanied at the time of the discovery, and afterward he is not bothered by jealous prior claimants or complications or controversy of any kind. Rather, the discovery remains a quiet private moment of inspiration and rejuvenation as Outland gazes reverentially upward from the canyon below, standing where Cather's Richard Wetherill had stood.

Tom Outland discovers Cliff City not on just any day in December but on Christmas Eve, suggesting the rebirth of an older, better world as well as a personal redemption for Outland himself.[35] Full of reverence for his discovery, Outland is tempted to preserve the secret. Not until several hours after his return to camp does he tell Roddy Blake and Henry Atkins. By contrast, Wetherill and Mason told the first people they saw as soon as they saw them, three acquaintances in another camp for whom Richard drew a map showing the location of Cliff Palace.[36] As Outland and Blake plan their excavation of Cliff City, they are still inclined to preserve the sanctity of the ruins: "We didn't want to make our discovery any more public than necessary. We were reluctant to expose those silent and beautiful places to vulgar curiosity" (*PH* 205). Richard Wetherill took the tourists there himself, and soon after their discoveries he and his brothers tried to impress collections of artifacts upon audiences in Durango and Denver, who remained uninterested until, in a move that P. T. Barnum would have admired, the Wetherills included the mummy of a child found by Clayton and Charlie Mason.[37]

Tom Outland disdains both money and museums. To Mrs. St. Peter he *gives* a complete pot, but he will not have any of his artifacts placed in a museum. Richard and his brothers sought museums (much to their credit, incidentally), conducted paid tours, and sold photographs and whole collections of relics.

Finally, in the aftermath of his discovery, Tom Outland, this "boy of such humble pretensions" (*PH* 231), goes to Washington to try to interest officials at the Smithsonian in excavating and preserving the ruins. The bureaucratic runaround and indifference that he encounters are now almost legendary. In actual fact, as noted in chapter 2, it was B. K. Wetherill, not Richard, who made the initial contact with the Smithsonian—and that through the mail, not in person. Also in actual fact, the Smithsonian was more interested in the project than Cather's version allows, even though it was several years before the institution took any action.

If Cather knew these facts, she chose to rearrange them. For her purposes, cold rejection in person is far more poignant than luke-warm encouragement through the mail. Furthermore, as John Murphy explains, Tom's trip to Washington allows Cather to contrast "the worst aspects of the city of the present . . . with the best aspects of the city of the past."[38] Finally, there is the built-in theme of West versus East, exemplified here with irresistible romantic opposition: little man from the West with a truly significant find meets "crushing indifference"[39] of large impersonal institution in the East. This was not the real story, but it certainly makes a better story. As Cather herself once remarked, "in novels, as in poetry, the facts are nothing, the feeling is everything" (*WCOW* 84).

That these divergences from fact are deliberate, calculated to heighten the qualities merely suggested by the historical incident, can be further demonstrated by noting the few significant compo-nents that Cather has left unchanged. It is still a humble cowboy, a sort of western Everyman, who makes one of the grandest archae-ological finds of the century. There is still a light snow falling that at once obscures and reveals the scene like a vision in a dream[40] (one thinks of the snowflakes in *One of Ours* that grace the Wheeler farm with a "faint purity, like a fragrance almost too fine for human senses" [*OO* 84]). And there is still the reverence for the ruins, irresistible and everlasting, a reverence not so much for the dead as for an abandoned way of life, ancient and honorable, whose most mundane possessions inspire awe.

Willa Cather found in Richard Wetherill's story a historical frame upon which to build her "old idea," the dramatization of that personal myth of discovery in the Southwest that had been haunting her for so long and that she had been trying to write at least since "The Enchanted Bluff." No doubt encouraged by the Wetherill story, Cather began in 1916 to write "Tom Outland's Story" itself under the title "The Blue Mesa."[41] True to form, however, she had to put the manuscript aside to allow time for the "shapes and scenes" to "get themselves rightly put down" (*WCOW* 48); therefore, it was not until 1922, apparently, that she finally completed the story[42] and not until 1924, it seems, that she renamed it.[43]

It now becomes clear that the moment when Tom Outland looks up from the canyon floor and sees "a little city of stone, asleep" is more than just a memorable scene in a good story; it is the culmination of years of thinking, feeling, and writing. Several stories and experiences fuse as yet another boy actually discovers, both for himself and for the world, such a place as those boys on the sandbar had only imagined and such a place as Thea Kronborg and Willa Cather herself were shown.[44] To borrow a phrase from Alexandra Bergson, it is a case of "the old story writing itself over."[45] For Cather, this scene must have been personally satisfying, especially as Tom Outland is Cather's "dream self."[46]

The vicarious pleasures do not end here, however. Cather adds yet another dimension to the relationship by having Professor Godfrey St. Peter, with whom she is often identified, himself identify with Tom Outland. Susan Rosowski offers this succinct account of the process: "In turning to Outland for his second youth years ago, St. Peter had found a surrogate, and in evoking his memory now [as he recalls Tom Outland's story and as he prepares to edit Tom Outland's diary], he gives himself up to the memory so completely that the surrogate (Outland) and the speaker (St. Peter) merge."[47] Therefore, in a scene rich with suggestive complexities, one character identifies with another, and the author identifies with them both, first individually and then collectively, as one narrative mask fits inside another. One sees here a telling instance of a technique that Cather herself once described:

> When a writer has a strong or revelatory experience with his characters, he unconsciously creates a scene; gets a depth of picture, and writes, as it were, in three dimensions instead of two. (*WCOW* 80)

Evidently, however, not even this richness was enough to satisfy Cather for long. She never reused the discovery story in any subsequent work, but she did rewrite some of its origin when, thirteen years after the novel was published, she described her Wetherill source as "a very old man." With this one stroke, Cather enhances the picturesque aura of his tale and gives the teller something of the status of an oracle, two more features characteristic of myth. It would seem that the "old idea" had continued to tease her; or perhaps, after all those years, she was just reluctant to let it go.

5 ❊ *In a World Above the World*

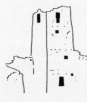*The myth of discovery* that had been working itself out for so long, encroaching first upon one story and then another, finally found its own vessel in "Tom Outland's Story." When Willa Cather claimed later that this discovery episode was historically authentic, she may not have meant to extend the claim to the rest of "Tom Outland's Story," but she could have: not because it is authentic but because it deviates from history in the same way and for the same reasons that Tom Outland's discovery of Cliff City deviates from Richard Wetherill's discovery of Cliff Palace. In fact, from its central position in the story, spatial as well as thematic, the discovery episode provides a compositional precedent for the rest of the narrative. The same creative rationale that transformed Richard Wetherill's story into a cleaner, simpler, and more ideal Tom Outland's story is also at work in virtually everything else Cather says about the Blue Mesa experience from beginning to end.

To perceive it rightly, one needs to read the story with this creative rationale in mind. Otherwise, the reader is likely to accept the historical, archaeological, and geological conditions at face value—the way, for instance, so many readers have done with Cather's portrayal of the Smithsonian Institution.[1] To do so is to miss both the departures from fact and Cather's reasons for making

102

them, and thus to miss the significance of "Tom Outland's Story" as a whole. As history, "Tom Outland's Story" is misleading; as archaeology, it is naive; and as geology it is exaggerated; but as art—especially as a demonstration of an artful imagination at work—it is rich and rewarding.

As soon as Cather hires out Tom Outland and Roddy Blake to the Sitwell Cattle Company, she begins enhancing the facts with her fiction. After riding the range with the cattle during the summer, Tom and Roddy are to take the herd to the winter camp, which "was down on the Cruzados river, directly under the [Blue] mesa" (*PH* 187). Bernice Slote suggests that the Cruzados is based upon rivers and creeks around Red Cloud and in Virgil's *Georgics*.[2] A more likely prototype, however, is the Mancos, originally called Rio de los Mancos, which Cather mentions in her 1916 essay and which parallels the Cruzados by running directly under the east side of Mesa Verde. Whether Cather knew anything about the origin of the name,[3] her well known fear of mutilation, especially the loss of a hand, must have made her take note of the word "mancos" itself, which means one-handed, or maimed or defective. For one of her stories that deal with mutilation, this name might have been just the thing; for this one, however, she needed something else, so she used another Spanish term, Cruzados.

Well chosen and illustrative like so many of the names in Cather's fiction, this one is even richer than most.[4] A form of the word *cruz,* or cross, the name Cruzados anticipates the religious significance that Tom Outland assigns to the cliff dwellings in Blue Mesa. It also calls to mind the patronymic of Godfrey St. Peter, the Biblical St. Peter, whose unusual crucifixion became part of Christian lore. Finally, it anticipates the burden that Tom Outland will eventually assume, a burden that finally proves too much for him.

Other meanings also apply. A *cruzado* is an old Spanish gold or silver coin. In this sense, the name of the river recalls the theme of corruption through money that Book I of *The Professor's House* has already defined so well, and it foreshadows Roddy Blake's resigned observation in Book II that everything comes "to money in the end" (*PH* 244).[5]

One more meaning of the word *cruzado* is particularly helpful in defining Tom Outland's character and in affirming the significance of his subsequent actions. A *cruzado* is also a crusader, quite literally, one who bears the cross. That Cather intends this association between Outland and a centuries-old romantic tradition becomes apparent through her use of the river that bears the name.

The Cruzados presents the first obstacle to the summer-long plans that Tom and Roddy make to "climb the mesa and be the first men up there" (*PH* 187), a plan that their foreman John Rapp is quick to discourage:

> The only way into it [Blue Mesa] is through that deep canyon that opens on the water level, just where the river makes the bend. You can't get in by that, because the river's too deep to ford and too swift to swim. Oh, I suppose a horse could swim it, if cattle can, but I don't want to be the man to try. (*PH* 191)

When Tom Outland announces his intention to be the man to try it, Rapp cuts him off with the promise of firing him for the attempt: "You'd break your bones and lose the herd for us" (*PH* 191). Obviously, in Rapp's estimation trying to climb the Blue Mesa is neither safe nor smart. Then later in the story Roddy reiterates this opinion, at least in part, when he cautions Henry about the venture that he and Tom are considering: "You may get a bad cold going over the river. . . . It's bad crossing—makes you dizzy when you take to swimming. You have to keep your head" (*PH* 205).

As is so often the case, however, the warnings fail to dissuade. Camped in the very shadow of the mesa, Outland and Blake cannot ignore their "tantalizing" neighbor (*PH* 191), "admirably inaccessible in its mystery."[6] Sometimes it is "red with sunrise," sometimes it blazes like a "volcanic mountain," and sometimes it looks "like one great ink-black rock against a sky on fire" (*PH* 192–193). "No wonder the thing bothered us and tempted us," Tom says; "it was always before us, and was always changing" (*PH* 193). Ironically, though, this siren's song is not so much seductive as threatening:

> I've never heard thunder so loud as it was there. The cliffs threw it back at us, and we thought the mesa itself, though it seemed so solid, must be full of deep canyons and caverns, to account for the prolonged growl and rumble that followed every crash of thunder. After the burst in the sky was over, the mesa went on sounding like a drum, and seemed itself to be muttering and making noises. (*PH* 193)

Even the skyline of the mesa seems forboding, "like the profile of a big beast lying down" (*PH* 191). This image recalls Thea Kronborg's Panther Canyon (the innocuous sounding Walnut Canyon rechristened) and evokes what Bernice Slote calls the "primitive, animal forces" that Willa Cather equated with creativity.[7]

Although it makes little impact upon Outland and Blake, Rapp's warning about the dangerous river serves Cather's purpose in another way by laying the romantic foundation for Outland's discovery: it becomes the harbinger of peril that typically introduces a quest narrative, like the cryptic message of Elijah in *Moby-Dick*. From a practical standpoint, of course, if there were no significant obstacle to challenge Cather's adventurer, someone else would have already found Cliff City. From a more romantic view, however, one to which Cather certainly subscribed, the value of a prize increases in proportion to the difficulty encountered in obtaining it; therefore, once Outland passes the test of the "bad crossing"—an intentional pun, probably, on the name of the river—he has proven his mettle and earned the right of discovery. All of this comes straight out of the tradition of romance literature. To use it, however, Cather had to embellish the facts of Mesa Verde topography.

The Mancos River does run "thru the middle of the town," as

Cather says in her 1916 essay, but it was never an imposing water-way like the Cruzados or even like the Mancos that Cather's Richard Wetherill had to swim. Nordenskiold calls it "a little stream" and never mentions any difficulty in crossing it.[8] Speaking more poetically, Frank McNitt describes it as "a twisting thread of blue silk" when seen from the mesa top and, like Nordenskiold, never mentions Richard or anyone else being particularly wary in crossing it.[9] William Henry Jackson had some difficulty at a point where the perpendicular banks presented "an extremely trouble-some matter to cross," but even at that point he described the current as "sluggish."[10] Moreover, the Mancos was so inconsistent in supplying water for irrigation that a priority system had to be established for water claims by ranchers;[11] and, according to a friend of the Wetherills, it was only during the winter and spring, thanks to melting snow, that the river might have achieved "really substantial volume," and even at that a horse and rider would have forded the river rather than swum it.[12] None of this mattered to Cather, of course, because even a sluggish little stream was more than enough to suggest the formidable river that her story needed.

Another obstacle that Cather puts in Outland's way, one that works in concert with the river, is the geologic formation of the mesa itself. In this case, the barrier is not an exaggeration of a natural formation, like the Cruzados, but a complete invention. Not long after settling into the winter camp and the routine of the work, Outland rides completely around the mesa to get "a better idea of its actual structure":

All the way round were the same precipitous cliffs of hard blue rock, but in places it was mixed with a much softer stone. In these soft streaks there were deep dry watercourses which could certainly be climbed as far as they went, but nowhere did they reach to the top of the mesa. The top seemed to be one great slab of very hard rock, lying on the mixed mass of the base like the top of an old-fashioned marble table. The channels worn out by water ran for hundreds of feet up the cliffs, but always stopped under this great rim-rock, which projected out over the erosions like a granite shelf. Evidently, it was because of this unbroken top layer that the butte was inaccessible. I rode back to camp that night, convinced that if we ever climbed it, we must take the route the cattle took, through the river and up the one canyon that broke down to water-level. (*PH* 195)

Mesa Verde is not crowned by a "great rim-rock" that projects over the edges like the top of a table. Certainly there are precipitous places, and in the canyons that house the cliff dwellings the harder rock does protrude like a roof over the places where the softer sandstone has been eroded; but the overall effect of the mesa and its canyons is that of a more tapering ascent than the one Cather ascribes to Blue Mesa. As one Mesa Verde historian has noted, from the point of highest elevation in the park (Park Point, at 8,572 feet) "one can easily see how the present plateau slopes gently to the south where the elevation is about 6,000 feet...."[13] There is one spot that corresponds somewhat to the geology of Blue Mesa, Park Point. But rather than a flat slab, it is a "huge jutting mass of rock"[14] that from a distance blends unnoticed into the Mesa Verde skyline; it is only as one approaches the mesa, particularly from the east, that the mass becomes distinguishable.

Obviously, when she came to the creation of her mesa, Cather rejected the topography she saw at Mesa Verde and formed instead a rock like the one in "The Enchanted Bluff." This barrier, together with the river so difficult to cross, further insures that Outland has not been preceded by a Moss, Jackson, Holmes, or McClurg. It also dictates that Cather's hero enter the mesa "through the river" (*PH* 195).

I strapped my blanket and my lunch on my shoulders, hung my boots around my neck to keep them dry, stuffed my socks inside my hat, and we waded in. My horse took the water without any fuss, though he shivered a good deal. He stepped out very carefully, and when it got too deep for him, he swam without panic. We were carried down-stream a little by the current, but I didn't have to slide off his back. He found bottom after a while, and we easily made a landing. I waved good-bye to Henry on the other side and started up the canyon, running beside my horse to get warm. (*PH* 199)

The mundane diction and details in this passage belie the greater significance of the experience. When he crosses the Cruzados, Outland receives his baptism and begins his crusade. This crossing also marks Outland's entry into a mystical realm to which he responds as if transfixed. When he makes his Christmas-Eve discovery of "a little city of stone, asleep," he finds it difficult to objectify the experience, as if he were a shepherd or a wise man finally standing before the stable in Bethlehem:[15] "I wish I could tell you what I saw there. . . ." (*PH* 201); "I can't describe it" (*PH* 202). Even so, Outland is certainly able to respond to it on its own mystical terms: "Such silence and stillness and repose—immortal repose. That village sat looking down into the canyon with the calmness of eternity. The falling snow-flakes, sprinkling the piñons, gave it a special kind of solemnity" (*PH* 201–2). This moment is the beginning of Outland's transformation, which is symbolized by his crossing the river. Cliff City may be asleep, but its discoverer experiences a profound awakening.

To facilitate this awakening, Cather makes Cliff City a much more habitable and inviting place than Cliff Palace or any of the other ruins in Mesa Verde. Small and intimate, it is not a simple reproduction of Cliff Palace but, like so many of Cather's characters, a composite, displaying features that Cather probably adapted from at least the three other ruins already discussed: Daniels House, Swallows Nest, and Spruce Tree House.

Once they enter the village, Tom and Roddy find it uncommonly pleasant and appealing. Tom says, "everything seemed open and clean, and the stones, I remember, were warm to the touch, smooth and pleasant to feel." Cliff City is also remarkably neat: "Here and there a cedar log in the ceiling had given way and let the second-story chamber down into the first; except for that, there was little rubbish or disorder. As Blake remarked, wind and sun are good housekeepers" (*PH* 208).

This may have been the way Cliff Palace looked when Cather and Lewis saw it, but it is hardly the way it looked when it was discovered. If Cather's own observation of Tower House did not reveal the true condition of an unexcavated and unstabilized ruin, the accounts in the park brochure and in Nordenskiold's book must have.

Notice in the park brochure of the debris found in the ruins is brief and matter-of-fact, as in the account of an ancient passageway, "hitherto unknown," that was found deep "under the debris which covered the lower terrace of Cliff Palace."[16] Such sifting through debris is hardly unusual. Jackson found rooms in several of the ruins he inspected to be half-filled with debris,[17] and Jesse Fewkes had to spend most of his time clearing away debris before the ruins could be stabilized and repaired and opened to the public.[18] No doubt Cather heard details of this kind of work during Fewkes's campfire talks.

More graphic images come from Nordenskiold, both in the photographs and in the text. Even if Cather had only thumbed through most of the book, she could not have missed the black and white images of ruined towers and walls protruding from piles of rubble. In the accompanying text, Nordenskiold speaks at one point of digging through "about half a metre of dust and rubbish";[19] at another site he and his crew faced about twice that thickness of debris, to their obvious discomfort:

> My two men worked hard; yet it took a day and a half completely to clear the estufa. The removal of the rubbish gave them little trouble; a single push of the spade sent it over the

precipice. Great inconvenience was caused, on the other hand, by the fine dust, which rose in dense clouds at each blow of the spade.[20]

For one of Nordenskiold's workers, the memory of these conditions was still fresh after sixty years when he recalled dust so fine and deep that the crews could work in it only twenty or thirty minutes at a time.[21] Cather must have heard similar stories from Clayton Wetherill too. Al Wetherill, for instance, remembered that practically all of Nordenskiold's collection "was made from digging in the refuse heaps, which covered the much desired information. Taking turns, Richard, John and I swallowed more quantities of mummy dust."[22] Another of the Wetherills' friends and clients, physician and Columbia University professor T. Mitchell Prudden, wrote about the "resolution" required "to be a voluntary scavenger in a prehistoric rubbish heap. The air is hot, the dust stifling, and you may be forced to ride for many miles before you find water enough to wash from your person these pulverized relics of humanity."[23]

Just how noxious this dust of ages can be is even more tellingly revealed in this account of the excavation of a small ruin in Fewkes Canyon directed by Jesse Nusbaum. Several years before, Fewkes had attempted the job himself but abandoned it because of the "darkness, dust, and deep deposits of rat nests and cactus":

> Nusbaum returned to the site equipped with lanterns and respirators, but even so the crew could bear the oppressive conditions only for thirty-minute intervals before they had to retreat for fresh air. There was room only for three men to work at a time, and the cave was in total darkness. They could only work a total of four hours per day before exhuastion made it impossible to continue. . . .[24]

Mercifully, Tom Outland and Roddy Blake are spared any exposure to such choking conditions.[25] All they must do is walk about

softly, trying "not to disturb anything," and observe the unbroken
water jars and bowls and the yucca-fibre mats (*PH* 208). The debris
of reality would only intrude upon the magic of this moment and
lessen the impact of the awe-inspiring scene.

In addition to a clean site, Cather provides more illumination
than reality would allow, even in "a kind of back court-yard"
behind the houses. Outland describes this area as

> a long, low, twilit space that got gradually lower toward the
> back until the rim rock met the floor of the cavern, exactly like
> the sloping roof of an attic. There was perpetual twilight back
> there, cool, shadowy, very grateful after the blazing sun in the
> front court-yard. (*PH* 209)

In this passage there is more of Cather's attic room in the house in
Red Cloud than there is of Mesa Verde cliff dwellings. For Jesse
Nusbaum's crews, the darkness at the rear of cliff dwellings necessi-
tated the use of lanterns; for Nordenskiold, it afforded an unexpected benefit: he found a room in the interior of Spruce Tree
House to be so devoid of light that he used it as a darkroom to
develop his photographs.[26]

Another amenity that Cather furnishes in Cliff City is water:

> When we entered it [the back court-yard] we heard a soft
> trickling sound, and we came upon a spring that welled out of
> the rock into a stone basin and then ran off through a cobble-
> lined gutter and dripped down the cliffs. I've never anywhere
> tasted water like it; as cold as ice, and so pure. Long afterward
> Father Duchene came out to spend a week with us on the
> mesa; he always carried a small drinking-glass with him, and
> he used to fill it at the spring and take it out into the sunlight.
> The water looked like liquid crystal, absolutely colourless,
> without the slight brownish or greenish tint that water nearly
> always has. It threw off the sunlight like a diamond. (*PH* 209)

If *agua es vida,* as a popular southwestern saying attests, then here is life at its purest. Here also is one of Willa Cather's richest departures from fact. Even during its ancient inhabitation there seems not to have been a spring of any consequence in Cliff Palace,[27] and during the irregular times when water appears there now, it does not well out or run but seeps or drips from cracks in the overhang.[28] The spring that Edith Lewis says she and Cather drank from[29] is evidently another of her fabrications. If she and Cather did have lunch at Cliff Palace, they brought their water with them. Conditions are not much, if any, better at other cliff dwellings. Superintendent Rickner dutifully cautioned tourists with a bent toward camping on their own that only at the spring below Spruce Tree Camp was there a reliable source of good water.[30] In 1923 just under a third of a $10,000 appropriation was earmarked to further develop this source of water. In the days before such modern enhancements, however, water was scarce, "the most scarce possession of the ancient Cliff Dwellers," one visitor surmised, "and they undoubtedly made a gallon go as far as our civilization does a hundred gallons."[31] As for the prospect of bathing, a tourist from the 1890s concluded, "even a prehistoric's unrushed life would be too short."[32]

Not only is water in short supply at Mesa Verde, most of what is there is unpalatable—and has been as long as people have been trying to drink it. In fact, its high alkaline content has inspired a number of colorful complaints. Al Wetherill said, "you can drink it if it is made up into strong coffee or tea, but even then it is villainous stuff."[33] In his book Nordenskiold displays some reserve in noting the "nauseous taste" of the water from a spring in Cliff Canyon and the "extremely injurious effect on the digestion" it would have over any lengthy period.[34] In one of his letters home, however, Nordenskiold vents his distaste: after sipping from "a spring of the most horrible, falsified water," he exclaims, "if we had swallowed half a stein full of turpentine . . . we would have had a hard time feeling any worse."[35] Finally, Chief Park Archaeologist Jack Smith suggests that, if Father Duchene had tried to fill his glass at Cliff Palace, not only would it have taken "the better part of a morning," but also the taste would have made thirst a "desirable alternative."[36]

Perhaps it is because they had an ample supply of good water that Cather's cliff dwellers were able to live "for something more than food and shelter." According to Father Duchene, their lives were enriched not just by "an appreciation of comfort" but also by a sense of architectural design:

> There is unquestionably a distinct feeling for design in what you call the Cliff City. Buildings are not grouped like that by pure accident, though convenience probably had much to do with it. Convenience often dictates very sound design. (*PH* 219)

Here again Cather enhances the facts as she saw them and read them. The impression created by most of the ruins is more a "jumble of houses," to borrow Tom Outland's phrase (*PH* 201), than the planned development described by Father Duchene. Moreover, Nordenskiold noted that "no premeditated design has been followed in the erection of the buildings [in Spruce Tree House]" and concluded that rooms were added with no other thought than to accommodate the increasing population, a circumstance that "may be observed in most of the cliff-dwellings."[37]

Another departure from fact occurs in Father Duchene's examination of the crania of the mummies, which was probably suggested by a section from Nordenskiold's *Cliff Dwellers of the Mesa Verde*. "He [Father Duchene] measured the heads of the mummies and declared they had good skulls" (*PH* 217). By contrast, Nordenskiold's colleague G. Retzius measured the heads of the Mesa Verde mummies and declared that they all exhibited an "artificial deformation . . . [that] has altered their natural form."[38] While certain skulls are "strongly developed" and "stoutly built," often with the teeth in an "excellent state of preservation,"

> we observe that in nearly all these crania an *artificial deforma-*
> *tion* has been caused in early infancy by the application of
> pressure to the *superior parieto-occipital region,* this part . . .
> having been depressed with some flat object. But this depres-
> sion *varies greatly in degree* . . . .[39]

The reason for this deformation, Retzius explains, can be found
in *Crania Ethnica Americana,* a contemporary publication by Rudolf
Virchow. According to Virchow, "this deformation may originally
have been caused not with a design to produce distortion, but from
a wish to protect the new-born child from violent concussion with
the board to which it was tied. . . ."[40] Evidently, Anasazi mothers
resorted to this arrangement out of sheer necessity. Gilbert Wenger
explains that women with tiny babies could work only if they took
their babies with them; to protect her baby's fragile neck, the
mother fastened the infant's head to a rigid, hard board cradle.[41]
Perhaps Thea Kronborg "could feel the weight of an Indian baby
hanging to her back as she climbed" (*SL* 376), but neither she nor
Willa Cather ever considered the life-long deformation thus produced, nor would either of them have been likely to agree with
these ancient people that a flattened skull was fashionable.[42]

Father Duchene also explains the fate of the people as a whole.
He concludes that they were exterminated by an uncultured tribe,
"some horde that fell upon them in their summer camp and destroyed them for their hides and clothing and weapons, or from
mere love of slaughter." Quite significantly, however, "these brutal
invaders never even learned of the existence of this mesa, hon-
eycombed with habitations. If they had come here, they would have
destroyed" (*PH* 221).

As she seems to have done with Father Duchene's other hypoth-
eses, Cather could easily have found scientific support for this one;
but the important point is that she chose this explanation for the
disappearance of the cliff dwellers over others that were also advanced by the people she read or met: simple migration, which

would have been too mundane; and a prolonged siege by enemies, which would have been too threatening to the sanctity of the mesa.[43] Cather chose instead to sacrifice the cliff dwellers but to leave the mesa inviolate so that, when Tom Outland finds it, it remains what for Cather it always has been, a holy place where ideals of all kinds—natural, physical, intellectual, and spiritual—can flourish and can inspire a receptive and harmonious soul.

Only after his return from Washington, a place as spiritually enervating as Cliff City is spiritually uplifting, is Outland able to articulate what the mesa means to him. But it is no doubt a strong intuition of this meaning that sends him to Washington in the first place, as Cather continues to develop her story along factual lines that she redraws to encompass her fiction.

"You must go to the Director of the Smithsonian Institution," Father Duchene tells Tom Outland. "He will revive this civilization in a scholarly work" (*PH* 222). The word "revive" is an ironic choice. For Outland and Blake the Blue Mesa civilization has already been revived—and they, Outland especially, have been revived in the process. But from his first contact with a Washington official, the congressman from his district, Outland finds that his Washington experience depletes rather than restores his life, an outcome foreshadowed, again ironically, by the hopeful and deliberative preparations for his trip.

Blake works on the railroad all winter to earn the money Outland will need; Outland carefully stores his diary in a niche in Eagle's Nest; they buy a trunk, "a supply of white shirts," two suits, and an outmoded clawhammer coat that a "conscienceless trader" convinced Roddy "was the proper thing for dress occasions" (*PH* 224). All this is the outfitting for Outland's crusade to Washington. There was certainly more trouble in outfitting their excavation of Cliff City, but that process Cather glosses over with a general reference to gathering "supplies." Here, the anticipation is more pronounced, in direct proportion to the disappointment that follows. "I think Roddy expected that I would be received by ambassadors," Tom says, adding that he must have thought so, too (*PH* 224).

Traveling in ambassadorial style with a berth on a Pullman,[44] Outland watches his mesa recede into the western sky-line:

> I hated to leave it, but I reflected that it had taken care of itself without me for a good many hundred years. When I saw it again, I told myself, I would have done my duty by it; I would bring back with me men who would understand it, who would appreciate it and dig out all its secrets. (*PH* 224)

He brings back, instead, a disillusioned view of Washington as an unscrupulous place that fosters all the petty, self-serving desires known to man, from the high level officials at the Smithsonian who snap at a free lunch as eagerly as they lobby for funds to attend an exposition, to the bloodless young couple, financially as well as socially bereft, who take his room-and-board money but insist that he pass as their guest, not their tenant.

For this "boy of such humble pretensions" (*PH* 231), the crusade to Washington is a dismal failure. After a bureaucratic run-around that sends him from his congressman, to the Indian Commissioner, then back to his congressman, he finally succeeds, through an elegant lunch that he can ill afford, in gaining a few minutes with the secretary to the Director of the Smithsonian.[45] This luncheon meeting provides nothing but another occasion for disappointment, however, as Outland finds the secretary more interested in vain boasting about his own experiences in the Southwest than in hearing about Outland's truly significant find.[46] Even so, the secretary does arrange a meeting with the Director, who three days later introduces Outland to Dr. Ripley, the "authority on prehistoric Indian remains . . . [who] had excavated a lot of them." Even with him, however, the pattern of Outland's rising then falling hopes continues:

Dr. Ripley asked the right sort of questions, and evidently knew his business. He said he'd like to take the first train down to my mesa. But it required money to excavate, and he had none. There was a bill up before Congress for an appropriation. We'd have to wait. . . . But I soon found that the Director and all his staff had one interest which dwarfed every other. There was to be an International Exposition of some sort in Europe the following summer, and they were all pulling strings to get appointed on juries or sent to international congresses. . . . There was, indeed, a bill before Congress for appropriations for the Smithsonian; but there was also a bill for Exposition appropriations, and that was the one they were really pushing . . . in the end it came to nothing. (*PH* 234–35)

This exposition, according to the "nice little Virginia girl" (*PH* 227) Virginia Ward, who worked as the secretary's stenographer, was to be held in Paris. The prize behind the conniving of Cather's Smithsonian officials, it may have two real-life prototypes. The more likely is the International Paris Exposition of 1900, for which Cather's cousin Howard Gore served as a juror and as a director (see chapter 1). The great haste with which the reports of the exposition were prepared may have been enough by itself to suggest to Cather the obsessive attitude of her Smithsonian officials; or she may have found some handy suggestions in the several pages of Volume Six that describe with barely veiled disgust the political maneuvering in the selection of jurors;[47] or she may simply have observed people like the characters she later described. In any event, for the real Smithsonian officials, unlike Cather's, the Paris Exposition was just one of many, not a preoccupation at all. Under the heading "Expositions," the 1898 report of the United States National Museum previews some upcoming events, devoting fourteen lines to the Tennessee Centennial Exposition, twenty-six to the Trans-Mississippi and International Exposition, and four each to the International Fisheries Exposition at Bergen, Norway, and the

International Exposition in Paris.[48] In subsequent annual reports, the Paris Exposition shares attention with many others, including the Louisiana Purchase Exposition, the Lewis and Clark Centennial Exposition, and the Jamestown Tercentennial Exposition.

The other possible prototype, which Cather could have learned about either from John or Clayton Wetherill or from her own reading, is the Paris Exposition of 1889. Because it had ended a month before B. K. Wetherill's first letter to the Smithsonian, it probably did not compete with the Wetherill correspondence for the attention of Smithsonian officials. Smithsonian anthropologist Otis T. Mason did attend the exposition,[49] but the Smithsonian was involved in so many other activities around that time that this event was not a preoccupation either.

Cather not only exaggerates the obsessive nature of her Smithsonian officials, she also misrepresents the Smithsonian's attitude toward Native American archaeology and anthropology. Trying to console Tom Outland, Virginia Ward evaluates her employers for him:

> She said the only thing Dr. Ripley really cared about was getting a free trip to Europe and acting on a jury, and maybe getting a decoration. 'And that's what the Director wants, too,' she said. 'They don't care much about dead and gone Indians.' (*PH* 235)

Just how familiar Cather was with the work of the Smithsonian is difficult to say. During her months in Washington she must have heard something about it, and at any time she could have read some of the frequent publications that detailed a long history of interest in ancient Indian artifacts and ruins, beginning with the Institution's very first publication, *Ancient Monuments of the Mississippi Valley,* in 1848. Thereafter, the record is full of similar work, financed by large portions of the institution's annual budgets. The Smithsonian helped support the numerous surveys and explorations of the

Southwest during the 1860s and 1870s, Smithsonian archaeologist William Henry Holmes saw parts of Mesa Verde thirteen years before the Wetherills did, and by 1922, when Cather probably finished writing "Tom Outland's Story," the Smithsonian had done or sponsored so much work at Mesa Verde that it took dozens of volumes to describe it.[50]

Clearly, Cather deliberately altered the actual role of the Smithsonian in southwestern archaeology in order to cast the institution and its people as unmitigated villains in their treatment of Tom Outland. His humility well in place, Outland says that Dr. Ripley and the other officials "were very kind to take so much trouble with a green boy" (*PH* 234), but it soon becomes apparent, both to Outland and to the reader, that he is little more than an entertaining diversion.

Outland is both demoralized and reaffirmed by this ill treatment. As Philip Gerber says, "Outland's depressing sojourn makes his return to the mesa particularly exhilarating."[51] He returns even more committed to protecting the Blue Mesa than he would have been had he brought back with him "men who would understand it, who would appreciate it and dig out all its secrets." The point, of course, is that Outland is the only one who can understand the mesa, at least in the way Cather would have it. When he learns that a profit-motivated foreigner, "the German, Fechtig," has been digging out all those secrets in his absence—and with Blake's blessing—he goes into a righteous rage made all the more vehement by the fresh memories of his time in Washington, memories of the eminent Smithsonian archaeologist who would rather go to Paris than to Blue Mesa and of the small-minded clerk at the Indian Commission who wanted a priceless ancient pot for an ashtray. In one of the novel's many ironies, the money that Blake earned from Fechtig pays Outland's way home (*PH* 236).

The story that Outland hears upon his return to Tarpin is dispiriting indeed. Like Outland's encounter with the Smithsonian,

it resembles a factual incident (this one involving Gustaf Nordenskiold) enough to indicate that the same creative rationale that
has directed the story so far is still at work.

"On the 14th of September [1891]," Nordenskiold writes,

> I gave orders for the removal of the camp. While three of my
> men were thus employed, I conveyed, with the help of the
> other two . . . a portion of my collections on pack-horses to
> Mancos and thence to the railway station at Durango. There I
> was disagreeably surprised. Some slight difficulties which had
> previously been thrown in my way on the part of the authori-
> ties, but which I had imagined were already obviated, were
> now renewed in a more serious form. I was compelled after a
> fortnight again to return to Durango, where the complaints
> that had been lodged against my operations were, however,
> formally abandoned.[52]

The disagreeable surprise to which Nordenskiold so cryptically
alludes is his arrest, apparently for trespassing on an Indian reservation.[53] His arrest was not prompted by this strict legality, however,
so much as it was by the general sense of outrage felt by Coloradans
over his removal of local artifacts and his plans to ship them out of
the country.

In August 1891 Nordenskiold became concerned that he had
been or soon would be doing work inside the Ute Indian Reservation. One reason for his concern, certainly, was a public notice in the
Mancos post office that proclaimed, "No foreigner is allowed on the
Indian land without permission . . . fine 1000 dollars." Nordenskiold
adds, " '1000 dollars' had a negative effect upon me."[54] Therefore, he
rode to reservation headquarters at Fort Lewis to obtain permission
to work on Indian land, which was granted with the stipulation that
he not damage any of the buildings in the process. Thus assured of
his legal standing, Nordenskiold resumed his work. Then early in
September he and John and Clayton Wetherill packed a collection of

artifacts, took it to the train depot in Durango (the railroad to Mancos was evidently still under construction), and arranged to have it sent to the Swedish consul in New York, who would in turn ship the collection to Stockholm. At this time, evidently, there were some murmurings of discontent among local authorities, identities unknown, but Nordenskiold seems to have been satisfied that he had assuaged their objections sufficiently. It was not until he returned to Durango later in the month with a second collection for shipment that he learned that the first had been impounded and that he himself was the object of an arrest warrant. Nordenskiold was released after posting $1,000 bail—"much trouble some expense no danger," he telegraphed his father—and when he returned in early October for the hearing the charges were dismissed. Before it was over, though, this confused incident had involved the mayor of Durango, the Swedish legation in Washington, the U.S. Attorney General, and the acting Secretary of State.[55]

The legal proceedings against Nordenskiold had always been tenuous at best because at that time there was no prohibition against removing artifacts or against sending them out of the country, the two activities that the locals sought to stop. The only infraction that would have stood up in court stemmed from the condition that Nordenskiold not damage the ruins during his excavations, a condition that he scrupulously upheld.[56] Rather, the formal accusation seems to have been nothing more than a desperate attempt to incriminate in some way this foreigner who had incited the local population by daring to take Colorado artifacts to Sweden. For weeks Nordenskiold was villified in the press, which gave voice to the righteous indignation of concerned citizens in Montezuma County and other parts of Colorado. "Baron Lordenskiold [sic] Arrested/Charged with Devastating the/Cliff Dwellings," proclaimed one headline, typical of several others. The story, a mixture of fact and misrepresentation, says that Nordenskiold's arrest at the Strater Hotel in Durango "has been the chief topic of conversation here to-day. . . . Much indignation is expressed by the people here, as it is believed that the baron's expedition was one of devastation, more than a mere pleasure jaunt."[57]

Although their information was skewed and their motives not necessarily scientific or even consistent, many of the people who objected to Nordenskiold's operation did so from a genuine and admirable desire to preserve the ruins. For quite some time these preservationists had been trying to curtail the frequently destructive removal of antiquities from ruins like those at Mesa Verde, and they "particularly abhorred the practice of some collectors who indiscriminately sold their accumulations of 'relics' to the highest bidder."[58] Evidently, these feelings came to a head with the Nordenskiold affair, which to the young Swede's dismay was simply a handy and particularly dramatic instance.

Undoubtedly, Cather knew enough about this historical incident to see its value to her story, once the details were rearranged in a manner consistent with her themes and with her other historical alterations. The source of her information was not Nordenskiold himself because his brief account provides scarcely a clue to what really happened; rather, she probably heard the story from John or Clayton Wetherill, two of the other participants, or she may have read some of the coverage in the press. In either event, she found in Nordenskiold's story the suggestion for another unpleasant surprise for Tom Outland.

When he returns from Washington, already depressed and dispirited, Outland is "terribly disappointed" that Blake is not at the depot to meet him. The liveryman Bill Hook explains that Blake has been "shy of this town lately" because of the animosity he has aroused. No one was bothered as long as Outland and Blake "were playing Robinson Crusoe out there, digging up curios. But when it leaked out that Blake had got a lot of money for your stuff, then they begun to feel jealous." Hook rather philosophically predicts that the uproar will "blow over in time; people are always like that when money changes hands. But right now there's a good deal of bad feeling" (*PH* 237).

Hook then proceeds to tell Outland about Roddy's "damnedest luck" with a foreign buyer:

> This German, Fechtig, come along; he'd been buying up a lot of Indian things out here, and he bought your whole outfit and paid four thousand dollars down for it. The transaction made quite a stir here in Tarpin. I'm not kicking. I made a good thing out of it. My mules were busy three weeks packing the stuff out of there on their backs, and I held the Dutchman up for a fancy price. . . . I lost one of my mules, too . . . but Fechtig paid for her like a gentleman. . . . He treated everybody well, though; nobody's sore at him. It's your partner they're turned against. (*PH* 237–38)

Clearly, Cather has rearranged the roles and motivations of her historically-inspired characters to coincide with the direction of her fiction. The townspeople have bad feelings toward Blake not because they object to the loss of artifacts from the ruins, as did the people from Colorado, but because they are "jealous" of the money he made selling commodities that belong to them just as much as to him.[59] They are not "sore" at Fechtig, however, because he "treated everybody well," despite the fact that he himself will turn a tidy profit on the sale of their heritage. Interestingly, Bill Hook is not sore at anybody because of the "good thing" he made out of the deal, nor does he appear to be the object of anyone else's wrath. Nonetheless, he is just as mercenary as his neighbors. His story about Fechtig, which occupies barely a page and a half, contains ten references to making money.

As for Fechtig, he is a mere collector, a buyer, without even the least pretension toward science or anything noble. His only contribution to the Blue Mesa is economic, which for Cather is a depradation not a benefit. Nordenskiold too was preoccupied with monetary matters—how much things cost, how much people earn, when money would arrive from home, how much his collection might bring[60]—but these concerns are mitigated somewhat by his scientific intentions. Otherwise, the only similarity between Fechtig and Nordenskiold is Fechtig's anxiety over taking artifacts out of the country. In several letters Nordenskiold alludes to his haste in shipping collections out of Durango before they can be confiscated. Fechtig takes this anxiety a step further: after hurriedly packing up the goods, he

> chartered a freight car, and travelled in the car with it [the collection]. I reckon it's on the water by now. He took it straight through into Old Mexico, and was to load it on a French boat. Seems he was afraid of having trouble getting curiosities out of the United States. (*PH* 239)

This news shocks Outland almost into stupefaction. "I had heard all I wanted to hear," he says. "I went to the hotel, got a room, and lay down without undressing to wait for daylight" (*PH* 239). There he experiences something akin to the mystical state of illumination and the dark night of the soul. "All I'd been through in Washington was nothing to what I went through that night" (*PH* 239). Outland begins by cursing Blake's "stupidity and presumption"; finally, though, he comes to a realization that had been only an intuition before, something he had never even attempted to articulate either to Blake or to himself:

> I had never told him just how I felt about those things we'd dug out together, it was the kind of thing one doesn't talk about directly. But he must have known; he couldn't have lived with me all summer and fall without knowing. And yet, until that night, I had never known myself that I cared more about them than about anything else in the world. (*PH* 239)

The long night over, Outland springs from his "damnable bed," endures an interminable wagon ride to the mesa, and finally sets foot on the trail leading home. To continue the mystical process, Outland is tempted toward a permanent union with his adopted home when, overcome by the aroma of the wild-currant bushes in bloom and the overbearing afternoon sun, he becomes "soft" and wants "to lie down and sleep" (*PH* 240). But more than this he wants to experience the mesa again, "to see and touch everything" (*PH* 240); therefore, he continues his climb to the top, where he feels a more invigorating union with his mystical realm, effectively conveyed by the use of synesthetic imagery:

> Once again I had that glorious feeling that I've never had anywhere else, the feeling of being *on the mesa,* in a world above the world. And the air, my God, what air!—Soft, tingling, gold, hot with an edge of chill on it, full of the smell of piñons—it was like breathing the sun, breathing the colour of the sky. (*PH* 240)

With this air in his lungs, Outland heads "straight for the cabin," about three miles away, and his confrontation with Roddy Blake.

One of the most poignant, and poisonous, scenes in "Tom Outland's Story," this confrontation seems to have no historical antecedent, at least among the sources known or suspected to have influenced other parts of the story. One critic, dividing the Wetherill brothers into two camps, has suggested that Roddy is a reflection of the attitudes of Richard and Al, whereas Tom represents the attitudes of John and Clayton.[61] Certainly the brothers had their differences, but they all seem to have operated from a similar set of motives, though multiple and subject to change. In fact, if a comparison must be made they all had a good deal more in common with Roddy than with Tom: all of them participated in Nordenskiold's activities, and none of them had any scruples about earning money from their work in the ruins, whether as guides, outfitters, or salesmen of photographs and artifacts. They were, after all, men of their time and place with a ranch to run and bills to pay. This mercenary interest notwithstanding, the Wetherills were more faithful caretakers than many of their contemporaries would have been.

Because the confrontation is told from Tom Outland's perspective and because Outland's motives seem so noble, the reader tends to see Blake as Outland sees him: as a betrayer, one who has sold out. This perspective, however, misses the point of the scene, which is to demonstate the extreme degree of Tom Outland's transformation.

Like so many crusaders, Tom Outland has crossed the line between devotion and obsession. Precisely when this happened is difficult to say, but the direction was established probably as early as Henry's death, which marked the beginning of the end of the "happy family" on the mesa. To have Henry suffer such a horrible and painful death—a rattlesnake "struck him square in the forehead," causing it to swell and to turn purple, the agony lasting "nearly two hours" (*PH* 217)—Cather again had to embellish the facts.

"From the first," Outland says, "we'd been a little bothered by rattlesnakes" (*PH* 216), but they do not seem to have been a problem for the Wetherills or any of the other early explorers. One almost never finds snakes even mentioned in any of the first- or second-hand accounts of exploration. Rattlers have been seen in Mesa Verde—it was to avoid them that Cather and Lewis climbed up on that large rock—but no member of any of the Wetherill expeditions was ever bitten;[62] and T. Mitchell Prudden assured his readers that they ran a greater risk "of being sandbagged on the streets some night in New York, or of contracting typhoid fever through the criminal carelessness of a New England dairyman, or of acquiring tuberculosis in a Pullman sleeper, or in the average hotel. . . ."[63]

Clearly, then, Cather chose an extraordinary means to dispose of Henry. Perhaps she intended to demonstrate the danger of the enterprise that Outland and Blake are engaged in and to underscore their determination to continue it, despite their sympathetic response to Henry's death. "We were so cut up [by it]," Outland says, "that we were almost ready to quit." But Father Duchene, who came for the funeral, "had been planning to come out to see our find for a long while, and he got our minds off our trouble" (*PH* 217). In a way, then, Henry is sacrificed to the cause, which must be sustained regardless of the price the family must pay.

Upon his return from Washington, Outland feels betrayed by the remaining member of the family; therefore, an orphan once again, he directs his familial affection toward the mesa itself and the people who once lived there.[64] It is their possessions—"the pots and pans that belonged to my poor grandmothers a thousand years ago" (*PH* 243)—about which he has come to care more "than about anything else in the world" (*PH* 239); and the remains of one of these people, Mother Eve, are so dear to him that he would have sold his own grandmother or "any living woman first" (*PH* 244). These are clearly the words of a man obsessed. Although one can sympathize with the circumstances that have driven Outland to this "myopically idealistic" extreme,[65] there is no escaping the uncomfortable fact that he now values the dead more than the living—at least he says he does. He values the dead so much, in fact, that he willingly sacrifices a friendship merely to make the point: "This painful interview went on for hours," Tom says. "I walked up and down the kitchen trying to make Blake understand the kind of value those objects had had for me. Unfortunately, I succeeded" (*PH* 245).

Ironically, Tom has succeeded in making Roddy understand something that he has only begun to understand himself. The people at the Smithsonian, with all their crass and petty obsessions, begin to seem a little less odious as Outland the victim becomes Outland the victimizer, berating his one true friend for actions taken under the name of friendship. Clearly, more is at stake than the disposition of archaeological properties.

For his part, Blake is as dumbfounded as Outland is outraged.

Once Outland's indignation has belied all of his assumptions—that they were partners in the enterprise, that they both had hoped and expected to "realize" something out of it—Blake can only offer a rueful bit of after-the-fact advice: "You might have given me some of this Fourth of July talk a little earlier in the game" (*PH* 245). As Blake also grimly observes, his motives, which were almost completely unselfish, count for nothing. The $4,000 from the sale to Fechtig was to pay for Outland's education, after which, Blake says, "you can divide with me" (*PH* 243–44).[66]

The rift between Outland and Blake is so wide that a reconciliation is impossible. "If it was my money you'd lost gambling, or my girl you'd made free with," Outland says, "we could fight it out, and maybe be friends again. But this is different" (*PH* 246). Blake's only recourse, then, is to leave, completing the dissolution of the family that had once been so happy. His final words are proof of his compassion: ". . . I'm glad it's you that's doing this to me, Tom; not me that's doing it to you" (*PH* 247–48). Outland probably has this benediction in mind when he tells Rosamond and Kathleen about "noble Roddy" (*PH* 124).

Roddy's departure complicates any Edenic symbols the Blue Mesa may have conveyed. Perhaps Mother Eve was a temptress, perhaps Henry Atkins offers the sacrifice of innocence;[67] but Roddy's expulsion hardly sets matters right. Even if, as Outland believes, Blake has done wrong in betraying an implicit trust, he has been more severely wronged by Outland's betrayal of an explicit trust.[68] Notably, Cather grants impunity to neither man. Blake, of course, suffers exile and disappears completely from the story, despite Outland's earnest attempts to locate him and, presumably, to make amends. Outland, on the other hand, remains on the mesa for a glorious summer, but one clouded by an occasional fright at his own "heartlessness" (*PH* 252) and by the melancholy prospect that colors the whole story by concluding it: "the older I grow, the more I understand what it was I did that night on the mesa. Anyone who requites faith and friendship as I did, will have to pay for it" (*PH* 253). Perhaps Cather's point is that, when an irreconcilable difference of values exists, matters cannot be set right. The result is a true dilemma, one beyond resolution—just the sort of dilemma, in fact, that Cather saw facing the artist perpetually at odds with the world.

When Outland warns Blake that the river is high, that it is "dangerous crossing," the story has come full circle. In one sense, the phrase recalls Outland's entry into the Blue Mesa several months before when he crossed the Cruzados for the first time and found his life irrevocably changed. In another sense, the phrase fulfills the prophecy of the "bad crossing" in an earlier warning. At that time it was Blake warning Henry Atkins, for whom events certainly turned bad. This time it is Blake receiving the warning and immediately throwing it back to Outland in a bitter retort: "I'm surprised at you, using such common expressions! . . . *Dangerous crossing;* it's painted on signboards all over the world!" (*PH* 247).

For Roddy Blake the phrase offers little more than a convenient but not terribly clever parting shot at the man who has assumed a superior position yet resorts to common language. For Cather—and for the reader—the significance is greater. Tom Outland has ignored warnings throughout the story, from the ominous thunder emanating from Blue Mesa, to Rapp's stern opposition to an exploration of the mesa, to Henry's death, and now to his own warning to Blake returned upon himself. Everywhere the world warns against dangerous crossings, yet the people who should heed the warnings seldom do.

It is dangerous for anyone with acute sensibilities to cross into an ethereal world, a mystical realm where the air is purer, the water colder, the colors more brilliant, and the ideals more sharply defined than anywhere else. "To arrive there," Cecil Moffitt explains, "one must have exercised extraordinary intellectual power and creative desire. But one must also have subordinated the claims of the human affections."[69] Moreover, a person who makes such a crossing will find a new way of seeing, both physically and ethically, that will invariably oppose the perceptions and values of others, like Plato's characters who emerge from the cave and then, upon their return, find themselves unable to cope with their former lives, "no longer at home in the ordinary world."[70] The experience is exalting, but the price is high: a friend, certainly—"There was an ache in my arms to reach out and detain him, but there was something else that made me absolutely powerless to do so" (*PH* 247); possibly even a life—"I went to sleep that night hoping I would never waken" (*PH* 248).

Crossing into this rarified world is both a blessing and a curse. Before he disappears below the rim rock on his way to the canyon below, Blake says "with grim cheerfulness, 'here's luck!'" an ironic echo of Bill Hook's earlier exclamation. The wish is probably sincere, however, because it precedes Blake's compassionate final words. Even so, Outland is "not very sanguine about good fortune" for himself (*PH* 253). Such is the blessing and the curse of one who lives in a world above the world. It is the damnedest luck.

6 ❋ A Glittering Idea

 *From the river* and overhanging ledge that protect it to the foreigner who invades it, Willa Cather's Blue Mesa is a thoroughly idealized version of Mesa Verde. Such a portrayal places "Tom Outland's Story"—if not *The Professor's House* as a whole—directly in the mainstream of American Romantic literature. One thinks, for instance, of Fenimore Cooper's insistence upon "the privilege of all writers of fiction, more particularly when their works aspire to the elevation of romances, to present the *beau-ideal* of their characters to the reader";[1] and of Nathaniel Hawthorne, who distinguished between the novel and the romance by asserting that the latter was obligated to present "the truth of the human heart" but permitted to do so "under circumstances, to a great extent, of the writer's own choosing or creation"[2]—in other words, idealized circumstances. This transformation toward the ideal is also strictly in keeping with both the artistic theory and the bulk of the fiction by that author whom Bernice Slote labelled "a passionate idealist."[3]

At least as early as 1896 Cather saw the value of idealization as a fictional device in her assessment of the essential weakness in a novel by Edgar Saltus: "He absolutely does not possess the power of idealization." She continues to say that the descriptions in his book are "effective and alluring," the characters "strongly drawn and cleverly treated"; but there is no "dominant character ... who shall embody the purpose of the book and justify its creation ... [no] character whom it would be a pleasure or a profit to know" (*KA* 416). In her own fiction, Cather idealized so many people, places, and events—created so many characters "whom it would be a pleasure or a profit to know"—that idealization has been recognized as one of her standard creative techniques.[4] In fact, it is such a prominent feature of the novels subsequent to *The Professor's House*—*Death Comes for the Archbishop* and *Shadows on the Rock* in particular—that one might see *The Professor's House* as a turning point toward the idealization of specific historical themes, characters, and situations, as opposed to the idealization of more representative people and conditions in *O Pioneers!, My Antonia,* and *The Song of the Lark.*

As an idealized place, the Blue Mesa is the proper home of "a superior people" (*PH* 219) who, with their sense of design and appreciation of comfort, built themselves into the mesa and humanized it. Their legacy to Tom Outland is an enchanted world full of superlatives: the most spectacular coloration, the loudest thunder, the most inaccessible places, the purest air, the cleanest and coldest water. Cather collected from a great variety of historical sources enough facts for a semblance of reality; then she either exaggerated or sublimated the facts as needed to achieve the desired effect. She thus created a place where ideals coexist gracefully, almost unobtrusively, with reality; where what was suggests what might have been—and what is, in the mind of the artist. As James Maxfield explains, Cliff City "symbolizes for Willa Cather much the same thing Byzantium does for Yeats: a moment in human history when 'religious, aesthetic and practical life were one.'"[5] In short, Cather designed the Blue Mesa to be a tangible yet mystical locale for her Kingdom of Art.[6]

Cather began building the Kingdom of Art in the early 1890s, the same period, incidentally, when many women writers found their careers vigorously or tacitly repudiated by their families.[7] Sometimes she called it by name; other times she simply delineated principles to define it. By 1896 this kingdom

> was clearer far than the land she was leaving, more precisely marked than the lines of earth and sky in Nebraska. She had described it in more than three hundred separate pieces in newspaper columns and reviews, through more than three years in which all the weathers of her mind and belief were marked, and in which she set down those principles of art which she finally considered to be absolutes.[8]

Cather conceived the Kingdom of Art as an allegorical means of collecting these principles, of housing them, so to speak. Although they are the product of an early stage in her career, these principles remained "unchanged through the years."[9] In fact, Cather's attitudes toward art, writing in particular, remain so consistent that "the 1920 and 1930 essays seem like afterthoughts or absentminded repetitions of the obvious." The pieces from 1895–96 especially provide "a documentary of the creative process,"[10] which Cather spent the rest of her career enacting.

Chief among Cather's aesthetic creeds is the unwavering belief that art is a religious experience, that through the act of creation the artist enjoys some of the creative power of God, whom Cather described in terms of the "Master Workman" and "this gigantic Artist of all art that is" (*KA* 178). Hence the name the Kingdom of Art, which, of course, is a deliberate echo of the Kingdom of Heaven. Significantly, in an essay entitled "Novels on the Christ and the Christ Period," Cather offers a full description of her Kingdom of Art.

To be sure, the analogy between the two kingdoms is not absolute, but there are enough elements in common to support Cather's concept. For example, Jesus often explains the Kingdom of Heaven through parables, stories in the oral tradition, and many of the parables—of the sower, of the mustard seed, of the leaven, and of the talents—convey positive images of productivity or achievement, goals shared by artists. Other parables of the Kingdom of Heaven illustrate the choices that people must make, giving up one thing to obtain another, the way an artist must give up the common life to pursue his craft:

> the kingdom of heaven is like unto treasure hid in a field, the which when a man hath found, he hideth, and for joy thereof goeth and selleth all that he hath, and buyeth that field. Again, the kingdom of heaven is like unto a merchant man, seeking goodly pearls: Who, when he had found one pearl of great price, went and sold all that he had, and bought it.[11]

Other parables highlight the process of selectivity, which also applies to the artistic life: "It is easier for a camel to go through the eye of a needle, than for a rich man to enter into the kingdom of God";[12] "for many be called, but few chosen."[13] One parable even sounds like a paraphrase of a major theme in *The Professor's House:* "He also that received seed among the thorns is he that heareth the word; and the care of this world, and the deceitfulness of riches, choke the word, and he becometh unfruitful."[14] Finally, in the Kingdom of Heaven, as in the Kingdom of Art, there is a special place for children: "Suffer little children, and forbid them not, to come unto me; for of such is the kingdom of heaven";[15] "a child's normal attitude toward the world is that of the artist, pure and simple" (*CSF* 275).

In keeping with her belief in the connection between art and religion, Cather includes in *The Professor's House* a priest, Father Duchene, to interpret the lifestyle of the ancient ones. After a week's study, Father Duchene concludes that the people "lived for something more than food or shelter" (*PH* 219); that they spent their time "making their mesa more and more worthy to be a home for man, purifying life by religious ceremonies and observances" (*PH* 220). Like Tom Outland, Father Duchene feels "a reverence for this place. Wherever humanity has made that hardest of all starts and lifted itself out of mere brutality, is a sacred spot" (*PH* 221).

Father Duchene also interprets Mother Eve, who "had greatly interested" him:

> "I seem to smell," he said slyly, "a personal tragedy. Perhaps when the tribe went down to the summer camp, our lady was sick and would not go. Perhaps her husband thought it worth while to return unannounced from the farms some night, and found her in improper company. The young man may have escaped. In primitive society the husband is allowed to punish an unfaithful wife with death" (*PH* 223)

Whether Cather intends Father Duchene's interpretation to be taken literally or ironically has been a matter of considerable disagreement.[16] Regardless of the moral or social issues involved, the diction in the passage cautions against wholehearted literal acceptance. Unlike the priest's other pronouncements, this one is offered "slyly," in an atmosphere of "pure supposition," as Margaret Doane calls it.[17] Four of the five sentences in Duchene's hypothesis contain qualifiers, two of them at the beginning: "seem," "Perhaps," "Perhaps," and "may," respectively. This string of uncertainties undermines the credibility of Duchene's theory. Moreover, the only sentence offered as a certainty is the last one, and it refers in a vulnerably broad way to "primitive society" as a whole.

Surely Cather intended an association with the biblical Eve, especially considering the probable origin of the mummy's name (see chapter 2). Perhaps she meant to suggest that even the Kingdom of Art, like this first Kingdom of Heaven, is susceptible to corruption; that even there faith and friendship can be betrayed. That Cather's priest (whose calling precludes one of those "cruel biological necessities") should fabricate an adulterous dimension to this betrayal probably says more about him, however, than it does about Mother Eve.

It is tempting to see in the Mother Eve episode a social commentary with a feminist bent; however, had Cather intended such a reading, she probably would have made use of the passage in the park brochure about the apparent social distinctions among the cliff dwellers[18] or of the lengthy discussion in Nordenskiold of the matrilineal and matrilocal aspects of contemporary pueblo society.[19] As Bernice Slote says, from the books that influenced her Cather "took what she could use and what suited her temper."[20] What Cather seems to use in this case are not the social implications but the artistic ones: the concept of an artistic genesis, the very first Kingdom of Art.

In the familiar story from the Book of Genesis, God's creation of woman is painless—even pleasant—for all involved:

> And the Lord God caused a deep sleep to fall upon Adam, and he slept; and he took one of his ribs, and closed up the flesh instead thereof; And the rib, which the Lord God had taken from man, made he a woman, and brought her unto the man. And Adam said, This is now bone of my bones, and flesh of my flesh: she shall be called Woman, because she was taken out of Man.[21]

Cather both alludes to and alters this metaphor of creation when she presents Mother Eve, her matriarch of the Blue Mesa, with a "great wound in her side," corresponding to the removal of Adam's rib. In this case, however, the process of creation was painful—even violent—and the flesh was not "closed up" but left open "through all those years"; hence the "terrible look of agony" (*PH* 214) still visible on that tormented face. For God, all things are possible; man, however, must make choices and suffer consequences. Evidently, Cather has combined in Mother Eve both the sacrifice of part of oneself to creation, made by Adam, and the everlasting punishment for presuming too much, suffered by both Adam and Eve. Such presumption is the occupational hazard of an endeavor that imitates the role of the Creator, the Master Workman. Witness Prometheus, another creator from ancient times whose daring led to a chronic wound.[22]

Whatever her actual or perceived transgression, Cather's Mother Eve, like her Biblical namesake, must have violated a personal trust and indulged herself in some way, achieving something that she would otherwise have been denied. "[T]hen your eyes shall be opened," the serpent in the garden insinuates, "and ye shall be as gods, knowing good and evil."[23] Placed in the context of the Kingdom of Art, Mother Eve is an ominous priestess, one whose fate foreshadows that of the artist who forsakes all others to follow his craft. Perhaps the scream that still seems to be emanating from that agonized face protests the fate that makes such sacrifice a prerequisite for creation. Perhaps it is also a warning to any who would be artists, creators—another of the book's warnings against the dangerous crossing.

Unlike her Biblical counterpart, however, Mother Eve is not banished; in fact, she is not permitted to leave: "She went to the bottom of Black Canyon and carried Hook's best mule along with her. They had to make her box extra wide, and she crowded Jenny out an inch or so too far from the canyon wall" (*PH* 244–45). As a symbol of the Kingdom of Art, Mother Eve must stay in Blue Mesa. At this point the Biblical parallel shifts to Tom Outland, the living artist, who has also entered the Kingdom and eaten of the tree. Like Adam and Eve, who "hand in hand with wand'ring steps and slow, / Through Eden took their solitarie way,"[24] Outland has little reason to feel "very sanguine about good fortune" for himself when he leaves the Kingdom for the other world.

In addition to his role as interpreter, Father Duchene also acts as a motivator. After Henry's horrible death, the priest encourages Tom and Roddy to continue with their work (*PH* 217); after Roddy's expulsion, he advises Tom to return to the mesa and continue his studies (*PH* 149); when Tom is ready to leave the mesa, Father Duchene recommends Godfrey St. Peter (*PH* 114); and just after Outland patents his invention, Father Duchene arrives in Hamilton "on his way back to Belgium, hurrying home to serve in any capacity he might" (*PH* 259–60). Like the military chaplain in Melville's *Billy Budd*, Father Duchene becomes the servant of Christ in the service of Mars.[25] Behind his genial facade, this "rugged old man" (*PH* 260) seems like a semi-sinister *deus ex machina*, prodding and manipulating his charge through the paces of life, art, and death.

The Blue Mesa exemplifies another of Cather's major tenets of art: the artistic life is not an easy one. Hence the Kingdom is sparsely populated, inhabited only by artists with the gift of expression, a gift that enables them to "keep an idea living," to retain "all its original feeling, its original mood, preserving in it all the ecstasy which attended its birth, . . . and [to] transfer it on paper a living thing with color, odor, sound, life all in it. . . ." Such artists reach the Kingdom through a "voyage perilous," a "short voyage from the brain to the hand" but one during which much might be lost. Many may attempt the voyage, Cather says, but most of them are as ill prepared for this allegorical crusade as the good men "many centuries ago" who, with "their wives and progeny set out [on a real crusade] for Palestine," only to find that they lacked the stamina to endure the high mountains, hot sands, and bitter water of the desert (*KA* 417). Even more formidable than the natural obstacles in Cather's parable, the Blue Mesa is utterly inaccessible, except by fording a river (suggestively named the Cruzados) that poses perils of its own. Until Tom Outland, no one from the modern world had entered the mesa at all. Once he does, however, he finds the essence of art, what Bernice Slote has called "the high, rare, splendid ideal that justifies the quest and the devotion." Moreover, Cliff City itself embodies the "earthly pattern or achievement" through which Willa Cather usually expressed her concept of the ideal.[26]

Like other aspects of "Tom Outland's Story," the allegorization of ancient cliff dwellings as the Kingdom of Art appears first in *The Song of the Lark*. In Panther Canyon Thea Kronborg finds the ultimate symbol of art in the pottery that the ancient people had so carefully and laboriously decorated but that "could not hold food or water any better for the additional labour put upon them" (*SL* 379). Indeed, what better example of art at its purest than a crucial utilitarian object made needlessly and unprofitably beautiful? Twenty-one years after *The Song of the Lark* was published, Cather again cited the decorated pots of the cliff dwellers as proof that the major arts "have a pedigree all their own," independent of "increasing the game supply or promoting tribal security. They sprang from an unaccountable predilection of the one unaccountable thing in man" (*WCOW* 19).

It is also in Panther Canyon that Thea realizes the essential purpose of art:

> what was any art but an effort to make a sheath, a mould in which to imprison for a moment the shining, elusive element which is life itself—life hurrying past us and running away, too strong to stop, too sweet to lose? The Indian women had held it in their jars. (*SL* 378)

This image is the Grecian Urn recast in a new setting. Elaine Smith Hawkins has already noted the similarity between Keats's ode and "Cather's vision of art" as depicted in *The Song of the Lark*, and E. K. Brown has seen the evocation of the Grecian Urn ideal in Tom Outland's description of Cliff City, specifically the passage beginning with "It was as still as sculpture."[27] The ideal appears again in the water jar "shaped like those common in Greek sculpture" that Outland gives Mrs. St. Peter (*PH* 118). However, in place of the "maidens loth" and the "happy, happy boughs" and the "Bold Lover" who can never kiss but never lose his love, the pots in Panther Canyon display "graceful geometrical patterns," "a crested serpent's head," or "a broad band of white cliff-houses painted on a black background" (*SL* 380–81). The images are different because the lives were different, but the theme of art saving life from time, paradoxically preserving it in static motion, is the same. In *The Song of the Lark,* Cather introduces this theme and explicates it, but not until "Tom Outland's Story" does she develop it fully, creating an entire landscape to contain it.

Thanks to the story of Richard Wetherill, Cather found at Mesa Verde not only the ancient setting she had wanted but also the realization of the myth of discovery that she had been trying so long to express. Now the importance of this myth becomes clear: at some early point Cather must have begun to associate it with her concept of the Kingdom of Art, the governing metaphor of her life. The nature of Outland's discovery points quite emphatically to this association. What Outland finds is indeed a sort of natural urn, "a memorial to man's thoughts and works which defy the ravagings of time and attain the immortality of art."[28] To borrow Ernest Becker's words, Outland's discovery testifies to the universal hope and belief "that the things that man creates in society are of lasting worth and meaning, that they outlive or outshine death and decay, that man and his products count."[29] Like Keats's speaker, Outland is enthralled by the images before him though the objects of his adoration again reflect the different lives: stone buildings, water jars, corn cobs, turkey feathers, and even mummies of the people who made and used these things—all of them preserved by the dry air and the sheltering rock, protected from the effects of time. It is life once again caught in static motion, "like a fly in amber" (*PH* 202).

Another important feature of this natural urn is that it is a vestige of indigenously American antiquity discovered by a truly American type—the cowboy, the Western Everyman. "These objects, these rooms, even the human remains, were elements distinctively our own, something that changed a new, raw country into one with cycles of civilization through an ancient past."[30] This fact helps explain Tom Outland's reaction to Fechtig: when he learns that a mercenary foreigner has removed "our things," Outland's rage is fueled by a sense of nationalistic possession:

> They belonged to this country, to the State, and to all the people. They belonged to boys like you and me, that have no other ancestors to inherit from. You've gone and sold them to a country that's got plenty of relics of its own. You've gone and sold your country's secrets, like Dreyfus.[31] (*PH* 243)

This resentment also lies behind Outland's response to Mrs. St. Peter's suggestion that the water jar he gives her belongs in a museum: "museums . . . don't care about our [that is, American] things. They want something that came from Crete or Egypt" (*PH* 119), two other countries with plenty of relics of their own.

The emphasis upon Americanism in these passages strongly suggests that Cather shared another interest with her predecessors in Romance, Poe and Emerson in particular. Like them, Cather was concerned about the state of American arts and letters, sometimes bemoaning the void and other times extolling the achievements.[32] For instance, in her 1895 essay on Poe, a writer "born into a country without a literature," Cather proclaims: "We lament our dearth of great prose. With the exception of Henry James and Hawthorne, Poe is our only master of pure prose. We lament our dearth of poets. With the exception of Lowell, Poe is our only great poet" (*KA* 382–83). Nonetheless, at the same time Cather saw signs of Americanism on the rise. Speaking of humorist Charles H. Hoyt, Cather says that his

> great hold on the people of this country lies in the fact that his humor is thoroughly American, just as much as Mark Twain's. It is not borrowed from England or stolen from France. It comes right up from the streets and the shops and the everyday life of the American people. (*KA* 241)

And if, "some day there will be born in America a man who can . . . [lose] himself in the greatness of his theme, [who] will work it through to its consummation without faltering . . . [t]hen the history of American drama will begin" (*KA* 237). As one of the early reviewers of *The Professor's House* observed, Cather believes what "no native novelist since Hawthorne has practised, that there is profundity in American life . . . a conscious spiritual profundity which poets like Robert Frost and Edwin Arlington Robinson have long seen."[33]

All of her comments about the state of American letters come from the same period when Cather was formulating her concept of the Kingdom of Art. By 1922, when she seems to have finished "Tom Outland's Story," Cather was either hopeful or confident enough about American literature to place the Kingdom in this country, to give it American roots and an American future—at the very time when American literature was receiving "almost no institutional recognition."[34] And if in the 1890s she was unsure of her own place in this kingdom,[35] by the 1920s that too was more clearly defined.

Finally, at this time Cather also felt more secure in her role as a woman pursuing a man's occupation. In 1925 she chided Fanny Butcher for a chauvinist remark in her review of *The Professor's House:*

> You made one terrible error in your review of the book. You spoke of me as a woman novelist. Woman novelist is as out of date as a phrase as woman musician or woman painter, or woman anything else that women do as professionally as men. There are so many women writing novels nowadays that very soon the critics will have to begin talking about prominent male novelists.[36]

If the Blue Mesa is the Kingdom of Art, Tom Outland is of course the artist, rhapsodizing over the natural urn the way Keats's speaker does over the Grecian Urn. As the first to enter Blue Mesa and as the discoverer of Cliff City, the central shrine in the kingdom, Outland is the only character with an original vision into the nature of art, or an original relation to the universe, to borrow Emerson's phrase. It is therefore through Outland's perspective that the reader gains entry into the kingdom, just as one reads a book or views a painting through the artist's perspective. When he crosses the Cruzados, Outland takes the voyage perilous; then he enters the kingdom and brings back news of discovery. In this role, Outland fits Ernest Becker's definition of the Hero as the one who, ever since primitive and ancient times, "could go into the spirit world, the world of the dead, and return alive."[37]

Tom Outland is perfectly suited for the role. A representative of the real world of railroad men and cowboys, he is unschooled in the ways of the artist; but his capacity for genuine feeling—his gift of sympathy—reflects Cather's "general tendency to invest the common man with instincts of appreciation and knowledge that are in many ways superior to those of the learned—superior, that is, in being closer to the 'real thing' of authentic response."[38] Tom Outland is also one who "idealized the people he loved and paid his devoir to the ideal rather than to the individual" (*PH* 172), one whose "fine long hand . . . had never handled things that were not the symbols of ideas" (*PH* 260). In fact, Outland himself is the symbol of an idea, "not so much a person as a personification, an embodiment of the ascendant intellect, the liberated imagination."[39]

With the single-minded devotion that Cather often ascribed to the true artist, Outland gives himself up to the mesa, his heightened sensibilities thrilling to the sights, shapes, colors, and myriad other stimuli he finds there. It is an experience not only in beauty but also in unity, "a sense of almost mystical exaltation"[40] reminiscent of Walt Whitman's in "Song of Myself," a fulfillment of the process described by Bernice Slote: "art is based in the physical, ends in the spiritual."[41] Upon his return from Tarpin, where he had gone to look for Roddy Blake, Outland notices the "glittering silveriness" of the moon, "the sign . . . of the voyage perilous,"[42] and he begins to articulate what before had been only an intuition. "I'll never forget the night I got back," he says:

> . . . that was the first night I was ever really on the mesa at all—the first night that all of me was there. This was the first time I ever saw it as a whole. It all came together in my understanding. . . . Something had happened in me that made it possible for me to co-ordinate and simplify, and that process, going on in my mind, brought with it great happiness. It was possession. The excitement of my first discovery was a very pale feeling compared to this one. For me the mesa was no longer an adventure, but a religious emotion. I had read of filial piety in the Latin poets, and I knew that was what I felt for this place. It had formerly been mixed up with other motives; but now that they were gone, I had my happiness unalloyed. (*PH* 250–51)

The key terms and phrases in this passage reflect the concerns of authorship: seeing the subject "as a whole," having the parts all come "together in . . . [the] understanding," achieving the ability to "co-ordinate and simplify." In short, it is "possession"—not physical possession of the sort coveted by Fechtig and the people of Tarpin—but imaginative, even spiritual, possession, an absorption of the ideas that the place conveys, a case of art being based in the physical and ending in the spiritual.

The concept of artistic possession was important to Willa Cather. Thea Kronborg finally achieves it the afternoon she performs *Sieglinde* before "an inspiring audience" (*SL* 565) that includes Fred Ottenburg, Dr. Archie, Mr. and Mrs. Harsanyi, and Spanish Johnny.

> That afternoon nothing new came to Thea Kronborg, no enlightenment, no inspiration. She merely came into full possession of things she had been refining and perfecting for so long. Her inhibitions chanced to be fewer than usual, and,

within herself, she entered into the inheritance that she herself had laid up, into the fullness of the faith she had kept before she knew its name or its meaning. . . . She felt like a tree bursting into bloom. (*SL* 571)

Cather experienced this excitement herself while she was writing *One of Ours*. In a letter to Dorothy Canfield Fisher in April 1922, Cather described that compositional circumstance as life at its best, complete possession.[43] Then in the following year Cather wrote again about artistic possession in her essay on Katherine Mansfield, a writer she admired: "She had not, as she said, the physical strength to write what she now knew were, to her, the most important things in life. But she had found them, she possessed them, her mind fed on them."[44]

As for Tom Outland, had his possessive nature taken the more customary turn, even without the pecuniary inclination, he would have hoarded all the artifacts he could find, built himself into the mesa, and dehumanized it. Instead, once he possesses the ideas, he can leave the physical mesa behind him, carrying always with him the meaning he has derived from it. It is for this reason that the excitement of the first discovery, only dimly understood, pales in comparison to this one, which is a moment of realization. What used to be a mere adventure (one aspect of a crusade) has become "a religious emotion" (the major goal of a crusade); and Outland actually lives the union of art and religion about which St. Peter so forcefully yet vainly lectures.[45] Cather carefully incorporates into the discovery scene a premonition of this reverential attitude when Outland's position in the bottom of the canyon forces him to look up, worshipfully, to find the shrine of Cliff City. Even at first sight it was a world above the world. Now, with Outland in full possession of this awareness and freed from other motives, his return assumes a "sacramental quality,"[46] and Outland has his "happiness un-alloyed."

As Susan Rosowski explains, however, this "unalloyed happiness of pure imaginative experience" is contaminated by "a troubling undercurrent of human values betrayed [that] runs through the story."[47] Indeed, none of this would have been possible without the rift between Outland and Blake. A patron but not an artist, Blake must be removed just as Ray Kennedy in *The Song of the Lark* had to be removed. Neither man is entirely forgotten, but each is left behind. During those moments when his "vitality is too high to be clouded, too elastic to stay down," when he hurries toward his study spot in Cliff City, Outland is sometimes "frightened at my own heartlessness." But, like Thea Kronborg, he finds solace in a "narrow moccasin-worn trail," so that he would "forget all about Blake without knowing it" (*PH* 252). In this way, Outland's behavior toward Blake can be explained in artistic terms, but it can never be defended in personal ones—still the dilemma still unresolved. Perhaps the blame can be mitigated somewhat by Cather's belief that the "true artist . . . cannot do what he will, but what he must" (*KA* 161), that he has "no choice since he himself was chosen";[48] but it still lies heavy on Outland's conscience. Moreover, the passage that concludes "Tom Outland's Story" presents a grim and succinct account of the high cost of a life devoted to art, a cost borne not only by the artist but also by those around him:

> the older I grow, the more I understand what it was I did that night on the mesa. Anyone who requites faith and friendship as I did, will have to pay for it. I'm not very sanguine about good fortune for myself. I'll be called to account when I least expect it. (*PH* 253)

Ultimately, however, the kind of payback that Outland contemplates is impossible because the currency honored in the Kingdom of Art is not accepted anywhere else. "One requites faith and friendship in a different coinage from that in which one makes a payment to the ideal."[49] And once one has paid his devoir to the ideal—has undertaken the solitary and essentially selfish act of creation—he has cut himself off even from the means of making amends. If Tom Outland were to find Roddy Blake, what would he say? He has not repented his actions, only regretted the consequences. Even so, it seems likely that he will be "called to account" when he least expects it: "[T]hen came August, 1914," and Father Duchene.

Ever since the 1890s, Cather was acutely aware of the dilemma facing the artist who felt dual obligations. On the one side, in May 1896 she wrote, "art itself is the highest moral purpose in the world, and when a man deserts it for another he pays money for that which is not bread and gets the worst of the bargain" (*KA* 378). On the other side is this statement from the year before: ". . . Our Lady of Genius . . . takes one from the millions, and when she gives herself unto a man it is without his will or that of his fellows, and he pays for it, dear heaven, he pays!" (*KA* 386).

With the distraction of Roddy Blake relegated to an occasional memory, Outland is free to indulge in his "high tide." "I can scarcely hope that life will give me another summer like that one," he says (*PH* 251). "Troubles enough came afterward, but there was that summer, high and blue, a life in itself" (*PH* 253). Notably, Outland spends his time not writing but studying—the Spanish grammar and the twelve books of the *Aeneid*—and he follows Cather's own habit of working in the morning and tending to other chores in the afternoon. That part of the day he spends mainly "clearing away the mess the German had made in packing" (*PH* 251)—in effect returning the mesa to the nearly pristine condition in which he and Blake had found it. Still in perfect harmony with his surroundings, Outland wakes each morning with the feeling that he had "found everything, instead of having lost everything" (*PH* 251). "Nothing tired me," he says. "Up there alone, a close neighbour to the sun, I seemed to get the solar energy in some direct way" (*PH* 251). The union is complete.

That summer on the mesa, "a life in itself," represents one dimension of Outland's art, and Cather's as well: it is the experience that must be stored and savored before it can be expressed. "The spontaneous untutored outpouring of personal feeling does not go very far in art," Cather wrote in 1936 (*WCOW* 117). Better, though more costly, results are achieved when one has allowed the mind to be "'teased' . . . for years" until the "shapes and scenes . . . do at last get themselves rightly put down" (*WCOW* 48). Cather practiced what she preached. Noting that "her best method . . . required the use of material that had long possessed her," James Woodress observes that almost all of her books "were made out of old experiences that had had time to season."[50]

In keeping with this creative process, Outland never even retrieves the diary he secluded in Eagle's Nest before his trip to Washington, never attempts to revise it or enhance it, for reasons that are quite revealing. "It would have been going backward," he realizes—backward to the time before he understood the mesa, when he did sense a "kind of composition" but before he was able to "co-ordinate and simplify," before it all came together in his understanding, before he had "possession." "I didn't want to go back and unravel things step by step. Perhaps I was afraid that I would lose the whole in the parts" (*PH* 252). Years later, Godfrey St. Peter would find the style of Outland's diary to be deliberately austere yet remarkably evocative—"almost beautiful" (*PH* 262)—but at this point Outland demonstrates the other side of the writer as defined by Cather, one who "must care vitally . . . about . . . the arrangement of words, the beauty and power of phrases," but who must also "get more out of life itself than out of anything written" (*KA* 82). In October 1915, shortly after her return from Mesa Verde, Cather told an interviewer, "If I hadn't again grasped the thrills of life, I would have been too literary and academic to ever write anything worth while" (WCP 15).

While he lives one of "the many lives that in themselves are art" (*KA* 178), Tom Outland fulfills the challenge issued by another literary pilgrim, Henry Thoreau, whose kingdom was meant to be, although probably never was, more populous than Cather's:

It is something to be able to paint a particular picture, or to carve a statue, and so to make a few objects beautiful; but it is far more glorious to carve and paint the very atmosphere and medium through which we look, which morally we can do. To affect the quality of the day, that is the highest of arts.[51]

Outland's high tide also calls to mind another of Thoreau's dictums: "My life has been the poem I would have writ / But I could not both live and utter it."[52] Of course, Tom Outland does tell his story eventually (just as Thoreau wrote *Walden* and a number of poems), but like his creator he must allow the experience to be seasoned before translating it into narrative.

Tom Outland's final qualification as an artist is his name, which "seemed to suit the boy exactly" (*PH* 114). Related to the German *Ausland,* meaning foreign country, his surname portrays him as one outside, one who never belongs; and it suggests the distance that often exists between artists and the world at large. A "foundling boy," he was "informally adopted" by a couple named O'Brien, "who took care of his mother in her last hours" before she died on the Kansas prairie (*PH* 115). As he grows and moves about like Melville's Ishmael (another orphaned American story teller), Outland joins in one way or another a succession of other families: Roddy Blake and Henry Atkins; the Bixbies in Washington; the Blue Mesa and Mother Eve; and finally the St. Peters, the first real family (parents and children) that he joins after the O'Briens. His unexpected arrival at the St. Peters' house is a variation upon the foundling theme, so that Outland joins his first and last families in much the same way: St. Peter "was working in his garden one Saturday morning, when a young man in a heavy winter suit and a Stetson hat, carrying a grey canvas telescope, came in at the green door that led from the street" (*PH* 112).

For various reasons, however, none of these families provide any lasting comfort; therefore, Outland remains an orphan, an outsider, to the end. His engagement to Rosamond, which would make him a legal and presumably permanent member of the St. Peter family, is thwarted by his decision to join instead the war in Europe. Thus, Tom Outland becomes the second of Cather's young men to escape a wife (or fiancée) by rushing off to war. For Claude Wheeler, the decision seems inevitable: there is such mounting anticipation in the early pages of *One of Ours,* and his marriage to Enid Royce—all the better, probably, because of the physical separation between them—is no inducement to stay home. For Tom Outland, on the other hand, the decision seems impulsive, at least as Louie Marsellus explains it, and nearly as mysterious as the disappearance of the ancient cliff dwellers:

> Before he dashed off to the front, this youngster had discovered the principle of the Outland vacuum, worked out the construction of the Outland engine that is revolutionizing aviation. He not only invented it, but, curiously enough for such a hot-headed fellow, had taken pains to protect it by patent. He had no time to communicate his discovery or to commercialize it—simply bolted to the front and left the most important discovery of his time to take care of itself. (*PH* 40–41)

What matters to Outland, whether in science or in art, is the divine act of creation itself, not the aftermath. He does secure a patent, the scientific equivalent of a byline; but he would have had no interest in trying to "communicate his discovery" at meetings of scientific societies like Louie's Association of Electrical Engineers, where "poor Tom [was] served up again" (*PH* 111), nor would he have known "the twists and turns by which the patent could be commercialized" (*PH* 137). Instead, he was content to leave his idea as "merely a formula written out on paper" (*PH* 138), just as he was content to seal his Blue Mesa diary in a rock and to tell his story to an audience of one or two. Drawing upon the philosophies of Otto Rank and Kierkegaard, Ernest Becker reaches a conclusion that applies to Tom Outland: "there is no way for the artist to be at peace with his work or with the society that accepts it. The artist's gift is always to creation itself, to the ultimate meaning of life, to God."[53]

After his entry into the Kingdom of Art, Outland also exists outside the realm of everyday life, inside an ethereal world. From this perspective he sees the mesas, the cliff dwellings, and the artifacts quite differently from the officials at the Smithsonian, to whom he was always an outsider, and even differently from his friend Roddy Blake, to whom he becomes an outsider.

For a while, Outland finds solace in his surroundings. Like St. Peter gazing out of his study window to the "long, blue hazy smear" that is the horizon of Lake Michigan (*PH* 29), Outland looks beyond the picture on the page of the *Aeneid* to the picture behind it:

> blue and purple rocks and yellow-green piñons with flat tops, little clustered houses clinging together for protection, a rude tower rising in their midst, rising strong, with calmness and courage—behind it a dark grotto, in its depths a crystal spring. (*PH* 252–53)

A spiritual high tide cannot be sustained forever, though, and no matter how much he vivifies the former inhabitants of Cliff City, Outland is still alone, living only half of the artist's life. The artist, Cather said, "should be among men but not one of them, in the world but not of the world" (*KA* 407). In other words, the artist must leave the kingdom simply for the sake of expression, for what Bernice Slote calls "the personal encounter" between the artist and his audience.[54] For all her idealism, Cather had a practical side too: the artist must not only feel, but also produce.

Like Thoreau leaving Walden, Tom Outland has "several more lives to live, and . . . [can] not spare any more time for that one."[55]

Perhaps also like Thea Kronborg and Fred Ottenburg, he has grown tired of "the dead races, of a world without change or ideas" (*SL* 408). At any rate, when he crosses the river for the last time— the "dangerous crossing"—he finds himself outside the mesa, beyond the protection of the sheltering rock, and back in a world that has become foreign to him. A stranger in a strange land, like Robinson Crusoe and Lemuel Gulliver,[56] Outland has reasons other than his remorse over Roddy Blake not to feel "very sanguine about good fortune" for himself (*PH* 253).

At first, Outland returns to his earlier life in Pardee, staying again with the O'Briens, "working on the section and studying with Father Duchene and trying to get some word of Blake." Once more things come to money in the end as Outland and Father Duchene offer a reward of a thousand dollars for whoever finds Blake, but this time the money itself "came to nothing" (*PH* 253). It comes to nothing again as Outland leaves his bank account untouched and, on the advice of Father Duchene, seeks out Professor Godfrey St. Peter, whose article about Fray Marcos de Niza is "the only thing with any truth in it" that Father Duchene had read about the Southwest (*PH* 114). Having entered Blue Mesa as little more than a curious cowboy and having emerged nearly two years later as a reluctant visionary from the Kingdom of Art, Outland finds himself a pilgrim on another crusade. This time he has a story to tell, and he seeks the right person to hear it. "And I only am escaped alone to tell thee."[57]

The relationship between Outland and St. Peter resembles a reunion between twins separated at birth. Outland finds in St. Peter a kindred spirit, someone who can not only share but also understand his enthusiasm for the mesa. For his part, St. Peter finds in Tom Outland a means to his own childhood, which he had virtually forgotten until he recalled Outland's story and began editing his diary. "But now that the vivid consciousness of an earlier state had come back to him, the Professor felt that life with this Kansas boy, little as there had been of it, was the realest of his lives. . . ." (*PH* 264). It is no accident that Willa Cather chose for her character a name whose full form, Thomas, means twin. Thus, Outland's name is a synopsis of his life: always on the outside, he continually tries to connect but continually fails until he meets someone very much like himself, his spiritual twin.

Among the St. Peters, Outland devotes his creative energies not only to art but also to science, the field that, according to the Professor, has contributed nothing but comfort and has actually detracted from life by making it seem less meaningful. With the aid of a tutor, Outland completes three years of work in mathematics in only four months, and he soon becomes "the most brilliant pupil" that physics professor Robert Crane ever had (*PH* 148). These developments would seem abrupt and unbelievable except that the reader sees them in reverse, meeting Outland the scientist in Book I before getting any glimpse of Outland the artist in Book II. Early in Book I, for the benefit of St. Peter's dinner guest Sir Edgar Spilling, Louie Marsellus identifies Outland as "a brilliant young American scientist and inventor. . . ." (*PH* 40). It is only later in the book, though earlier in the life, that Outland appears as a brilliant young American artist. Yet even in this role he displays significant signs of the other one. For example, Outland employs scientific terminology to describe his moment of artistic possession: "It all came together in my understanding, as a series of experiments do when you begin to see where they are leading" (*PH* 250). With the other motives gone, Outland's happiness on the mesa is "unalloyed" (*PH* 251). And his Blue Mesa diary is a model of the amateur archaeologist's record keeping:

There was a minute description of each tool they found, of every piece of cloth and pottery, frequently accompanied by a very suggestive pencil sketch of the object and a surmise as to its use and the kind of life in which it had played a part. (*PH* 262)

Susan Rosowski has called Outland's work in the ruins

> a modern version of the "brutal invaders" who ravaged the ancient tribe. He hired workmen to clear a road to Cliff City, excavated the ruins, numbered specimens, each evening wrote of an account of his work in "a merchant's ledger," and eventually went to Washington for others to "dig out all its secrets. . . ."[58]

There is an interesting irony in Outland's use of a merchant's ledger; however, from the standpoint of archaeology his actions are kindly and commendable, quite the opposite of the wanton removal or destruction of artifacts perpetrated by vandals or invaders. To the archaeologist, precise records of a find—condition, location, depth of burial, and proximity of other objects—are just as important as the find itself. Cather probably knew enough about archaeology, either from her reading or her contact with the Rickners, Jeeps, and Wetherills, to make Tom Outland a responsible caretaker of the ruins, an "incipient scientist," as Sergeant calls him.[59]

Furthermore, within himself there are two sides to Thomas, the twin, which Outland is apparently able to integrate with relative ease. Contrary to John Murphy's belief that Outland's "scientific career seems to have little to do with his true self,"[60] it actually reflects one side of his true self. All the while he conducts his experiments in Dr. Crane's laboratory, Outland also entertains Rosamond and Kathleen with stories of his life with "noble Roddy"; therefore, while inventing an engine to revolutionize the future, Outland busily crafts stories that rejuvenate the past.

Notably, only with the two daughters does Outland feel free at this point to tell his stories.

He would spend hours with them in the garden, making Hopi villages with sand and pebbles, drawing maps of the Painted Desert and the Rio Grande country in the gravel, telling them stories, when there was no one by to listen, about the adventures he had had with his friend Roddy.[61] (*PH* 122)

When Mrs. St. Peter asks to know all about his pots and where he got them, Outland's reply is "courteous but final": "Maybe some day, Ma'am, I can tell you" (*PH* 120). Never again, though, does he take up "the story of his own life . . . either with the Professor or Mrs. St. Peter, though he was often encouraged to do so" (*PH* 124). This audience discrimination probably reflects Willa Cather's faith in the romantic nature of children and a continuation of the theme that started several years earlier with a group of boys on a sandbar dreaming about the Enchanted Bluff.

Outland integrates science and art in another way too, for his success in the one field complements his failure in the other. In a practical sense, Outland fails as an artist.[62] He makes little impression upon the Smithsonian officials, despite the heart-felt rightness of his crusade; his impression upon Roddy Blake comes too late to do any good, either in preventing the abduction of the artifacts by a foreign buyer or in maintaining the friendship with Roddy; and he even leaves his one composition sealed up in rock where no one would ever find it (if Cather had espoused the theory of art for art's sake, this would be the perfect demonstration). As a scientist, however—a "theoretical physicist," James Schroeter calls him— Outland is immensely successful.[63] His invention earns him a patent, immortalizes his name, and brings a fortune to his heirs—all this in spite of a "careless" laboratory technique (*PH* 146) that contrasts sharply with the meticulous care he bestows upon his first science, archaeology.

To return to an earlier point, Tom Outland, like the Blue Mesa he discovers, is an ideal: a young man with an irregular background who is somehow able to synthesize what for most people—Godfrey St. Peter included—are two irreconcilable disciplines. People like that have existed in real life, but rarely—less often, probably, than exceptional students appear in the classes taught by professors St. Peter and Crane. With his ability to see the ruins and artifacts at Mesa Verde in these two ways—to describe them poetically and to analyze them scientifically—Gustaf Nordenskiold was such a person; with her botanist's knowledge of plants and her child's love of wildflowers, Willa Cather was another.[64] If Fenimore Cooper could portray "a being removed from the every-day inducements to err which abound in civilized life, while he retains the best and simplest of his early impressions,"[65] Willa Cather can extract elements from history, autobiography, and imagination to create her own *beau-ideal*, Tom Outland. As one who often longed for "wholeness," for the union of opposites,[66] Cather must have found this creation especially appealing, perhaps even more so than the many professional artists in her other works.

Throughout *The Professor's House*, Tom Outland's presence is so keenly felt that one can easily forget that he is not a character, but a memory. When the novel begins, Outland has been dead for at least four or five years (see the Appendix). He has been gone for so long, in fact, that Scott McGregor confesses to St. Peter, "You know, Tom isn't very real to me any more. Sometimes I think he was just a—a glittering idea" (*PH* 111). McGregor's comment underscores one of the novel's overlooked themes, how profoundly the dead can affect the living.

The legacy of the cliff dwellers, which Tom Outland, Roddy Blake, and Henry Atkins fall heir to, is received with mixed motives. Outland hopes to preserve the find, Blake to realize upon it, and Atkins merely "to share your fortunes" (*PH* 205). For all three, however, the outcome is quite different than expected—and much unhappier—because even in a world of superlatives things seldom turn out as planned. Certainly the same is true in the mundane world, as St. Peter points out (cf. *PH* 23). Indeed, Tom Outland's legacy, divided into two parts according to his dual nature, is just as glittering and just as damaging to its inheritors as the one the cliff dwellers, his "poor grandmothers" (*PH* 243), left him. As Lillian Bloom says, Tom Outland's "real bounty creates discontent and tension."[67]

The more apparent of Outland's legacies is the scientific one, the "formula written out on paper" that had lain for two years in Dr. Crane's laboratory (*PH* 138), awaiting discovery much like Cliff City in Blue Mesa. Perpetuated in the will drawn in Rosamond's favor, this legacy produces substantial monetary rewards but even greater costs: the disruption of social and familial units. The will turns sister against sister: "she's entirely changed," Kathleen complains of Rosamond. "She's become Louie. Indeed, she's worse than Louie" (*PH* 86); brother-in-law against brother-in-law: ". . . Marsellus had never so much as seen Tom Outland, while he, McGregor, had been his classmate and friend" (*PH* 42); father against daughter: "This calling it [the Marselluses' house] after him passes my comprehension. And Rosamond's standing for it! It's brazen impudence" (*PH* 47); and colleague against colleague: Professor Crane says to St. Peter, "You, of course, do profit—indirectly, if not directly. . . . That's as it should be. But your claim was less definite than mine" (*PH* 148).

The interview between Crane and St. Peter, precipitated by the profit-motivated visit of Crane's wife, brings the issue into focus. After Crane admits that he never tried to capitalize on Outland's idea or even to make the gas itself, St. Peter asks him point blank, "Then it's only since this patent has begun to make money that it does interest you?" Uncomfortably, Crane replies, "Yes. It's the money" (*PH* 147). Once this painful interview is over, St. Peter makes this assessment: "If Outland were here to-night, he might say with Mark Antony, *My fortunes have corrupted honest men*" (*PH* 150). Cather's point is that anybody's fortunes would have the same effect.

It would seem that Outland anticipated this development. "When he was working on that gas," St. Peter tells Rosamond,

> he once remarked to me that there might be a fortune in it. To be sure, he didn't wait to find out whether there was a fortune, but that had to do with quite another side of him. Yes, I think he knew his idea would make money and he wanted you to have it, with him or without him. (*PH* 61)

And several times during their work together, according to Dr. Crane, Outland "spoke as if there would be something in it for both of us if our gas became remunerative" (*PH* 145). In these instances, Outland sounds like Roddy Blake expecting to realize on a project. Perhaps it was a premonition of history repeating itself in another legacy begetting discord that made Outland bolt to the front and leave his invention to take care of itself.

In August 1914 the United States had not yet become embroiled in the war in Europe; therefore, like over a thousand young American men, Outland enlists in the French Foreign Legion, certainly a fitting regiment for someone with his name and background. He joins not only with the intention of fighting for "a humanitarian cause he believes in,"[68] but also with the hope of locating Roddy Blake, who he suspects has joined the Legion, too (cf. *PH* 131), having become an outsider himself. In either event, Outland dies as he had lived, for an ideal.[69]

For Rosamond and Louie, the principal heirs to the scientific legacy, Tom Outland has "all turned out chemicals and dollars and cents," Kathleen says to her father. "But not for you and me! Our Tom is much nicer than theirs" (*PH* 132). It is a telling distinction between the two daughters that Kathleen recognizes this difference on her own, whereas Rosamond must have it explained to her in fairly forceful terms. When Rosamond tells her father of the plan that she and Louie have devised to "settle an income" on him so he can devote his time to research, St. Peter says flatly, "I couldn't possibly take any of Outland's money" (*PH* 61). When Rosamond persists, so does he, distancing himself as emphatically as he can from any direct benefit from this side of Outland's legacy:

> Once and for all, Rosamond, understand that he owed me no more than I owed him. . . . And there can be no question of money between me and Tom Outland . . . I'm purely selfish in refusing your offer; my friendship with Outland is the one thing I will not have translated into the vulgar tongue. (*PH* 62)

The "nicer" Tom Outland that Kathleen recognizes is the "quite another side of him" that St. Peter mentions rather cryptically in the earlier part of his conversation with Rosamond. This other side leaves the other legacy, the artistic one, which St. Peter alone inherits.

Notably, the artistic legacy is documented not by a will, which is the means of disseminating the remnants of a life once lived, but by a diary, a daily record of a life in the fullness of being lived. It also takes some important intangible forms: shared interests, sympathies, and enthusiasms; Saturdays spent sailing together on the lake; stories told after a shared meal of leg of lamb and steaming asparagus; a trip together to the Southwest to retrace a missionary's route and to retrieve a boy's past.[70] Like the scientific legacy, however, it too bears the strain of corruption because it contributes to the family's monetary success by enhancing the latter volumes of St. Peter's history, the ones that attracted public notice and eventually brought him the prize that bought him the new house. For St. Peter, the real contribution, though, is in the quality of the work, not the money it brings. As he tells his wife, if he could trade the money for the fun he had writing his history, she would never have gotten her house. "But one couldn't get that for twenty thousand dollars. The great pleasures don't come so cheap" (*PH* 33). Ironically, even in repudiating the translation of his work into the "vulgar tongue," St. Peter uses that tongue himself.

The artistic legacy also causes a familial disruption of its own. Early in their association with Outland, "Mrs. St. Peter saw more of their protégé than her husband did" (*PH* 122), partly because St. Peter at first "held the boy at arm's length," having been fooled before by a student who seemed extraordinary but was really quite common (*PH* 121–22). Mrs. St. Peter helped Outland with domestic and social adjustments and made him feel welcome in their home. By the time Outland became a senior, however, ". . . Lillian began to be jealous of him," (*PH* 172–73), "fiercely jealous" (*PH* 49). Loretta Wasserman makes a good point in saying that Lillian's jealousy of Tom Outland "arose from her justified fear that St. Peter was using him in a vain attempt to hold on to his own youth."[71] However, there is even more at stake:

> He had been almost a member of the family for two years, and she had never found fault with the boy. But after the Professor began to take Tom up to the study and talk over his work with him, began to make a companion of him, then Mrs. St. Peter withdrew her favour. (*PH* 173)

Because she sees Tom Outland as a rival for her husband's "mental companionship" (*PH* 50), Mrs. St. Peter also begins to find fault where before she had found none. Sensitive to the change in her demeanor, Outland begins "to make his work a pretext for coming to the house less often," preferring to meet the Professor at the university (*PH* 173). Thus, Outland is on the outside again.

This time, however, he has a companion, one who would not sell his country's secrets but who would be glad merely to travel to the Blue Mesa and "to look off at those long, rugged, untamed vistas dear to the American heart" (*PH* 270). To this companion Outland entrusts his more valuable legacy by taking him to the Blue Mesa, by giving him his diary, and by telling him his story: in short, by inviting him into the Kingdom of Art.

Granted, St. Peter's daughters were the first to be told about Outland's adventures on the Blue Mesa, the first to whom Outland spoke "freely and confidentially about himself" (*PH* 124); but in those stories, which St. Peter overheard "through the open windows" (*PH* 125), "there were no shadows" (*PH* 123). Not until one summer evening three years after his arrival in Hamilton, one summer when the rest of the family is away, does Tom Outland finally tell the whole story, shadows and all. Cather calls it "Tom Outland's Story," with the emphasis upon possession. Even with all the shadows in place, however, the story is "nothing very incriminating"—except to the teller; "nothing very remarkable"—except to the listener; "a story of youthful defeat, the sort of thing a boy is sensitive about—until he grows older" (*PH* 176)—until he is at last able to tell it.

It is both natural and significant that Outland uses the ancient oral form,[72] which connects him to a long line of story-tellers, and that he selects an archetypal setting: "It was on one of those rainy nights, before the fire in the dining-room, that Tom at last told the story he had always kept back" (*PH* 176). The thematic and compositional unity achieved by this setting is remarkable.

The fire is the eternal flame of narrative, a dreamy, flickering backdrop to the stories of one generation after another, a manifestation of Cather's "absolute, lifelong vision" of "preserving through history some sacred fire . . . the quest and the voyage perilous."[73] Hundreds of years ago the cliff dwellers told the first stories of life in a world above the world while they crouched around their own fires: fires that left soot on the walls of Panther Canyon—"They were that near!" Thea Kronborg exclaims (*SL* 375); and fires that charred the bottoms of their cooking pots—"Nothing [else] makes those people seem so real to me," Tom Outland confesses (*PH* 119). Willa Cather probably had the same feeling as she listened to the stories of Jesse Walter Fewkes around a campfire at Mesa Verde one late summer evening in 1915. Perhaps it was then, among the homes of an ancient people whose fires she could see burning still, that Cather conceived her glittering idea and found a home for her Kingdom of Art. "Come . . . inherit the kingdom prepared for you from the foundation of the world."[74]

7 ✳ *The World of Men and Women*

*When Willa Cather* was naming the two major characters in *The Professor's House* and conceiving the relationship between them, she probably had in mind a familiar passage from the Book of Matthew: "Upon this rock," Jesus said of Simon Peter, "I will build my church. . . . And I will give unto thee the keys of the kingdom of heaven."[1] Tom Outland does not build a church in the usual scriptural sense, of course, but he does discover and comprehend the Kingdom of Art, the world of ideals where art and religion merge into a grand harmonious whole; and he leaves to his own disciple, Godfrey St. Peter, the keys to this kingdom. Just as allegorical as the ones in the passage from Matthew, these keys take the form of an artistic legacy, a legacy that began with a primitive, rock-dwelling people; that was passed on to a boy who discovered "a city of stone, asleep"; and that was finally entrusted to one whose name, St. Peter, perpetuates the symbol of the rock and whose nature perpetuates the ideal. Through his own gift of sympathy, St. Peter is able to take up the cross first borne by Tom Outland. Moreover, their lives become so intertwined that each complements the other and each is reflected in the other, like the ideal of twins.[2] The two men are alike in another way, a darker one, in that their efforts on behalf of the Kingdom of Art lead to personal ruin.

For years, long before he ever met Tom Outland, the "artist-historian"³ Godfrey St. Peter had demonstrated his gift of sympathy by championing the integrity of the university against the onslaught of those philistines of academia: enrollment-conscious deans, watered down courses, and trade school mentality. Even so, he reaches out to the world at large by writing not only for academic journals but also for popular magazines, a practice that usually gets him "into trouble" (*PH* 114) but that at least in Outland's case leads to a happy result. Thus, he has often taken that voyage perilous between the brain and the hand.

Both Outland and St. Peter are realistic enough about their skills to recognize their shortcomings. During their first meeting, the Professor asks Outland, "what are your deficiencies?" The young man replies simply and directly: "I've never had any mathematics or science, and I write a very bad hand" (*PH* 114).⁴ St. Peter wastes no time in arranging for Outland's remediation. Likewise, St. Peter acknowledges his own "lack of early association, the fact that he had not spent his youth in the great dazzling South-west country which was the scene of his explorers' adventures" (*PH* 258); yet he is sensitive enough to benefit from one who possesses what he lacks— "a boy who had grown up there, a boy with imagination . . . who had in his pocket the secrets which old trails and stones and water-courses tell only to adolescence" (*PH* 259). The result is a perceptible enhancement of the volumes written under Outland's influence, under the inspiration, albeit vicarious, of a vision of the Kingdom of Art. The complementary relationship between Outland and St. Peter is so close that what one character lacks, the other supplies; or, as John Randall says, each one "knows the world which is a mystery to the other."⁵

Through Outland's influence, the alignment of sympathies grows even closer. St. Peter assumes the intimate task of editing Tom Outland's diary and writing for it an introduction that will complete the story. This introduction is the problem, the "bother":

To mean anything, it [the diary] must be prefaced by a sketch of Outland, and some account of his later life and achievements. To write of his scientific work would be comparatively easy. But that was not all the story; his was a many-sided mind, though a simple and straightforward personality. (*PH* 171–72)

St. Peter must do what Cather tried to do with her characters, to get inside another person's skin, which even in this case is a perspective not easily achieved.

Beyond even this intimate literary relationship, St. Peter also assumes the burden of guilt that Outland carried to his death over his treatment of Roddy Blake: "Do you know, Kitty," he says to his younger daughter, "I sometimes think I ought to go out and look for Blake myself. He's on my conscience. If that country down there weren't so everlastingly big—" (*PH* 131). This guilt over Blake is Outland's other cross, the one he must bear because he took up the first one for the Kingdom of Art. One thinks again of the relationship between Jesus and Simon Peter.

Even in a familial sense, St. Peter is the reflection of Tom Outland. He too is an orphan, at least at times. During the reverie of his childhood inspired by memories of Tom Outland, St. Peter thinks in terms of "his adoption into the Thierault household" when he was a young student who had gone to France "to try his luck," leaving behind him in the Solomon Valley a "twin," another childhood that he remembered only rarely, "in moments of homesickness" (*PH* 264). Then as he contemplates, or dreads, the return of his family from France, St. Peter yearns to remain utterly alone, an orphan. Ironically, this desire comes just as the family shows signs of growth, returning earlier than planned "to prepare for the advent of a young Marsellus" (*PH* 273).

He loved his family, he would make any sacrifice for them, but just now he couldn't live with them. He must be alone. That was more necessary to him than anything had ever been, more necessary, even, than his marriage had been in his vehement youth. He could not live with his family again—not even with Lillian. Especially not with Lillian! (*PH* 274)

For Cather this is the old dilemma: family versus art; the World versus the Kingdom. It erupted before in the conflict between Tom Outland and Roddy Blake, and it has governed the way St. Peter has lived his life. Nowhere is the dilemma better illustrated than in the physical circumstances in which St. Peter had worked in the old house, described in Book I. In his attic study, he preferred to write by the light of "a faithful kerosene lamp." But when the oil ran out, rather than risk going downstairs for more, he jammed an eyeshade on his forehead and worked by the glare of a "tormenting pear-shaped [electric] bulb, sticking out of the wall on a short curved neck just about four feet above his table." Otherwise, on his way downstairs to refill the oil can,

> he would almost surely become interested in what the children were doing, or in what his wife was doing—or he would no-tice that the kitchen linoleum was breaking under the sink where the maid kicked it up, and he would stop to tack it down. On that perilous journey down through the human house he might lose his mood, his enthusiasm, even his temper. (*PH* 27)

Now, in Book III, fresh from his work on Outland's diary and the recollection of his story, St. Peter seems determined to retain his connection to the Kingdom of Art despite the consequences of "falling out of love," "falling out of all domestic and social relations, out of his place in the human family, indeed" (*PH* 275): in other words, in spite of being on the outside; in spite of being an orphan.

St. Peter and Outland are also alike in their attachments to women, almost to the point of being involved with the same woman under two guises. In one of those inexplicable twists of fate, Tom Outland, "a young man who saw a great deal," saw in his fiancée

Rosamond only what other people saw: "her rich complexion, her curving, unresisting mouth and mysterious eyes" (*PH* 59). To St. Peter, this older daughter is his own wife's "second self," the daughter for whom the mother "always worked things out" (*PH* 66). As John Murphy explains, Rosamond is indeed "her mother all over again, hard to the touch like seamstress Augusta's first form and imprisoning like the wire bird cage bosom of the second"—at least as St. Peter perceives her.[6]

Finally, through the recollections of his boyhood, St. Peter develops the capacity to respond to the facts and scenes of nature in the same elemental, emotive way in which Tom Outland responds to the Blue Mesa during that summer of his high tide. As Susan Rosowski explains, "Tom Outland's Story," which for Godfrey St. Peter is an "extended memory," rekindles St. Peter's own "youthful imagination" and anticipates the " 'new friendship' with 'the original, unmodified Godfrey St. Peter' that follows":[7]

> The Kansas boy who had come back to St. Peter this summer was not a scholar. He was a primitive. He was only interested in earth and woods and water. Wherever sun sunned and rain rained and snow snowed, wherever life sprouted and decayed, places were alike to him. He was not nearly so cultivated as Tom's old cliff-dwellers must have been—and yet he was terribly wise. He seemed to be at the root of the matter; Desire under all desires, Truth under all truths. He seemed to know, among other things, that he was solitary and must always be so. . . . He was earth, and would return to earth. (*PH* 265)

Like the corresponding passage in Tom Outland's experience, this one echoes Thea Kronborg's revelation upon her entry into Panther Canyon: "She was getting back to the earliest sources of gladness that she could remember. She had loved the sun, and the brilliant solitudes of sand and sun, long before . . . other things had come along. . . ." (*SL* 369).

According to Richard Giannone, St. Peter achieves his insight "in a pre-literate, auditory way," a fundamental means of identifying his own birth with that of all life.[8] If this is the case, then the same process also connects St. Peter with the ancient oral tradition of story-telling that Tom Outland continues.

St. Peter is well suited as the inheritor of an artistic legacy for another reason: he has the writer's interest in hands. More than an implement of manual dexterity—even though St. Peter "had a deft hand with tools" (*PH* 11)—the hand is for St. Peter and Willa Cather alike the image and agent of creativity. Bernice Slote calls the hand the "personal metaphor which was to haunt her [Cather] all her life. . . . The hand is the ultimate port, the instrument of birth, the ship of impossibilities."[9]

Although she took a particular interest in actual hands themselves—for instance, she admired the hands of Charles Gere, publisher of the *Nebraska State Journal,* because they were "dark and sinewy and so much alive," full of "a singular elegance" (*WCP* 181)[10]—it was the hand as metaphor that Cather frequently invoked in her praise of other writers. To describe Thomas Mann's power as a writer, Cather refers to "the strong feeling under the strong hand" (*NUF* 100); in her tribute to Émile Zola, she extols "the courage of the hand that penned *J'Accuse*" (*WP* 724); to illustrate the long apprentice period of "writing for writing's sake," which both she and Katherine Mansfield served, Cather affirms that it is only "the practised hand that can make the natural gesture,—and the practised hand has often to grope its way" (*NUF* 144); just when Robert Lewis Stevenson's life and career seemed at an end, "all his ancient cunning of hand returned to him, and he died in the high tide of a great novel, producing magnificently . . . as such a man should die" (*KA* 315); finally, *The Scarlet Letter* owes its wealth of "material investiture" to "the reserved, fastidious hand of an artist" (*WCOW* 41)—a phrase echoed three years later in *The Professor's House.*

Although the source of a powerful metaphor, the physical hand is always susceptible to injury and disability, in which case the catastrophe is compounded by the metaphorical association. According to Edith Lewis, "the greatest working calamity of her career" was a painful swelling in Cather's wrist, "a serious inflammation of the sheath of the tendon" that would recur from 1933 throughout the rest of her life.[11] And James Woodress notes that a horror of mutilation, especially of the hand, obsessed Cather from the beginning to the end of her career, from "The Clemency of the Court" (1893) to the unfinished Avignon manuscript, "which she was writing when she died."[12]

Reflecting Cather's own association, St. Peter recalls "those golden days" at the beginning of his work on the *Spanish Adventurers* as a time "when he could feel his hand growing easier with his material" (*PH* 32). He attributes also to the "hand, fastidious and bold, which selected and placed," the pleasing effect of bringing autumn indoors and thereby enhancing that "bright October afternoon" (*PH* 75)— not by manipulating and improving nature but by engaging in a responsive unity with it: "the seasons sometimes gain by being brought into the house, just as they gain by being brought into painting, and into poetry" (*PH* 75). Later, however, the hand image darkens, as St. Peter considers his resistance to the "difficult" task of editing Tom Outland's diary and writing an introduction to it: "It was a little thing, but one of those little things at which the hand becomes self-conscious, feels itself stiff and clumsy" (*PH* 171).

St. Peter's interest in hands extends to the actual hands of those people closest to him. A large part of Lillian's attraction is her "[n]ice hands . . . always such nice hands" (*PH* 48). When Tom Outland offers the two turquoises to Rosamond and Kathleen, it is not the stones that catch St. Peter's interest but "the hand that held them: the muscular, many-lined palm, the long, strong fingers with soft ends, the straight little finger, the flexible, beautifully shaped thumb that curved back from the rest of the hand as if it were its own master. What a hand!" (*PH* 121).

Hands reflect relationships, too. During a rare moment of close-
ness between St. Peter and his wife, at the opera *Mignon,* St. Peter
does not take his wife's hand but "one of her gloves," which he
draws "out through his fingers" (*PH* 95). This image continues the
hand motif but injects into it an unmistakable distance, like the
"separation" that St. Peter teasingly alludes to while bantering with
Augusta about his dual residence. Granted that "tender moment[s]
of conjugal affection" are rare in Cather's fiction generally,[13] this
scene is still significant because it shows St. Peter toying with a
symbol twice removed rather than responding to the "something
lonely and forgiving in her voice, [the] something that spoke of an
old wound, healed and hardened and hopeless" (*PH* 94). If Lillian
then turns away and says nothing more, if she withdraws from him
and toward her sons-in-law, it is at least partly because St. Peter
withdraws deeper and deeper into himself. "I wonder what it is,"
Lillian asks him, "that makes you draw away from your family. Or
who it is." "You are not old enough for the pose you take," she tells
him. "You're naturally warm and affectionate; all at once you begin
shutting yourself away from everybody" (*PH* 162). By the end of the
novel, this process is too far advanced to reverse.

Eventually, St. Peter reverts to a primitive state and pictures
himself utterly alone, almost a pre-human removed from personal
contact altogether. Susan Rosowski sees this transition as a positive
one, a "letting go of ties to the external world and releasing the
truths of his own heart" that allows St. Peter to reach a dream state
in which Cather saw "a redemption for the human soul":[14]

> by casting off everyday preoccupations and detaching himself
> from others' worries, [St. Peter] becomes the author of his own
> solitude and feels a being opening within. In his daydreams St.
> Peter enjoys a timeless peace and communication with his
> world so close that he does not distinguish between himself
> and it. He was, Cather wrote, not a scholar but a primitive....

St. Peter ceases to be a perceiver and his world ceases to be an other; there is no distance.[15]

This may be, but it is accomplished at the loss of St. Peter's identity with "the world of men and women" (*PH* 279), a loss greater than any gain from a complete union with nature or even a merging "with all life"[16] because it leaves him powerless to act. As Ernest Becker points out, "[i]ntroversion is impotence."[17] Furthermore, as James Maxfield has noted, this state of inactivity contrasts sharply with the "compulsively hard worker" that St. Peter had been.[18] Alone with his dreams, St. Peter is like Hamlet, for whom there was no good or bad except as "thinking makes it so." Also like Hamlet, St. Peter indulges in excuses for not acting, for not rejoining the world of men and women: he would look for Blake if the country were not so large; he would revisit the monument to Delacroix except that "chance, in one great catastrophe, [had] swept away all youth and all palms, and almost Time itself" (*PH* 260). Before the moment of letting go, St. Peter considers driving "up in front of Notre Dame, in Paris, again, . . . [to] see it standing there like the Rock of Ages, with the frail generations breaking about its base." Or perhaps he will go "down into Outland's country, to watch the sunrise break on sculptured peaks and impassable mountain passes" (*PH* 270). Of course, he does neither. His name having become an ironic symbol, St. Peter himself has already broken against the rocks. Such is the consequence of his desire to free himself of entanglements with the world of men and women.

Had he lifted his hand at an earlier time St. Peter probably could have salvaged any one of several compensations that, taken together or even separately, would be the envy of almost anyone, even other professors whose opinions he would respect. Somewhat astonished at the Professor's dismay, Leon Edel summarizes the things that should make him happy: "he is a prize-winning historian, his work is recognized, he is about to become a grandfather."[19] To this list one might add fine memories of a happy life. However, St. Peter's withdrawal from other people, for which he is mostly to blame, has transformed these achievements into trifles, which he regards with indifference rather than satisfaction.[20] St. Peter is like Hawthorne's Wakefield, another "Outcast of the Universe" who, through his own volition, caused a "perilous . . . chasm in human affections," so that "an almost impassable gulf divides his hired apartment from his former home."[21] Readers are not likely to feel sympathetic toward Wakefield's isolation because it is capricious and self-determined; and to the extent that they see St. Peter as the author of his own discontent—hoist with his own petard—they will be impatient with him too.

Once St. Peter decides that he can no longer live with Lillian, he pictures her hand as the symbol of that "intense and positive" nature that he cannot endure: "If her character were reduced to an heraldic device, it would be a hand (a beautiful hand) holding flaming arrows—the shafts of her violent loves and hates, her clear-cut ambitions" (*PH* 275).

It is also in terms of the hand that St. Peter contemplates the fate that Outland was spared, a fate strikingly similar to the one he himself has endured:

> What change would have come in his blue eye, in his fine long hand with the backspringing thumb, which had never han-dled things that were not the symbols of ideas? A hand like that, had he lived, must have been put to other uses. His fellow scientists, his wife, the town and State, would have required many duties of it. It would have had to write thousands of useless letters, frame thousands of false excuses. It would have had to 'manage' a great deal of money, to be the instrument of a woman who would grow always more exacting. He had escaped all that. He had made something new in the world—and the rewards, the meaningless conventional gestures, he had left to others. (*PH* 261)

These applications—perversions, even—of the hand constitute the "imperfect practice" to which the Blue Mesa ideal would have been reduced if Tom Outland had lived.[22]

Just as the hand image dominates St. Peter's ultimate thoughts of Lillian and Tom Outland, so it becomes the controlling metaphor for the Professor's ultimate experience of letting go. Alone in his old study, with all its associations of death—no longer terrifying but strangely consoling—St. Peter finally reads the two letters he has received from his family, "one addressed in Lillian's hand and one in Louie's" (*PH* 273). The burdens they imply have made him "drop his shoulders and look woefully tired" (*PH* 273). Even as early as Book I, St. Peter had told his wife, "now I seem to be tremendously tired. One pays, coming or going. A man has got only just so much in him; when it's gone he slumps" (*PH* 163). At this moment, however, a sense of his family's imminent arrival seems to seize him, and he grabs up his hat and light overcoat to rush downstairs on some unindicated mission; but half-way down,

> he stopped short, went back to his study, and softly shut the door behind him. He sat down, forgetting to take off his overcoat, though the afternoon was so hot and his face was damp with perspiration. He sat motionless, breathing unevenly, one dark hand lying clenched on his writing-table. (*PH* 274)

Both the image of the clenched hand and the progression leading up to it are unmistakable. Early in his career, when the design of his work was unfolding before him, when he had his own perception of the Kingdom of Art, St. Peter could feel his hand "growing easier" with the material (*PH* 32). Then just as he was beginning his third volume, aware of his "great drawback," "into his house walked a boy . . . with imagination" and his pockets full of secrets to make the last volumes "more simple and inevitable than those that went before" (*PH* 258–59). In other words, at the very time "when the morning brightness of the world was wearing off for him, along came Outland and brought him a kind of second youth" (*PH* 258), that "ceremonial youth" whose "constant turning inward and expulsion of disturbances and grown up obligations" is so necessary to creativity.[23] In her fifties, the age at which she completed *The Professor's House,* Cather "believed in youth, its creativeness and its fecundity. . . ."[24] Also its energy.

Now, with Outland gone and his family removed from him physically and spiritually, St. Peter tries again to find solace in his work, his art. It is symptomatic of his enervated condition that the Professor does not attempt anything even remotely as ambitious as *The Spanish Adventurers.* Rather, the project at hand is merely the annotation of and introduction to the diary of a friend. James Maxfield believes that, were it not for the loss of the inspiration Tom Outland provided, St. Peter could devote himself to another grand, multi-volume history, perhaps *French Explorers in the Northwest.*[25] One must remember, however, that long before Tom Outland appeared St. Peter found his own inspiration for his work and that it was well underway by the time the two men met in the garden. Certainly St. Peter feels the loss of his kindred spirit, but the silence into which he has lapsed comes from a different, a deeper, malaise, one that has turned his hand "stiff and clumsy" and made the work, even writing about Outland, a "bother," which St. Peter approaches not with the focus and energy of his earlier work but "in a desultory way" (*PH* 262). Tillie Olsen has pointed out that, for a variety of reasons, periods of silence often follow a writer's completion of a truly fine work.[26] In the case of Godfrey St. Peter, the silence may well be permanent.

While trifling away two months at a task "which should have taken little more than a week" (*PH* 263), St. Peter is also reflecting, which he has done before; but this time he sees his life for what it has been. The more he reflects—the closer he comes to the elemental truths of life and art—the more he realizes that "the most important things in his life . . . had been determined by chance" (*PH*

257); that all the years since his childhood "had been accidental and ordered from the outside" (*PH* 264); that ever since Lillian and his conjugation of the verb "to love," "existence had been a catching at handholds" (*PH* 264); that "the design of his life had been the work of this secondary social man, the lover" (*PH* 265); and that even his histories "had no more to do with his original ego than his daughters had" (*PH* 265). These last two realizations in particular make one wonder whether St. Peter ever had a clear view of the Kingdom of Art. Still, he "did not regret his life, but he was indifferent to it. It seemed to him like the life of another person" (*PH* 267).

For a while, these reflections seem as desultory and trifling as his work with Outland's diary; and for the first time in his life St. Peter is able to loaf, to day-dream, to enjoy "doing nothing" (*PH* 269): in other words, to enjoy being free of all the duties—personal, domestic, social, academic, and creative—to which his life had always been committed. But then comes that moment in the study.

The dark hand lying clenched on the writing table is a double symbol, a paradox. In one sense it shows the hand no longer able to write, having degenerated inexorably since those early days of feeling easy with the material, so that it now displays what Michael Klug has called a "paralysis of the creative spirit."[27] As long as St. Peter can maintain his desultory attitude, as long as he can enjoy doing nothing, he will not mind the loss. But the habits of a lifetime are not easily abandoned. Just as the world makes it "hard to hold fast to art pure and simple" (*KA* 406), so the exhilaration of art is difficult to let go. In its other sense, then, the dark hand is clenched in a vain effort to hold onto a dream that St. Peter has already lost— or even worse, a dream that he may never have fully grasped at all. For a writer, or for any artist, this is as grim as it gets: either to lose the gift in the end or to realize finally that one has never had it, never had possession. St. Peter "has consumed himself. His fire is out."[28] In the context of art that is religion, St. Peter's experience is "the loss of the gods themselves," another of Cather's lamentations over the theme of "lost divinity, or lost belief."[29]

David Stouck correctly calls Leon Edel to task for objecting that St. Peter's despair lacks clear motivation. Stouck counters by insisting,

> specific motives are hardly essential to great art; if so what do we make of *Hamlet*? Surely it is precisely because the professor's depression and despair are not literally accounted for (as that of Ishmael in *Moby Dick* or the narrator of *Walden* are not) that they assume the dimensions of a universal experience.[30]

Yet when St. Peter's despair is shown to stem from the loss of the very forces and desires that have motivated his life, it becomes all the more tragic.

At first, St. Peter successfully diverts his attention from the major cause of his despair to a lesser one, his family. "There must, he was repeating to himself, there must be some way in which a man who had always tried to live up to his responsibilities could, when the hour of desperation came, avoid meeting his own family" (*PH* 274). He stays in his study the entire afternoon, sitting "at his desk with bent head, reviewing his life, trying to see where he had made his mistake," trying "to account for the fact that he now wanted to run away from everything he had intensely cared for" (*PH* 275). And for a while he feels safe, even from Augusta, who surely will not come on such a stormy night to retrieve the keys to the new house, which Lillian had assigned her to do. Finally, he falls asleep, perhaps, as one critic suggests, sharing Outland's desire never to waken.[31] But he does awaken later with the realization that the "long-anticipated coincidence had happened. . . . The storm had blown the stove out and the window shut" (*PH* 276), putting St. Peter's life in imminent peril. The danger of asphyxiation is ironically reminiscent of the stuporous effect upon Tom Outland of the scent of wild-current bushes in the sun that "made [him] want to lie down and sleep" (*PH* 240). As St. Peter debates what to do, the hand is again the central image:

How far was a man required to exert himself against accident? How would such a case be decided under English law? He hadn't lifted his hand against himself—was he required to lift it for himself? (*PH* 276).

After his own long night of the soul, St. Peter learns that Augusta, who came after all, has saved him by pulling him out into the hall. The illumination that follows is St. Peter's realization that Augusta is essential to his salvation, both now and in the future. A "corrective, a remedial influence"; "the bloomless side of life" (*PH* 280); and one "seasoned and sound and on the solid earth" (*PH* 281); Augusta is the one character in the novel completely unaffected by Tom Outland and his vision of the Kingdom of Art. Frank W. Shelton suggests that in her new relationship to St. Peter, Augusta parallels what Mother Eve had meant to Tom Outland, the embodiment of "an extended family to which he can relate."[32] Certainly she is the embodiment of the new direction in his life, for it is toward her—not toward Outland or Roddy Blake—that the Professor begins to feel "a sense of obligation . . . instinctive, escaping definition, but real. And when you admitted that a thing was real, that was enough—now" (*PH* 281).

This new sense of obligation is possible because St. Peter has let go of his old ones, his family and the Kingdom of Art. "He didn't, on being quite honest with himself, feel any obligations toward his family. Lillian had had the best years of his life . . . and joyful years they had been. . . . But they were gone. His daughters had outgrown any great need of him" (*PH* 281). Thanks to Rosamond, St. Peter has also learned "how painful the paternal relation could be" (*PH* 155). Partly because it has been underway for years, the release of familial obligations is not very difficult; the other, however, St. Peter mightily resists.

In that moment of crisis, he did lift his hand to save himself after all, though the feeling he recalls is one of "acute, agonized strangulation" (*PH* 282), which suggests that in the very act of saving his life he must also lose it. This image turns Cather's artistic creed completely around. Echoing Scripture once again, Cather believed that the artist must lose his worldly life in order to save the artistic one, as if to suggest that the one were the mortal enemy of the other; St. Peter, however, having lost his artistic life, must try to save what is left of the other one. Even so, the life of art is still too "precious" for him to have relinquished it "consciously" (*PH* 282), for him to have willingly unclenched his hand. Therefore, his "temporary release from consciousness" (*PH* 282) has the beneficial effect of permitting an artistic suicide and providing a worldly salvation. As Cather said in her inscription to Robert Frost, *The Professor's House* "is really a story of 'letting go with the heart,'"[33] but the release is accomplished through the medium of the hand.[34]

Sister Peter Damian Charles has identified the inscription to Frost as an allusion to one of his poems, "Wild Grapes": "nothing tells me / That I need learn to let go with the heart."[35] Because of the similarities between Frost's poem and Godfrey St. Peter's condition, this allusion bears a closer look.

"Wild Grapes" is a woman's recollection of a childhood experience when she and her older brother were out picking grapes. Their method has the brother climb to the top of a white birch tree, on which the grapes are growing, and bend the tree with his weight until his sister can grasp it. The plan is foiled, however, because the sister weighs so little that the tree lifts her like a fish caught on a pole. Although her brother shouts "Let go!" the girl, "with something of the baby grip / Acquired ancestrally in just such trees," clings to the tree "uncomplainingly for life." Finally, her brother climbs the tree again and bends it to let her down. Once her feet "felt ground. . . . / And the world came revolving back to me," the speaker says, "I know I looked long at my curled-up fingers, / Before I straightened them and brushed the bark off." "Try to weigh something next time," her brother instructs her.

The poem concludes with the adult speaker's assessment of her situation, then and now:

I had not learned to let go with the hands,
As still I have not learned to with the heart
And have no wish to with the heart—nor need,
That I can see. The mind—is not the heart.
I may yet live, as I know others live,
To wish in vain to let go with the mind—
Of cares, at night, to sleep; but nothing tells me
That I need learn to let go with the heart.[36]

This passage presents an affirmation of life that is beyond St. Peter's grasp. As another who had taken the voyage perilous, who had had his own lover's quarrel with the world, Robert Frost would have well understood the significance of letting go with the heart.

In a reversed way, St. Peter's experience of letting go parallels Tom Outland's experience of possession, pointing to a way in which the novel comes full circle. During that memorable summer, Outland would awaken every morning with the feeling that he "had found everything, instead of having lost everything" (*PH* 251). In other words, for the loss of his one true friend, as well as the hundreds of Blue Mesa artifacts, Outland finds more than ample compensation in the life of the Kingdom of Art. One might well wonder at the abrogation of human ties that permits this feeling, but it is there nonetheless, almost to excess: "at night, when I watched . . . [the sun] drop down behind the edge of the plain below me, I used to feel that I couldn't have borne another hour of that consuming light, that I was full to the brim. . . ." (*PH* 251–252). St. Peter, however, has let go of "something very precious," and "it was gone" (*PH* 282). He has not lost everything either, but what is left hardly threatens to overwhelm him, as the sun does Tom Outland. St. Peter may have achieved the state implied in his given name—Godfrey, or God's peace—but it is an empty peace achieved through an absence of vitality rather than a resolution of conflict, an abandonment rather than a setting free.[37] To call St. Peter's condition a "triumph of the individual," as one early critic did,[38] or to see it as an achievement of "psychic composure," as a more recent critic has,[39] is to miss the point entirely. In exchange for "joy . . . [and] passionate griefs" (*PH* 282), both familial and artistic, St. Peter now has "a world full of Augustas" (*PH* 281). One pays, coming or going.

The novel has come full circle in another way, too. No longer grasping at the world above the world or seeing designs of books unfolding in the air above him, St. Peter now feels "the ground under his feet" (*PH* 283), like the speaker in Frost's poem, and feels himself "outward bound" with this world full of Augustas (*PH* 281). And for good reason. Before, when Tom Outland offered him the keys to the Kingdom of Art, St. Peter felt even more torn between two worlds just as he was torn between two houses. Now, the Kingdom of Art is "gone," and Augusta holds "the keys of the new house" (*PH* 277). As Lillian tells her husband, Augusta "would be the best person to open the house and arrange to have the cleaning done. She would take it entirely off his shoulders . . ." (*PH* 273). She is also the person whom St. Peter would "rather have . . . with him just now than anyone he could think of" (*PH* 281). Augusta has even supplanted his memories of Tom Outland, who is not mentioned again.

There was a time when St. Peter's personal and social lives were happily intermingled, when "the most important chapters of his history were interwoven with personal memories" (*PH* 101). But that was a long time ago, before the little girls had grown up, before husband and wife had grown apart, and before Tom Outland's money had worked its insidious destruction. John Gleason attributes St. Peter's "baffling sense of defeat" to the fact that "every character in his world, himself not excepted, has had his life distorted by money."[40] Certainly the corruption of money is a factor, but St. Peter's condition is far more serious.

The novel ends with St. Peter suffering the ultimate despair, virtually total isolation. Rather than having "heeded too exclusively the call of the false god of the intellect,"[41] or having "made his ultimate commitment to art instead of life,"[42] his problem is one of overextension. Having tried for so long to live in both worlds, the one above and the one below, St. Peter ultimately lives in neither. He has lost possession of the kingdom, the old house has been moved out from under him, he has eluded the house that was made for him "ere thou wast born," and he is now dispossessed of the new house to which Augusta holds the keys. The title of the novel, *The Professor's House,* is almost mocking in its irony in that St. Peter, having rejected the new house and having made the old uninhabitable, now owns no house at all. St. Peter is the ultimate orphan, dispossessed of house, of love, of family, of the secondary self he had become, and of the primary self he had rediscovered. Not only does St. Peter have the dubious distinction of being the first "major male character" in Cather's fiction to face "reality and the unidealized life,"[43] he is also the only major character, male or female, to be so completely deprived of identity and place. To describe St. Peter's condition in literary terms, the "interior monologue" that occupied most of Book III has become "a progression toward muteness."[44]

Augusta misses the irony, of course, but her remark hits home: when St. Peter confesses that he feels "rather lonely—for the first time in months," she explains, "That's because your family are coming home" (*PH* 279). What would be a comfort to any other man is to St. Peter an irritation of an old wound, a painfully close-up view of an unbridgeable distance. While the orphaned Ishmael could look with hope toward the *Rachel,* the outcast St. Peter must face with fortitude the *Berengaria* and a world devoid of delight.

If any hope remains for Godfrey St. Peter at the end of the novel, it comes from the simple fact that he is still alive—"to bear is to conquer our fate," Cather once wrote—and from the feeling that he is "outward bound" (*PH* 281) with a world full of Augustas. The word "outward" suggests a reversed direction for one whose inclinations had been mostly inward, especially during these last months. Furthermore, there is at least a hint of redemption in St. Peter's seeing "humankind" in Augusta, "as if after a definite absence from the world of men and women" (*PH* 279). "He thought he knew where he was," Cather says, but it is a place he has never been, with a self he has never known.

8 ❈ *The First Book I've Ever Written With Any Irony In It*

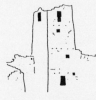 *In their biography* of Willa Cather, E. K. Brown and Leon Edel point out several similarities between what Godfrey St. Peter expects Tom Outland would have been required to do and what Cather herself refused to do: "She never became an official personage. . . . She declined to join societies. . . . If a letter appeared useless, she did not write it; and instead of a false excuse she preferred a frank explanation. . . ."[1] In his biography of Willa Cather, James Woodress draws extensive parallels between Cather and St. Peter:

> The same age as Cather, the professor was born on a farm on the shores of Lake Michigan, which has for him the same emotional pull as the mountains of the Shenandoah Valley had for Cather. He had a strong-willed Protestant mother, a gentle father, and a patriarchial grandfather, all of which Cather had. When he was eight, his parents dragged him out to the wheatlands of Kansas and 'St. Peter nearly died of it.' As an adult he went back to the region of his childhood for his professional career, just as Cather did. After he had been teaching a number of years, he conceived of his plan for a great historical work and then devoted fifteen years of his life to writing it. 'All the while that he was working so fiercely by night, he was earning his living during the day,' as Cather

earned her living as journalist and teacher while she wrote fiction in her spare time. . . . The first three volumes of his history made no stir at all, just as Cather's first three books . . . brought her little acclaim. With the professor's fourth volume (for Cather it was *O Pioneers!*) he began to attract attention; with the fifth and sixth (for Cather, *The Song of the Lark* and *My Antonia*) he began to be well known; and with the last two volumes (for Cather, *One of Ours* and *A Lost Lady*) he achieved an international reputation. . . . Then the professor won the Oxford Prize for History, which brought him five thousand pounds. Cather's Pulitzer Prize was a modest sum, but her royalties from Knopf the year before writing *The Professor's House* were close to the equivalent of five thousand pounds.[2]

In addition, both Cather and St. Peter develop strong attachments to houses,[3] and each works in a combination sewing room and study.[4]

Considering these autobiographical parallels, it is easy to see that Cather put a good deal of herself in the characters Tom Outland and Godfrey St. Peter. "More than most writers," James Woodress says, "Cather presents readers with the chance to compare biographical data with its transmutation into art."[5] Therefore, it is especially tempting to see Godfrey St. Peter's condition at the end of *The Professor's House* as a representation of Willa Cather's condition at the time she was completing it—and to wonder if perhaps Cather sensed her own fire going out, if she contemplated letting go of the kingdom, and if she might have considered whether to lift her hand in one way or the other.

At age thirty-five, before she made the break from journalism into fiction, Cather had wrestled with a similar dilemma, even to the point of wondering whether she had a split personality.[6] Perhaps at the time of *The Professor's House,* sixteen years later, with her career in fiction writing firmly established, she came to another crossroads at which she debated not only which direction she should follow but whether she should proceed at all.

Before making further autobiographical assumptions, however, one should realize that Cather does not, ultimately, identify very closely with either of her artist figures, Tom Outland or Godfrey St. Peter. The numerous similarities cannot be denied, but one also senses a careful detachment that allows the similarities to go only so far. Perhaps it is this detachment that Cather had in mind when she called *The Professor's House* "the first book I've ever written with any irony in it."[7] At any rate, the result of Cather's personal and artistic distance is what Wayne Booth calls "an inescapable ironic invitation."[8]

The first clue to this ironic invitation to *The Professor's House* is a very simple one: the fact that, to one degree or another, for one reason or another, neither Tom Outland nor Godfrey St. Peter is particularly likable.

In general, readers have sympathized with the plight of Godfrey St. Peter, finding it reasonable to blame his failings upon the deterioration of the university, the corruption of society, or the disintegration of his family. James Woodress's assessment is representative: "His [St. Peter's] problem is the problem of every thinking person: how does one live in a world of change? How does one face the future when the old verities have been blown away, and the world has entered a new era of chaos and uncertainty?"[9] Along the same lines Margaret Doane compares St. Peter with Jean Latour: their "isolation and reserve [do] not make the two men unlikable . . . for both arouse our sympathy and admiration";[10] and Richard Giannone confirms that readers admire St. Peter "because he grapples heroically with darkness and because Willa Cather implicitly esteems his struggle. . . ."[11]

Readers have been even more profuse with their praise of Tom Outland. James Woodress calls him "that uncorruptible youth";[12] David Stouck says that he and Augusta both lead "exemplary," unselfish lives;[13] James Maxfield also compares Outland to Augusta, saying that he too "most nearly embodies . . . Cather's values" in that he "does not negate the human bond," even though he does forget it from time to time;[14] Glen Lich calls him "the novel's touchstone of quality . . . , a central character by whom most others are judged";[15] and Leo Jacks says that, despite all he has suffered, Outland's "essential goodness never altered."[16]

These paens notwithstanding, however, a close reading of the motivations and behavior of Godfrey St. Peter and Tom Outland in light of the artistic theme suggests that Cather may have meant to create different impressions. Certainly she has undermined these two characters in ways more subtle and pervasive than she has applied to any other major characters thus far. In this sense, the irony in *The Professor's House* is indeed a "first."

To begin with Tom Outland, his deplorable treatment of Roddy Blake has already been discussed. It is mitigated by the guilt that Outland carries to his death in the war, but other personal failings, though of a lesser offense, remain unexpiated. One is Outland's excessive pride, which one reader has identified as his "sin."[17] The best example is his response to a question from St. Peter during their first meeting. When the Professor asks, "How are you fixed for money?" Outland offers a brief explanation that ends with, " 'I'll do anything but wait table. I won't do that.' On this point he seemed to feel strongly" (*PH* 115). For a boy with little money and an uncertain future, this position is strangely inflexible, suggesting a superior attitude out of keeping with his circumstances.

When St. Peter asks Outland if a call boy is a messenger boy, Outland promptly corrects him: "No, sir. It's a more responsible position." Perhaps it is, but the job was so simple that even a child could do it. In fact, as Cather must have known, the position was usually filled by "youngsters . . . below the age of ten."[18] In his early teens when he was a call boy (see the Appendix), Outland was a few years older than the average. Thanks, probably, to her brother Douglass, who worked for the Southern Pacific, Cather was familiar with the duties of the job, which she presents in realistic detail.[19] She probably also knew, however, that the call boy position was the very "depths of railroading," the bottom rung on the rags-to-riches ladder that was the railroad's version of the American dream.[20] Therefore, to have Outland boast about his "more responsible position" is to set him up for ironic undercutting. The railroad boys who said *The Professor's House* was "the best picture of old railroad days that they'd ever read"[21] probably saw through Outland's vanity.

From his position as call boy, Outland quickly makes moral judgments of the people he worked with: "Sometimes you have to get a man when he isn't where he ought to be. I found there was usually a reason at home for that" (*PH* 116). Outland also sits in judgment of the Bixbys, his landlords in Washington. Their lives probably are just as slavish and miserable as he depicts, but the Bixbys are victims more than villains who deserve better than the haughty contempt in which Outland portrays them. Finally, Outland's condescending account of Mr. Bixby's accompanying his wife when she shops for the material to make a new dress reveals another dimension to his superior attitude: "In New Mexico the Indian boys sometimes went to a trader's with their wives and bought shawls or calico, and we thought it rather contemptible" (*PH* 233).

Another problem with Outland's behavior is his social irresponsiblity. Three years of college and three more of laboratory work (under the careful guidance of a supportive but disinterested professor) have done little to instill in him a sense of obligation. Even if Outland was genuinely unaware of how much aid he received from his mentor Dr. Crane, it still seems thoughtless for him to leave the patent for his invention entirely to his fiancée (not yet his wife), who had nothing to do with it, and to disinherit utterly the man who helped him and who desperately needed the money. Perhaps, as St. Peter believes, Outland never expected the will to be probated because he "expected to come back from the war and develop the thing himself" (*PH* 137); however, even this explanation disenfranchises Robert Crane. It seems as if Outland chose to leave his corrupting fortune where it would do the most harm, St. Peter's allusion to Marc Antony notwithstanding.

Godfrey St. Peter fares no better when his attitudes and actions are scrutinized. He possesses, even cultivates, a strain of selfishness bordering on spite that often makes him insensitive to the feelings of others and that tends to justify the nickname given him by his students, Mephistopheles (*PH* 13).[22] In her recent study, Merrill M. Skaggs goes so far as to say, "Cather permits her Godfrey to be as wicked as he pleases."[23] Even Rosamond, who has an active strain of selfish spite herself, admits to being "a little afraid" of him (*PH* 60).

One example of St. Peter's attitude is his surprise upon learning that Augusta had never expected to "grow grey" in her service to Mrs. St. Peter. "He started. What other future could Augusta possibly have expected? This disclosure amazed him" (*PH* 23). St. Peter's reaction in this instance indicates his attitude in general. As Susan Rosowski says, "he is deeply ignorant of the private fears and aspirations of others in his family and college."[24] James Maxfield carries St. Peter's exclusivity a step further by saying that, for the most part, "he is concerned only with those individuals who he finds attractive, entertaining, or intellectually stimulating."[25]

Another example, ironically, is a cherished memory of his younger daughter, Kathleen: the summer morning when she sat outside his study for hours nursing a bee sting that had caused her fingers to swell like sausages. Granted, six-year-old Kathleen was "independent," and she "took pride in keeping her part of the contract" that left her father to his work in the mornings—that afforded him the isolation necessary to creation—but the scene reveals more about St. Peter's inaccessibility and his subordination of common familial priorities than it does about Kathleen's "square-dealing" nature (*PH* 88–89). Even when he recalls it years later, St. Peter regards it as a demonstration of how considerate Kathleen was, not how unapproachable he was (*PH* 127).

St. Peter's spiteful strain is more evident in his private delight in abstruse jokes at the expense of unwitting victims. The way he teases Augusta about the composition of the Magnificat is one example. Casual and unplanned, the episode demonstrates St. Peter's readiness to bait Augusta simply because of her sincere and unquestioning faith. Afterward, if both characters continue on their way "more cheerful than when they met," it is because Augusta, "the unquesting and unquestioning,"[26] has been duped into thinking that she has enlightened a man whom she regards as "knowing everything" and because St. Peter has been able to revel in one of his private jokes: "(Surely she had said that the Blessed Virgin sat down and composed the Magnificat!)" (*PH* 100).

A better illustration, one that a lawyer might label "with malice aforethought," is the anachronistic tableau that St. Peter devises for the student pageant commemorating an aspect of local history. In an irrelevant historical joke, St. Peter poses his two sons-in-law "in a tapestry-hung tent, for a conference between Richard Plantagenet and the Saladin, before the walls of Jerusalem" (*PH* 73). As one critic has pointed out, "the picture mocks Scott's frustration and Louie's 'foreign' craftiness in a way that they cannot understand."[27] Lillian understands, however, and disapproves. "But the Professor liked his picture, and he thought it quite fair to both the young men" (*PH* 74). The self-absorption that allows St. Peter to enjoy "his little joke" that "nobody saw" (*PH* 74) is probably his most unlikable trait—and also the most self-destructive.

Readers have sometimes had difficulty recognizing the shortcomings of Outland and St. Peter as human beings, partly because most of the other characters are equally, if not more, unlikable. Doris Grumbach aptly labels the St. Peter household "an unsavory tangle of persons."[28] Indeed, Rosamond is hardened by snobbery, Kathleen by jealousy; Scott is given to moping and sophomoric acts of retaliation, Louie to "heedless enthusiasm" that prevents any consideration of his effects upon others; and Lillian, her mistreatment at the hands of her husband notwithstanding, is prone to snobbery, jealousy, and contentiousness. Furthermore, even the characters beyond the St. Peter household are markedly disagreeable. Dr. and Mrs. Crane are petty, grasping, and desperate; Professor Horace Langtry is small-minded and vengeful.

In a case of poetic justice that would gratify Roddy Blake, the only

major characters in the novel who are not essentially unlikable are
Augusta and Blake himself. Neither one is perfect by any means—
Roddy's behavior during the card game in Tarpin could only be
described as surly, and Augusta's world view could charitably be
described as somber—but each one comes as close to selflessness as a
human being can. Roddy nurses Tom through a serious bout of
pneumonia, works on the railroad to stake Tom's trip to Washington, and works in the ruins for Fechtig to accumulate money to
send Tom to college. That the surprise horribly backfires is Tom's
fault much more than his. Augusta routinely stays overtime when-
ever there is illness or death in a household where she is working,
and she braves a severe storm merely to do Mrs. St. Peter's bidding. If
Roddy is commercially minded and Augusta "bloomless," these are
deficiencies that can readily be excused.

Roddy and Augusta also have forgiving natures. Painfully aware
of his ill treatment by Tom Outland, Roddy accepts the sacrificial
role: "And I'm glad it's you that's doing this to me, Tom; not me that's
doing it to you" (*PH* 247–48). If Augusta ever realizes how the
Professor has mocked her, she never lets it show. While St. Peter is
recovering from his brush with death, she tells him, "I can stay till
morning, if you prefer" (*PH* 279). Here is further poetic justice in
that St. Peter now relies upon a practice that, in earlier days, he
had ridiculed. That both of these likable characters are Philistines
makes an interesting commentary on the Kingdom of Art.

Readers also seldom see Outland and St. Peter in unfavorable
lights because each character is the hero of his own story. The first-
person narration makes this obvious in "Tom Outland's Story." Even
though the story is recalled by St. Peter as an extended memory, it is
still clearly told in Outland's voice. Naturally, the reader tends to see
characters and events as Outland sees them, although that troubling
undercurrent of betrayed values lurks like a quiet but nagging
wound behind the narrative.

Technically, books I and III are third-person omniscient narratives, but the principal point of view is still St. Peter's. The brief and

infrequent lapses into true omniscience or into the perspectives of other characters give Cather some freedom of movement but do not substantially detract from the impression that these two parts of the novel are Godfrey St. Peter's story, an impression reinforced by the title of the book, of course. Aside from the sympathy that St. Peter arouses for himself, probably the greatest effect of this narrative stance is the villification of Lillian's character. Certainly she can be unlikable entirely on her own, but the qualities that make her intolerable—her "vehement likes and dislikes" (*PH* 50) and her "violent loves and hates . . . [and] clear-cut ambitions" (*PH* 275)—mostly result from the perspective from which they are viewed: that of a shrinking husband whose energy is on the wane. Furthermore, as James Maxfield remarks, if Lillian "has withdrawn from her husband, her view of the situation is undoubtedly that he drove her away."[29]

Certainly enough of the author appears in the circumstances of her two artist figures Outland and St. Peter to induce readers to make autobiographical connections. As James Woodress succinctly explains, "the professor reflects Cather's thoughts and feelings at the age of fifty-three, [and] Tom Outland is her youthful other self."[30] Likewise, there is enough reality in the details of Cliff City for readers to make the historical connection with Cliff Palace (supplemented by two or three other ruins), so that Tom Outland's discovery seems like a real place rather than some imagined faerie kingdom. But at the same time that Cather replaces the reality of Cliff Palace with the idealism of Cliff City, she also undercuts her artist figures, first by making them unlikable human beings and then by confounding their motives as artists. In other words, the narrative fallacy that casts Tom Outland and Godfrey St. Peter as heroes causes the reader to perceive the novel in one sense, while Cather's undercutting offers another. When this alternative is recognized, the reader sees another dimension to the artistic theme. To use Tom Outland's word, nothing is truly "unalloyed."

One way that Cather undercuts her artist figures is through subtle yet incriminating echoes in diction. In each case a gesture, remark, or idea associated with Outland or St. Peter, ostensibly in a positive sense, is undermined as it is echoed by someone whose motives or character has already been impugned. The result is a sort of guilt by association.

After that first lunch with the St. Peters, the "poor perspiring tramp boy" Tom Outland departs, "leaving princely gifts" (*PH* 121); then years later, after dinner at the Marselluses', the St. Peters receive Louie's "princely invitation" for a trip to France in the summer (*PH* 161). During his stay in Washington, Tom Outland learns that the self-serving bureaucrats at the Smithsonian "will do almost anything for a good lunch" (*PH* 229), but "when was a professor known to refuse a good dinner?" (*PH* 96), particularly when he "had forgotten his scruples about accepting lavish hospitalities" (*PH* 92). When Tom Outland chides Roddy Blake for selling artifacts that belong "to all the people" (*PH* 242), he is merely echoing the argument, if not also the motives, of the people of Tarpin, who said "them ruins didn't belong to Blake any more than to anybody else" (*PH* 237). In fact, Thomas Strychacz sees this remark, together with Outland's numbering the specimens and keeping a daily ledger, as proof of "economic and acquisitive motives."[31]

Three characters decide to use a Mexican port as a way of avoiding paying the duty on imported or exported goods. The German collector Fechtig, after indulging in his own orgy of acquisition, ships his collection of Blue Mesa artifacts "straight through into Old Mexico . . . to load it on a French boat. Seems he was afraid of having trouble getting curiosities out of the United States ports. You know you can take anything out of the City of Mexico" (*PH* 239). Anything can be brought in, too. Louie's plan for the trip to France, as Rosamond explains it, is to buy lots of antiques and to have the Professor's friend in the shipping business "send our purchases from Marseilles to the City of Mexico for us. They would go in without duty, and Louie thinks he can get them across the border as household goods"

(*PH* 159). St. Peter's import scheme seems almost innocent by comparison. On his last trip to Spain, he bought "a dozen dozens of a sherry that went very cheap." However, like Fechtig and the Marselleuses, he "came home by the City of Mexico and got the wine through without duty" (*PH* 98); therefore, his action is tarred with the same brush.

For a professor so insistent upon upholding standards, St. Peter's beliefs are suspiciously inconsistent, almost to the point of self-parody. Clive Hart cites two examples. In his lecture, St. Peter repudiates the value of science, but in references to Dr. Crane he affirms the value of science; St. Peter disapproves of Crane's disregard for personal comfort but overlooks the same attitude in himself.[32] In addition, Jean Schwind labels St. Peter's diatribe against commercialism a glaring hypocrisy because he is dependent for his luxuries not upon the "petty economies" with his own salary but upon the incomes of the women in his family, Lillian and Rosamond.[33]

Even the title of St. Peter's opus, *Spanish Adventurers in North America,* is tainted by its subtle association with Louie's profiteering: Mrs. Crane tells St. Peter that her husband "was done out of it [his share in the Outland fortune] by an adventurer, and his friendship for you tied his hands" (*PH* 138). Finally, "that perilous journey down through the human house," which St. Peter must make to replenish his lamp, satirically echoes the writer's voyage perilous in the opponents it pits St. Peter against: his children, his wife, and the kitchen linoleum.

Cather also creates irony by undercutting some of her symbols. The title of St. Peter's life's work illustrates this point, too. Because it may simply be a casual word choice with nothing behind it, one should not make too much of it; but the word "Adventurers" is a curious choice for the Spaniards in North America. Surely they were on an adventure, but this is not the label by which historians have known them. Rather, they are called explorers, discoverers, *conquistadores,* pioneers, and even settlers. By calling them adventurers, and by associating the word with Louie Marsellus, Cather seems to be undercutting the integrity of St. Peter's work in a particularly subtle, perhaps even a private, way.[34]

Cather also undermines the color symbolism in the novel. David Stouck describes the pattern of favorable and unfavorable connotations of the colors blue and green: whereas green is "the color of envy and greed," blue is "the color of innocence and vision," a representation of "the idyllic experiences and reveries of both the Professor and Tom Outland."[35] The key passage in this interpretation is the moment when Outland presents to the St. Peter girls "two lumps of soft blue stone, the colour of robins' eggs, or of the sea on halcyon days of summer." When the children ask what they are, Outland replies, "Turquoises, just the way they come out of the mine, before the jewellers have tampered with them and made them look green" (*PH* 120). As Cather must have known, however, turquoise in its perfectly natural state can be either green or blue, depending upon where it is mined. Furthermore, if Cather had meant the symbolism to be consistent, it is unlikely that Tom Outland would say that visiting Baltimore when he was in Washington "always made me blue" (*PH* 175), or that, since his disillusionment in Washington, his "letters to Blake had been pretty blue for some time back" (*PH* 236).

Another ironic symbol is the Marselluses' Norwegian manor, Outland. As a demonstration of tasteless incongruity, presumptuous and ostentatious, it has attracted a good deal of comment, mainly about the irony in the name. As Brown and Edel point out, the house holds "no reminiscence of the village in the canyon" and no "vestige of American feeling,"[36] two qualities associated with Tom Outland. St. Peter is bitterly aware of this irony too, of course. He initially responds to Louie's announcement of the name by lifting "his heavy, sharply uptwisted eyebrows" (*PH* 40); then the next morning he expresses his opinion more precisely: Rosamond and Louie, he says, have everything that Outland should have had, "and the least they can do is to be quiet about it and not convert his very bones into a personal asset" (*PH* 47). What critics and St. Peter alike overlook, however, is that the Outland manor has been designed to be "very harmonious with its setting, just the right thing for rugged pine woods and high headlands" (*PH* 39). Whether this end has been accomplished is perhaps another matter, but at least the thought of environmental harmony influenced the design. The same cannot be said, however, for St. Peter's "French garden in Hamilton" (*PH* 14).

One of the first things the reader learns about the Professor, his garden helps define his character. Usually it is praised by critics: one sees it as a comforting retreat from the evils of the present,[37] another as "an aesthetic triumph which does not produce marketable goods,"[38] and a third as "an ordering of his [St. Peter's] soul."[39] However, a different image emerges when the garden is examined as the scene of another ironic invitation. Then it becomes a virtual study in incongruity. In a distant way it reflects the French Canadian side of St. Peter's ancestry; but, like the Marselluses' Outland, it has "no vestige of American feeling," certainly no vestige of Hamilton feeling. "A completely alien imposition on the prairie landscape,"[40] St. Peter's garden is as out of place in this midwestern American town as Bishop Lamy's French cathedral in the heart of the Spanish Southwest, "and it was the one thing . . . [St. Peter's] neighbours held against him" (*PH* 14).

Not only is the Professor's garden esthetically out of place, it fairly reeks of sterility. "There was not a blade of grass; it was a tidy half-acre of glistening gravel and glistening shrubs and bright flowers" and, as Appelhoff remarks, of "trees what don't bear not'ing" (*PH* 51). In this sense the garden holds "no reminiscence of the village in the canyon" either. Despite their artistic impulses, the ancient cliff dwellers cultivated only what they could eat: squash, corn, and beans; therefore, they would have thought a purely ornamental garden like St. Peter's a thing out of harmony with nature, and they would probably have held it against him too, seeing, as Appelhoff does, "the good ground wasted behind his stucco wall" (*PH* 52).

Certainly the garden serves what to the Professor are laudable purposes: it affords a place where he can work off his "discontent," a place where he can repose when his family is away; and there is, after all, "a bed for salad herbs" (*PH* 15). But beyond these pleasantries, the Professor's "walled-in" garden really grows the seeds of his separation; it therefore symbolizes the isolation of his life and art.[41] Moreover, that it exists at all is a consequence of St. Peter's missing a point. "He started to make it soon after the birth of his first daughter, when his wife began to be unreasonable about his spending so much time at the lake and on the tennis court" (*PH* 14). What Lillian surely had in mind is that St. Peter spend more time with his family, but that purpose was thwarted, whether deliberately or not, by the Professor's very attempt to fulfill it. A meaningful silence follows St. Peter's question about the fate of his "other-house garden": "What am I to do about that garden in the end, Lillian? Destroy it? Or leave it to the mercy of the next tenants?" (*PH* 77). Bette Weidman's description of the garden that Fr. Baltazar Montoya exacts from the Indians in *Death Comes for the Archbishop* applies to St. Peter's garden too: "made for the pleasure of only one owner, it does not outlast his lifetime."[42]

The reader is now left with a puzzling question: if Willa Cather undercuts her artist figures so thoroughly, revealing "the inescapable canker of negation at the heart of [almost] every affirmation,"[43] how closely is she to be identified with them?

Except as a dramatic stance to call the reader's attention to the undercurrent of irony, the fact that Cather's artists are unlikable is probably irrelevant—or merely a statement of frequent fact. There is no correlation between an artist's talent and personality, and even if there were it would likely be inverse. As Cather herself said, "very few of the world's great artists have been desirable acquaintances."[44] A case in point is Willa Cather herself, who was a difficult person to like sometimes and who "became increasingly prickly as she grew older";[45] but unlike Tom Outland she remained true to her old friends, and unlike Godfrey St. Peter she maintained close ties to her family.[46] If other artists do not, that is just part of the price of devotion to the craft. The sad part, Cather seems to imply, is that other people, like Roddy Blake, sometimes have to pay too; and if an artist's sensibilities even occasionally encompass a devoir to the human, the double cross may be too much to bear.

On this point, it is significant that, once he leaves Blue Mesa, Tom Outland never again experiences happiness. The "gravity" that St. Peter detects in his voice during their first meeting seems indicative of his general demeanor during the rest of his life: reserved, secretive, and serious. In this respect, Augusta is his complement rather than his foil. Probably both of them "had reflected deeply upon irregular behaviour" (*PH* 116). For his part, Outland seems determined not to come too close to anyone again: "One of his sentimental superstitions was that he must never on any account owe any material advantage to his friends, that he must keep affection and advancement far apart, as if they were chemicals that would disintegrate each other" (*PH* 172). Once burned, twice shy, so the saying goes. Perhaps this is one reason why Outland overlooks his obligation to Robert Crane.

The artists' mixed—or, to use a harsher word, impure—motives are more difficult to explain. During that summer of his high tide on the mesa, Tom Outland's devotion to the Kingdom of Art is complete, unalloyed. His only companions are ideas—his books and visions beyond them—and things that are the symbols of ideas—ruins, artifacts, the mesa itself. Except for this mental and spiritual stimulation, the world around him is dead, and has been dead for centuries, despite the teasingly fresh appearance of the vestiges of lives once lived. Even Mother Eve has been lost to him although she refused to leave the mesa. It is highly ironic that at this time, in this place, Outland "got the better of the Spanish grammar" (*PH* 251): he has learned a new language, but he has no one to talk to. As a consequence of his isolation from fellow human beings, Outland "began to commit long passages of Virgil to memory—if it hadn't been for that," he says, "I might have forgotten how to use my voice, or gone to talking to myself" (*PH* 252). However, little is gained in this endeavor either because both of the alternatives and the prevention as well are still symptomatic of a life apart from other people: a denial of communication. Hence Outland's dangerous crossing back into the world of men and women.

In a more positive sense, Outland's experience on the mesa can be seen as preparation, for it is his recitation of some fifty lines from Virgil that convinces St. Peter that he is a boy of exceptional abilities, that refutes the skepticism in St. Peter's reply to Outland's telling him that he had read all the books of the *Aenid*: "Oh, you did" (*PH* 113). But even this positive side is undermined by Outland's discomfort in the world at large. His sweating under heavy clothes and slipping in his new shoes on the St. Peters' stairs are minor, even comical, manifestations of a major maladjustment that produces more serious consequences: he picks the wrong woman, he remains aloof from people in general, and he seizes an opportunity to escape, to bolt to the front as he had tried years earlier to bolt through the St. Peters' garden gate to escape the terrifying prospect of a family meal. St. Peter thinks him lucky.

If Tom Outland demonstrates the disastrous consequences of a life totally devoted to the Kingdom of Art, Godfrey St. Peter dramatizes the tragedy of a divided commitment. The poses demanded of him—"of concerned father, of sympathetic host, of brilliant scholar, of devoted husband"[47]—require that he be among people despite his frequent attempts at separation, and they exact a heavy toll.

Of course, the most obvious of these attempts is St. Peter's attic study, which at one time had sat atop "the domestic drama . . . beneath him" (*PH* 101) but that now crowns a "dead, empty house" (*PH* 15–16). One may be tempted to see this attic study as St. Peter's version of the kingdom—as "the spiritual equivalent of the cliff-dwellers' cave in the Southwest"[48]—but Cather undercuts that interpretation too. Although it corresponds in several ways with Cliff City, the Professor's attic study is not a second locale for the Kingdom of Art. In the sense that it is built over the rest of the house, it is a world above the world. It is also a sort of sanctuary for creativity, both for the domestic arts practiced by Augusta and the more literary arts of St. Peter: witness the deference shown by other family members before entering (cf. *PH* 88 and 165). But it inspires none of the exuberance so characteristic of the Blue Mesa, nor does it encourage one to breathe deeply in pure air. Rather, the air is foul and stifling, and the light poor and dim. As Cather herself says, the place requires "the fresh air that blew off the Blue Mesa" to invigorate it (*WCOW* 31–32). In short, the Professor's study is the result of his attempt to pay his devoir to both worlds, a place actually ill suited for either.

Finally, it is only when he is alone—when he feels himself an orphan or a primitive—that St. Peter is able to connect with the kingdom. Yet as he succeeds in that direction he fails in the other by withdrawing farther into himself and farther away from his family. The final letting go of the one has been precipitated by the loss through erosion of the other.

Ultimately, both Tom Outland and Godfrey St. Peter fail as artists. Their downfall is their inability to resolve the very dilemma that seemed to occupy so much of Willa Cather's thought, the survival of the artist in the world. Outland can synthesize two opposing disciplines, art and science, but he never integrates his life with the lives of those around him. Rather, he "fails miserably with living men."[49] Almost in spite of himself, St. Peter has been more successful at social integration, but the symbolic mingling of his notebooks and Augusta's patterns foreshadows the secondary personal attachment that will replace the primary one with his family. Moreover, the constant juggling of so many roles has ennervated him to the point that he finally collapses in physical and mental exhaustion. "A man has got only just so much in him," he tells his wife; "when it's gone he slumps (*PH* 163).

Another dimension to the autobiographical question is the distinct possibility that Cather directs some of the satire in the novel toward herself. In a letter to Dorothy Canfield Fisher in 1933, Cather tried to put to rest "the legend that she had sacrificed herself to art." Rather, she saw herself (like Godfrey St. Peter) "as always avoiding what was less agreeable and actually leading a life of indulgence."[50] Perhaps Professor St. Peter cannot afford to buy a winter coat for himself, but he provides one for his creator: Cather wrote to Irene Weisz in January 1926 that her professor had bought her a mink coat, which was the first valuable thing she had ever owned.[51] Ironically, the very ship that St. Peter dreads is the one that Cather especially enjoyed. Speaking of Cather's upcoming trip to Italy on the *Berengaria,* an interviewer for the *Hastings Daily Tribune* says that Cather did not select this boat because it is "palatial or because it happens to be going at the time she wishes to leave." Rather, "she remembers that once before when she crossed the Atlantic on that boat the passengers were notably of good spirit and congenial. The boat is then associated in her mind with pleasant voyage companionship" (*WCP* 97).[52]

There may be some self-satire in the depictions of other characters, too. If, as James Woodress says, Cather was "a person of strong loves and equally strong hates,"[53] Lillian St. Peter may owe that aspect of her personality to the author. When Tom Outland declares that he will do anything but wait table, he may be echoing the attitude of the young Willa Cather. Mildred Bennett says that after Cather graduated from the University of Nebraska, she was unwilling "to support herself through any commonplace occupation."[54] Finally, Outland's bitter rejection of Roddy Blake may be a reflection of an attitude that Cather displayed early in her career. Witter Bynner tells of a debate among the members of the *McClure's* staff over whether Cather should withdraw her short story "The Birthmark" because of the personal injury it might cause the people upon whom it was based. "I can hear her now," Bynner recalls, "saying briskly: 'My art is more important than my friend.' "[55] The statement is a neat summary of the attitude that Tom Outland comes to regret. One wonders, then, if *The Professor's House* may be Willa Cather's effort at atonement.

Beyond the possibilities of self-satire, one can see Tom Outland's heedless enthusiasm for the ruins in Blue Mesa as a reflection of Willa Cather's heedless enthusiasm for art when, in the 1890s at approximately Tom Outland's age, she defined the Kingdom of Art and the absolute, exclusive allegiance it requires. In 1915, with *The Song of the Lark,* Cather could still celebrate the triumph of the artist over the other demands and expectations of life. But by 1925, when she completed *The Professor's House* and when she and St. Peter were the same age, Cather seems to have developed second thoughts about the severity of the commitment that severs other ties. She seems, in fact, to have realized that absolute allegiance to the kingdom is impossible—even undesirable—and that mixed allegiances can be troublesome—even disastrous. Then by 1936 Cather had reached the conclusion that "human relationships are the tragic necessity of human life" (*WCOW* 104). The process is a familiar one—the enthusiasm of youth tempered by the wisdom of age—but it does not necessarily lead to a resolution of the artist's dilemma. Perhaps the disappointing outcome of these two approaches to the Kingdom of Art made Cather regard *The Professor's House,* "certainly not her favorite among her books," as "a nasty, grim little tale."[56]

At any rate, the fates of Tom Outland and Godfrey St. Peter are definitely not autobiographical. However appealing she may have found the concept of the athlete—or artist—dying young, Cather certainly did not rush off to die for an ideal.[57] Probably, though, there were moments when letting go of the kingdom seemed to her, as it does to St. Peter, a life-saving act, a release from the demands imposed by the life of writing, a way of ending the separation from family and friends, or a means of curing the homesickness that made her physically ill. Anyone sensitive and perceptive enough to be an artist is likely, at some point, to question the validity of the life devoted to art. However, Cather's sense of separation was probably not as great as St. Peter's; and throughout her life, of course, Cather found considerable satisfaction in writing, so much so that she kept writing until she died. According to her friend and reviewer Fanny Butcher, Cather was "nourished spiritually" and "truly fulfilled" by her writing.[58] "Once she said to me that nothing mattered to her but writing books, and living the kind of life that makes it possible to write them. I never forgot those words, for they were her credo."[59]

Even so, Cather knew an author who deliberately halted her career and who "found life full enough without it," Sarah Orne Jewett. "Some six years before [Cather met her], she had been thrown from a carriage on a country road . . . and suffered a slight concussion. She recovered, after a long illness, but she did not write again—felt that her best working power was spent" (*NUF* 85).[60] If, in 1908 and 1909, Cather wondered how an artist could become so easily reconciled to life without art, by the 1920s she must have seen. Lillian Bloom says that as Cather "grew older—overwhelmed by a sense of mortality or the disappearance of her own desire—she began to question if the sacrifice [for the life of art] were not exorbitant. Certainly the attraction of life was as forceful as that of art, even more so."[61]

Clearly, then, Cather backs away from a complete endorsement of either of her artist figures, creating what Wayne Booth calls "stable irony," in the interpretation of which "there is a strong sense of rejecting a whole structure of meanings, a kind of world that the author himself obviously rejects."[62] There is, however, a larger autobiographical sense in which Cather embraces the prospect offered by the novel as a whole, an affirmation of hope that transcends individual despair. The critics who, largely on the basis of *The Professor's House,* accuse Cather of a "bitter negativism,"[63] who say that she "felt that human creativity was doomed,"[64] and who see in her work a foreshadowing of the present demise of traditional literary genres[65] have all missed this larger meaning. As Bruce Miller says, Cather may not have been a joyous artist, but she was at least a hopeful one.[66] For Cather, hope was a matter of time.

9 ❋ *The Design of Life*

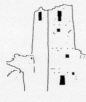*For Robert Frost*, to whom Cather presented an inscribed copy of *The Professor's House*, writing poetry served as a "momentary stay against confusion." For Willa Cather, writing short stories and novels served the same purpose,[1] but never so deliberately or effectively as in "Tom Outland's Story" and the novel that encompasses it. Begun in 1916 as a historically inspired narrative to articulate a long-standing personal myth, the story became for Cather a bulwark against the sundering of the world that occurred for her about the same time that she finished writing the story. With her celebration of an idealized primitive life, Cather blends history and imagination to create an exemplary society to contrast markedly with the disintegration of modern life. Many readers have commented upon this contrast. The important point, however, is to see the two worlds not as static and mutually exclusive, the one enshrined in the past and the other condemned in the present, but as related points along a continuum that defies the customary limitations of time. This theme is conveyed by almost every aspect of the novel, from the chronology of composition to the rhetorical devices that unify the final form. When read with these points in mind, *The Professor's House* becomes an effective demonstration of Willa Cather's "flat refusal to accept the dictatorship of time."[2]

The sequence of composition is important. As earlier chapters have shown, the story, as well as the novel as a whole, was written in a concentric rather than linear fashion, a movement from the inside out. In short, a myth grew into an episode, an episode into a story, a story into a novel. Glen Lich states the case exactly when he says, "the central location of 'Tom Outland's Story' suggests that structurally this brief first-person episode is somehow the ordering principle of the novel itself."[3] It is as if Cather began with a small house and gradually expanded it on all sides in a broadening perspective reminiscent of the interior and exterior views of the Dutch paintings that she said influenced her concept of the novel.

When the novel is examined from the outside, this concentric layering is evident in the repetition of the basic tripartite structure. Of course, the largest and most obvious instance is the division of the one novel into three books, which approximate the three movements in a sonata. Beyond this arrangement, however, the central book of the three, "Tom Outland's Story," is itself divided into three parts, which Clive Hart delineates as follows: "(1) the discovery and exploration of the mesa; (2) experiences in Washington; (3) the return to solitary life on the mesa."[4] Then in thematic rather than logistical terms, the central event in Book II is the discovery episode, which itself displays a tripartite structure: the anticipation of the discovery, the discovery of Cliff City itself, and the response to the discovery. Finally, one is drawn further inward, to the center of centers, by the chief symbol in the story, the "beautifully proportioned" round tower, itself a concentric structure located "in the middle of the group" of stone houses (*PH* 201). With good reason, David Stouck has called this group of houses "a curious kind of pastoral center in the novel—a world transcending place and time, fixed in 'immortal repose.'"[5] For Tom Outland, it is this round tower, with its "symmetrical and powerful" swell of masonry, that "held all the jumble of houses together and made them mean something," houses that "hung together, [that] seemed to have a kind of composition" (*PH* 201). In other words, the "aesthetic harmony of the cliff city enables it to transcend time."[6]

For Cather, this tower is the center that can hold. With its ascending design and its supposed use as an astronomical observatory, the round tower represents the harmony between man and nature that Cather imputed to the cliff dwellers, a harmony that Cather herself valued and enjoyed.[7] With its concentric shape, the tower suggests the continuity of life, an upward, hopeful spiral toward the heavens. This is also the direction of Outland's gaze the night he returns to the mesa from Tarpin, where he had gone to find news of Roddy Blake: "I lay down on a solitary rock that was like an island in the bottom of the valley, and looked up." What he sees are striking images full of light and color, a brilliance full of promise: canyon walls "dyed flame-colour with the sunset," the Cliff City "in a gold haze," the rim rock holding "red light," and a "copper glow in the piñons. . . . The arc of sky over the canyon was silvery blue, with its pale yellow moon, and presently stars shivered into it, like crystals dropped into perfectly clear water" (*PH* 250).

The tower symbol is repeated in the cedar tree, a natural tower, whose growth rings give Father Duchene an idea of the antiquity of Cliff City—how far back in time one must go to find the people whose houses have revitalized the lives of their present-day discoverers. With the construction imagery of the round tower and with the growth imagery of the cedar tree, Cather presents symbols that suggest the continuum of life and of time.

Other aspects of the writing reinforce these symbols. For instance, almost without exception the chapters of all three books begin with some reference to time: time of day, day of the week, month, season, or, in its sense of academic time, semester.[8] Also, as events in the lives of the characters are related, there is a casual and unobtrusive blending of different times, a technique that transforms years of separation into moments in common. All this happens as easily and naturally as one season follows another, as one generation is succeeded by another.

Joseph Hinz was perhaps the first to remark that the time span of the novel "is exactly one year."[9] More specifically, Book I begins in September of one year and Book III ends in September of the next year. In between, the seasons are defined by their natural manifestations and colored by events that happen during those times. Beyond this annual cycle, Cather gives each season its share of pleasant and significant associations. Tom Outland discovers Cliff City in the winter; he arrives in Hamilton in the spring; and it is on a bright October afternoon that "a rich, intense effect of autumn" fills the St. Peters' drawing room through an arrangement of seasonal flowers (*PH* 75). Yet it is during the summer, when life usually seems at its richest and fullest bloom, that most of the good things happen: when St. Peter develops his "special kind of affection" for Kathleen (*PH* 88); when he spends three weeks with Charles Thierault before sailing along the coast of Spain and finding that "the design of his book [has] unfolded in the air above him" (*PH* 106); when Tom Outland has his high tide; when he and St. Peter "sit and talk half through the warm, soft nights" (*PH* 15); and when Tom Outland finally tells his story. As Cather had written many years earlier in "The Treasure of Far Island," "the beauties of vanished summers were everywhere" (*CSF* 276). It is partly through these summertime associations that one perceives an expansion of time beyond the academic year, a single unit of time that seems to represent all time. This perception is sharpened as one becomes aware of the complex weaving of times past and present, accomplished in large measure by the presence of Tom Outland. In fact, the novel actually encompasses some sixteen or seventeen years in the lives of its characters.

The precise extent of this broadened time span is not readily discerned. Cather supplies only one specific time, August 1914, the month when Father Duchene arrives in Hamilton and he and Outland leave for the front; but she includes enough references to datable historical events—the hanging of the anarchists in Chicago, the Dreyfus case, and the battle of Flanders during the second year of WWI—and so many references to relative time—for instance, Outland's arrival in Hamilton "a year after I quarreled with Roddy" (*PH* 253) and his being "almost a member of the family for two years" (*PH* 173)—that one can work backward and forward from that one month and year to create an approximate chronology of the novel. Doing so, one discovers that Book I is set in 1919 or 1920 and Book III a year later; and that the events in "Tom Outland's Story" probably occurred from 1903 to 1907 (see the Appendix). However, the specific years are not as important as the realization that many more years than one are covered because it is through this realization that one sees another instance of Cather's outward narrative expansion. And once again "Tom Outland's Story" is the key.

The telling of the story takes only a summer's evening, or rather two evenings: the first when Outland tells it to St. Peter (before the time of the novel) and the second nine or ten years later when St. Peter recalls it while his family is away. Cather thus achieves an intriguing narrative stance. One hears Outland's first-person voice telling his own story through the recollection of Godfrey St. Peter, the principal third-person point of view character in the novel. The story is not a flashback in the sense that it resurrects Tom Outland himself to do the telling; rather, Outland lives again in the memory of another character who tells what he has heard in the words in which he heard it,[10] just as oral narratives have been repeated for generations, forever bridging gaps in time, like the ladder that Cather provides for Outland and Blake to climb into Cliff City. Of course, the story is a flashback in the sense that it returns the reader to an earlier time, but it does so for the interesting purpose of fulfilling the foreshadowing incorporated throughout the structurally earlier yet chronologically later Book I: in this way, the present anticipates the past and the past completes the present. "Why do you mix us all up?" Kathleen impatiently asks Tom when he too seems to be confusing times deliberately.

Loretta Wasserman has aptly called "Tom Outland's Story" the "jewel" of *The Professor's House* because it shows how Tom Outland "learned to allow past time to flow into the present."[11] In this story, three distinct times merge into one: that of the events themselves, approximately 1903 through 1907; that of the rainy summer night around 1910 when Outland finally tells "the story he had always kept back" (*PH* 176); and finally that of the summer evening in 1920 or 1921 (the novel's present) when Godfrey St. Peter, contentedly alone in the old house, recalls the story in Outland's words. As in *The Song of the Lark,* "we see past and present simultaneously."[12] If, in this merging of times and story tellers, it becomes difficult to discern what happened when—or even who is who—Cather has achieved her desired effect. She has created a story that revolves upon itself, just as one course of stone in the round tower leads to another, as one growth ring in the cedar tree leads to the next. So completely does one character tell what another has told (the speaker, St. Peter, having become the surrogate, Outland), that only one voice is heard, and it speaks for Willa Cather to one generation of readers after another.[13] Therefore, at the same time in the present that it delves further and further into the past—first a decade or two to find Tom Outland's discovery and then several centuries to find Mother Eve and her people—the novel also reaches indefinitely into the future through the simple fact of successive readers, whose lives are increasingly distant from those of the cliff dwellers yet whose sympathies, as activated by the novel, can overcome the effects of time.[14] In this way, the myth of discovery is continually retold and renewed, so that in the Kingdom of Art "the soft pipes . . . play on . . . / Forever piping songs forever new." What Stephen Tennant says of Willa Cather's art as a whole applies especially well in this case: it is "essentially one of gazing beyond the immediate scene to a timeless sky or a timeless room, in which the future and the past, the unspoken and the unknown, forever beckon the . . . reader."[15]

Cather may have borrowed the concept of simultaneous times from Henri Bergson, a writer she admired. As Loretta Wasserman explains Bergson's idea, "there are two times":

'Clock' time, or chronological time, which we conceive of as a line of measured, separate units, is time spatialized, or geometrized, the time of science and practical affairs. This time is useful but essentially artificial. The other, Bergson's 'duration,' is experienced, or lived time, the ceaseless flow of qualitative change; not a series, but layered, simultaneous moments. The reality of evolution lies in the creative surge of life, the *elan vital,* binding the universe, including human consciousness, into a dynamic, indeterminate cosmos. Spatialized, time past lies in inert, dead units; as lived time, it moves by 'reciprocal interpenetration' into the present.[16]

Through this interpretation, one begins to suspect another reason for Cather's fascination with the myth of discovering an ancient city. Not only does it provide an ideal setting for the Kingdom of Art, it also offers incontrovertible proof of the durability of man's creations, an artistic immortality that joyfully repudiates the dictatorship of time. "By analogy, Cather seems to be ensuring, or hoping for, the long future of her own designs."[17] As Rosowski and Slote point out, the image of the fly in amber appears first in the 1916 essay then again, unchanged, in "Tom Outland's Story."[18] Clearly, then, the idea of preserving life in static motion was part of Cather's early design.

To many of the tourists at Mesa Verde in August 1915, the ruins were probably little more than ruins: the long abandoned homes of a people long dead. If the stories of Jesse Walter Fewkes brought these ancient ones back to life, most of his audience doubtless pictured them in a remote past unrelated to modern times. Willa Cather, however, saw more. To her the cliff dwellings were not an isolated phenomenon, nor were they curiosities essentially without meaning to the modern world. Rather, she saw them as points along a continuum of creativity in which she herself was a participant; and she probably applied to herself what she had just written about Thea Kronborg, that she felt "bound . . . to a long chain of human endeavour" (*SL* 380), felt "older and higher obligations" (*SL* 383).

When one is connected to "a long history of human achievement, and to a larger community of shared values . . . idealism may defeat time."[19] This is what happened in the summer of 1915, when a twentieth-century novelist visited the scene of the nineteenth-century discovery of a thirteenth-century world.

This chain of endeavor and these obligations are the unheard melody that plays only to the ear of the imagination. Despite his chestful of relics and his knowledge of Panther Canyon, old Henry Biltmer does not hear it; nor does Roddy Blake or any one of the Professor's family. Nevertheless, the melody resounds throughout *The Professor's House* in the form of the legacy of an artistic life, of a story told and retold; and it strikes a responsive chord in the person of Godfrey St. Peter. Readers of the novel may hear it too, according to their own gifts of sympathy, thereby participating to a greater or lesser degree in the continuum of life, of time, and of story.

Like the image of static motion conveyed by Cliff City and its prototype Cliff Palace, *The Professor's House* maintains a place in the continuum of creativity, and at the same time it represents, as a thing created, the continuing act of creating. Each generation must write its own books, Emerson said; and those who do so, Cather said, must "do our work, our best work, until our tools break in our hands" (*KA* 393).[20] This is precisely what happened to Willa Cather herself.

Unlike her professor, Cather "sensibly dealt with her own crisis by continuing to write novels,"[21] although during those last years her real-life version of the clenched hand often interrupted the voyage perilous. Perhaps, as John Gleason believes, "the bold formal experiment" of *The Professor's House* helped Cather to work "her own way out of despair" and to find "the courage to go on."[22] She died with her final manuscript still unfinished, her final story untold.

Rather than an end, however, this accident of fate symbolizes a continuation, the very continuum of art and life that *The Professor's*

House has described. If the fire goes out in one writer, it will reignite in another at another time, "have another show," as Cather said, "sometime, somewhere" (*KA* 315).[23] If one artist embraces the kingdom but neglects mankind and then dies for an ideal, if another tries to live in both worlds but loses his place in each one, the kingdom is still there to be discovered, even if it has "to wait another hundred years, maybe, for the right explorer" (*PH* 251). Despite the warning issued by *The Professor's House*—one pays, coming or going—the inducements are great enough, it seems, for someone else sometime to risk the bad crossing going in and the dangerous crossing going out. The soft pipes play on, the final story is never told.

Until 1922 or so, Cather had applied this optimistic view to history as well as to art. As David Stouck explains, Cather had believed that if one civilization declines, "another will be born in which humankind's energies are renewed." But in *The Professor's House,* her first book after 1922, Cather's attitude has changed toward a "despairing view of history after the Renaissance, a rejection of the age of progress dependent on science and technology, with no reassurance any longer that history is cyclical."[24] Perhaps it was to compensate for her loss of hope in history that Cather built this house for the Kingdom of Art, detailing the lives of those who occupy it for a time and then move on in an unending stream of legators and legatees.

As a critique of contemporary society, *The Professor's House* has much in common with *The Waste Land,* published three years earlier; but as a statement of artistic principles, it corresponds to "Tradition and the Individual Talent": "No poet, no artist of any art, has his complete meaning alone. His significance, his appreciation is the appreciation of his relation to the dead poets and artists,"[25] to those others bound to a long chain of human endeavor, honoring older and higher obligations.

For Cather, this relation is "the design of life," the principal ingredient that she "tried to get into *The Professor's House,*" a quality so pervasive, she suggests, that it even "flows by a cashier's window" in her brother's bank. "That's what I want to do," Cather told Fanny Butcher, "the kind of thing that gets the design of life, not just the picture."[26] The design of life is the artistic impulse, that "unaccountable predilection of the one unaccountable thing in man." It "springs out of the very stuff that life is made of" (*WCP* 47). Ideally, it manifests itself in a design of art perfectly suited to its subject, one that controls and guides,[27] that comes "out of the truth of [one's] being"[28]: like the design of his books that St. Peter saw in the air above him; or the "explosion" that produced *O Pioneers!* by "bring[ing] with it the inevitable shape that is not plotted but designs itself[29]; or the "design [that] is, indeed, so happy, so right, that it seems inevitable; the design is the story and the story is the design" (*NUF* 77–78). This same artistic impulse compelled those ancient potters to decorate, to design, the vessels that contained the very water of life; prompted the hand, "fastidious and bold," to bring autumn indoors and to arrange it. "In Nature there is no selection," St. Peter realizes (*PH* 75); and so does Willa Cather.

When Richard Wetherill and Charlie Mason caught their first astonished glimpse of Cliff Palace at Mesa Verde, it was in its natural state: the remnants of rooms and towers poked through piles of rubble, every step raised dust centuries old, and the only water around was unfit to drink. But according to Willa Cather's design, Cliff City in Blue Mesa becomes something different, idealized, on the day of its discovery: the clean, sparkling legacy of a people who breathed pure air and drank crystal-clear water; who built their homes not in any desultory way but according to a sense of design—whether dictated by esthetics or convenience.

It now appears that Cather worked the design of life into her book by crafting *The Professor's House* as a metaphor for the art of composition, for the life of writing from beginning to end.[30] Through its dramatization of the thrill of discovering the Kingdom of Art, the often tragic costs of allegiance to it, and the anguish over losing it, the novel illuminates the whole range of emotions that characterize the artistic life.[31] It also shows the progress of that life, from the exuberant youth to the despairing older man; and it demonstrates the serious consequences that can arise along the way. Finally, as it reveals the process of its own composition—from inside out, from history to fiction, from personal myth to universal theme—*The Professor's House* demonstrates how good books can be written, all the while emphasizing and illustrating the artist's irresistible urge to write them, to brave the risks of participation in the continuum of creativity, the very stuff that life is made of. It is this impulse that guides the hand, that turns the head toward old ways, that makes the heart resist letting go.

A Chronology of *The Professor's House*

(TO is Tom Outland; RB is Roddy Blake;
HA is Henry Atkins; StP is Godfrey St. Peter.)

(Numbers in parentheses refer to pages in the novel.)

1886	Hanging of anarchists in Chicago, stemming from the Haymarket Riot in May, which RB "could just remember" (187).
1894	Dreyfus convicted of treason.
1899	Dreyfus tried and convicted a second time; pardoned by French president.
1903 Fall	TO and RB meet (179).
1903–4 Winter	TO catches pneumonia (185).
1904 Spring	TO getting around, recovering (186).
Summer (May)	TO and RB join Sitwell Cattle Company (186).

Late Oct.   TO and RB go to winter camp (188).

Late Nov.   TO and RB bring cattle to winter range (196).

Early   Foreman Rapp brings supplies and HA (196).
Dec.

Late Dec.   "four fine young steers" get away into Blue Mesa "a few days before Christmas" (198).

Dec. 24   TO goes after the cows, finds Cliff City, returns and tells RB and HA. ("We talked and speculated until after midnight. It was Christmas eve, and Henry said it was but right we should do something out of the ordinary" [203]. Thus, the "It" seems to refer to the evening of the discovery, not the day that technically began after midnight.)

Late Dec.   RB crosses the Cruzados "before New Year's day" (204).

1905
Early   TO and RB enter Blue Mesa "together for the first
May   time" (207).

Early   With their road and cabin built, TO and RB are
July   ready to begin "excavating" (211).

Early   Work is going well until HA is killed (216–17).
August

August   Father Duchene stays a week (217).

Fall   "beautiful autumn" that year (222); TO and RB prepare for TO's trip to Washington.

After Dec. 25	TO and RB leave Blue Mesa at first snow; go to Tarpin (222–23).

1906
January	TO arrives in Washington (225).
Feb. [?]	TO takes the secretary of the Director of the Smithsonian to lunch (230).
Mar. & Apr.	TO is kept "hanging on" (235).
May	TO stays in Washington (236).
June	TO returns to Tarpin; learns of Fechtig, who "cleared out three weeks" earlier (238); TO and RB quarrel, and RB leaves (241–48).
July	Dreyfus's conviction set aside by a civilian court of appeals. Had his innocence been finally settled any earlier, RB's assertion (243) would be pointless.
Jul. to Nov.	TO's "high tide" summer on Blue Mesa (251).

1906–07
Winter	TO back in Pardee (253).
Spring	"a year after I quarrelled with Roddy," TO arrives in Hamilton (253); StP recalls "that bright, windy spring day when he first saw Tom Outland" (112); TO, unsure of his age, says he is twenty (115).

Summer   "those first few months" when Lillian saw more of
             TO than StP did (122).

1907–09   TO "almost a member of the family for two years"
             (173).

1909–10   TO's senior year, time by which Lillian had become
             jealous of TO (172).

1910
Spring   TO's graduation.

Summer   "During that summer after Outland's graduation,
             St. Peter got to know all there was behind his re-
             serve" (175); StP's family in Colorado; TO tells his
             story and continues experiments in physics lab
             (176).

1910–13   The "three years" after TO's graduation when TO
             and Crane worked "side by side" in Crane's lab (145,
             142); one of these winters TO spent at Johns Hopkins
             (149).

1912
Summer   "Two years after Tom's graduation they took the copy
             of Fray Garces' manuscript . . . and went down into
             the South-west together. By autumn they had been
             over every mile of his trail on horseback" (259, 25);
             TO and StP retrieve TO's diary (259).

1913
Summer   TO and StP go to Mexico (259).

1914

Summer   *Would* have been TO's and StP's third summer outing (presumably consecutive), this time to Paris; "but it never came off. Outland was delayed by the formalities of securing his patent, and then came August, 1914" (259). By that time (the patent process), TO and Crane had "finished the experiments" (146).

August   Father Duchene stops in Hamilton (259); TO leaves for the front (260); TO "barely" thirty (40).

Oct. to   First Battle of Ypres, in Flanders; Allied victory.
Nov.

1915

Apr. to   Second Battle of Ypres; Central Powers victory; TO
May   "killed in Flanders, fighting with the Foreign Legion, the second year of the war" (40).

Spring   Louie Marsellus arrives in Hamilton "just at the time the city was stirred up about Outland's being killed at the front" (136).

1914–16

Aug. to   The two years when TO's papers lay in Crane's lab
Aug.   (138, 147).

1916

Summer   Louie Marsellus and Rosamond St. Peter become
or Fall   engaged; Louie takes TO's papers (136).

1917–18 Louie and others begin to sense the importance of
[?]   TO's invention "toward the close of the war" (41).

1918–19 Louie calls in experts and gets TO's idea "over from
[?]   the laboratory to the trade" (41).

[Book I and Book III must be set in 1919 or 1920 because TO's idea
is already "revolutionizing aviation" (40) and because Louie and
Rosamond seem recently married: Louie says they will move their
wedding presents to Outland before their trip to Paris (160).]

1919 or
1920
Sept.   Book I opens (11)

Dec. 25   StP spends the day in his old attic study working (98
       ff.).

1920 or
1921
Winter   Meeting of Association of Electrical Engineers in
       Hamilton (111); Scott McGregor says TO "isn't very
       real to me anymore" (111).

End of   StP goes to Chicago with Rosamond (151) for the
Semester "orgy of acquisition" (154).

March   "the dreariest and bleakest of the year in Hamilton";
       Louie announces plans for the family trip to France
       (157).

May   Louie, Rosamond, and Lillian leave for France (171).

June   StP's garden is especially beautiful (171).

Early   StP has spent almost two months on TO's diary (267).
Aug.

Before   StP goes to see Dr. Dudley (268).
Fall Term

Fall Term   Classes resume (271).

Sept. 17   StP receives letters saying his family will leave France
            "on the sixteenth, and this was the seventeenth" (273–
            74). StP's near asphyxiation (276); his obligation to
            Augusta (281); his determination "to live without
            delight" (282); his experience of letting go (282); his
            resolve to face "with fortitude the *Berengaria* and the
            future" (283).

✳ *Notes*

Introduction

1. Willa Cather, *Willa Cather on Writing,* ed. Stephen Tennant (1920; Lincoln: Bison-U of Nebraska P, 1988) 32. Subsequent citations will appear in the text, with the abbreviation *WCOW* substituting for the full title.

2. Susan J. Rosowski and Bernice Slote, "Willa Cather's 1916 Mesa Verde Essay: The Genesis of *The Professor's House,*" *Prairie Schooner* 58.4 (Winter 1984): 87–88.

3. James Woodress, *Willa Cather: A Literary Life* (Lincoln: U of Nebraska P, 1987) 282, 284 and 323.

4. Cather may have renamed the story in the summer of 1924. Edith Lewis recalls that after attending commencement at the University of Michigan in June of that year, she and Cather went to Grand Manan, where Cather "wrote that part of *The Professor's House* called *Tom Outland's Story* [sic]" *(Willa Cather Living: A Personal Record* [1953; Lincoln: Bison-U of Nebraska P, 1976] 137).

5. Bernice Slote, "Introduction," *Uncle Valentine and Other Stories: Willa Cather's Uncollected Short Fiction, 1915–1929* (1973; Lincoln: Bison-U of Nebraska P, 1986) xv; and David Stouck, *Willa Cather's Imagination* (Lincoln: U of Nebraska P, 1975) 108.

6. Stouck, *Imagination* 100; David Stouck, letter to the author, 31 Jan. 1989. Both of these stories, however, were preceded by another one, "The Professor's Commencement" (1902), which, as Joseph P. Hinz was perhaps the first to notice, presents a forerunner to Godfrey St. Peter ("A Lost

Lady and *The Professor's House,*" *Virginia Quarterly Review* 29 [Winter 1953]: 79). Moreover, Bruce P. Baker has pointed out that this early story anticipates one of the major themes of the novel, beauty and truth versus materialism ("*The Professor's House:* An Early Source," *Willa Cather Pioneer Memorial Newsletter* 24 [Summer 1985]: 13–14). Even so, the design of *The Professor's House* as a whole is derived more directly from the other two stories, and Willa Cather's interest in cliff dwellings like those at Mesa Verde predates 1902.

7. James Schroeter, "Willa Cather and *The Professor's House,*" in *Willa Cather and Her Critics,* ed. James Schroeter (Ithaca: Cornell UP, 1967): 373.

8. For illustrations of this practice as it applies to *The Professor's House,* see Cynthia Chaliff, "The Art of Willa Cather's Craft," *Papers in Language and Literature* 14.1 (Winter 1978): 63; J. M. Ferguson, Jr., "'Vague Outlines': Willa Cather's Enchanted Bluffs," *Western Review: A Journal of the Humanities* 7 (Spring 1970): 61–64; Philip L. Gerber, "Willa Cather and the Big Red Rock," *College English* 19 (Jan. 1958): 152–57; Meredith R. Machen, "Carlyle's Presence in *The Professor's House,*" *Western American Literature* 14.4 (Winter 1980): 285; Wallace Stegner, *The Sound of Mountain Water* (Garden City, New York: Doubleday & Company, 1969) 239; and Woodress, *Literary Life* 220 and 278.

9. Chapel Petty-Schmitt, "Patterns in Willa Cather's Fiction." Diss. U of New Mexico, 1989.

10. Patrick Sullivan, "Willa Cather's Southwest," *Western American Literature* 7 (Spring 1972): 31. See also Lillian D. Bloom, "The Poetics of Willa Cather," in *Five Essays on Willa Cather : The Merrimack Symposium,* ed. John J. Murphy (North Andover, Massachusetts: Merrimack College, 1974): 106; and Loretta Wasserman, "The Music of Time: Henri Bergson and Willa Cather," *American Literature* 57.2 (May 1985): 234.

11. Bernice Slote, ed., *The Kingdom of Art: Willa Cather's First Principles and Critical Statements, 1893–1896* (Lincoln: U of Nebraska P, 1966) 18.

12. In 1925 this view was far from unanimous. For instance, Joseph Wood Krutch called "Tom Outland's Story" the "initial mistake" in the novel ("Second Best," in *Willa Cather and Her Critics,* Schroeter, 56). By 1960, however, opinions had begun to change, as reflected in John H. Randall's assertion that the inserted story "contains the core of the book's

meaning" (*The Landscape and the Looking Glass* [Boston: Houghton Mifflin Company, 1960]: 204).

13. See L. Brent Bohlke, "Godfrey St. Peter and Eugene Delacroix: A Portrait of the Artist in *The Professor's House, Western American Literature* 17.1 (May 1982): 21–38; Paul Comeau, "*The Professor's House* and Anatole France," in *Critical Essays on Willa Cather,* ed. John J. Murphy (Boston: G. K. Hall, 1984); John B. Gleason, "The 'Case' of Willa Cather," *Western American Literature* 20.4 (Feb. 1986): 279–80; Alice Bell Salo, "*The Professor's House* and *Le mannequin d'osier:* A Note on Willa Cather's Narrative Technique," *Studies in American Fiction* 8 (Autumn 1980): 229–31; and Patricia Lee Yongue, "Willa Cather's *The Professor's House* and Dutch Genre Painting," *Renascence* 31 (Spring 1979): 155–67.

14. See Marilyn Arnold, "The Function of Structure in Cather's *The Professor's House,*" *Colby Library Quarterly* 11.3 (Sept. 1975): 169–78; E. K. Brown and Leon Edel, *Willa Cather: A Critical Biography* (1953; Lincoln: U of Nebraska P, 1987) 240–47; Margaret Doane, "In Defense of Lillian St. Peter: Men's Perceptions of Women in *The Professor's House,*" *Western American Literature* 18.4 (Feb. 1984): 299–302; Leon Edel, "A Cave of One's Own," in *Critical Essays on Willa Cather,* ed. John J. Murphy (Boston: G. K. Hall, 1984) 200–17; Gleason 275–99; Missy Dehn Kubitschek, "St. Peter and the World All Before Him," *Western American Literature* 17.1 (May 1982): 13–20; James F. Maxfield, "Strategies of Self-Deception in Willa Cather's *The Professor's House,*" *Studies in the Novel* 16.1 (Spring 1984): 72–86; Randall, *Landscape* 217 ff.; Susan J. Rosowski, *The Voyage Perilous: Willa Cather's Romanticism* (Lincoln: U of Nebraska P, 1986): 130–43; and Stouck, *Imagination* 96–109.

15. Several other works not yet in print examine other southwestern origins of *The Professor's House*. John March makes an intriguing case for Santa Fe writer Haniel Long as one of the prototypes Cather used in creating Tom Outland (see his *Handbook to Willa Cather,* a typescript currently being edited for publication by Marilyn Arnold); Constance Mierendorf illustrates how Cather's knowledge of Indian art adds authenticity to the novel (see "The Turquoise and Silver Bracelet: An Indian Perspective on *The Professor's House,*" ts., Minneappolis Community College, 1988); Jean Schwind proposes that the modern pueblo customs of matrilineal descent and matrilocal residence give a new meaning to

Mother Eve and thus to "Tom Outland's Story" and the novel as whole
(see "Pictorial Art in Willa Cather's Fiction," diss., U of Minnesota, 1983,
92 ff.); and Patricia Lee Yongue suggests that Cather's familiarity with
several early works on southwestern archaeology influenced parts of the
novel (see "Godfrey St. Peter: Willa Cather's Cliff Dweller," ts., U of
Houston, 1988).

16. James Woodress, "The Uses of Biography: The Case of Willa
Cather," *Great Plains Quarterly* 2.4 (Fall 1982): 202.

Chapter 1

1. Fanny Butcher, "Willa Cather Tells Purpose of New Novel," *Chicago Daily Tribune* 12 Sept. 1925: 9. Early in 1988 my wife, Yolanda,
happened upon an excerpt from this interview in *El Palacio,* the magazine
of the Museum of New Mexico. Then late in 1989 I finally located the
interview itself. It should also be noted, though, that Mary Miritello made
her own discovery of the interview after seeing a reference to it in a
dissertation. See "The 'design of life' in Willa Cather's *The Professor's
House,*" Fourth National Seminar on Willa Cather, Santa Fe, New Mexico, 21 June 1990.

2. Lewis, 81.

3. Woodress, *Literary Life,* 25.

4. Willa Cather, *Willa Cather in Person: Interviews, Speeches and Letters,*
ed. L. Brent Bohlke (Lincoln: U of Nebraska P, 1986) 10. Subsequent
citations will appear in the text, with the abbreviation *WCP* substituting
for the full title.

5. Woodress, *Literary Life,* 5. It was this very terrain that, more than
three hundred years before, had prompted Coronado to assign a man to
count the number of steps that the army took on its eastward march to
Quivira. Things had not changed much in three hundred years. When he
approached that unending expanse of plain from the east, Willa's uncle
George Cather "measured the circumference of one of the back [wagon]
wheels, tied a rag on the rim so they could more easily count the
revolutions and started across the prairie. George had a compass to keep
him going in the right direction. His wife sat in the back of the wagon,

counted revolutions and computed mileage" (Mildred Bennett, *The World of Willa Cather,* new ed. [Lincoln: Bison-U of Nebraska P, 1961] 12).

6. Richard C. Overton, *Burlington Route: A History of the Burlington Lines* (New York: Alfred A. Knopf, 1965) 186–87.

7. Bennett, *World,* 43–44.

8. Slote, *Kingdom of Art,* 35.

9. Slote, *Kingdom of Art,* 42.

10. Edward and Lillian Bloom, "The Genesis of *Death Comes for the Archbishop,*" *American Literature* 26 (Jan. 1955): 488.

11. Woodress, *Literary Life,* 49–51.

12. Jack L. Benham, "Publishers Preface and Introduction," *Mesa Verde and the Four Corners* (Ouray, Colorado: Bear Creek Publishing, 1981) N. pag.

13. Even so, it might be interesting to mention a few of the similarities between Cather's story and Holmes's essay: "Report on the Ancient Ruins of Southwestern Colorado, Examined During the Summers of 1875 and 1876," 1878, reprinted in *Hayden Survey, 1874–1876: Mesa Verde and the Four Corners* (Ouray, Colorado: Bear Creek Publishing, 1981): 383–408. Like Cather in "Tom Outland's Story," Holmes discusses the secure positions of the cliff dwellings (384), the possibility that the towers were used for religious ceremonies or as watch towers (384–85), the skill displayed in the masonry (385), the presence of springs in some of the cliffs themselves (396), and the ample evidence of the cliff dwellers' "art of ornamentation" in the bowls and other pottery, some perhaps of "foreign origin" (403).

14. Kathleen D. Byrne and Richard C. Snyder, *Chrysalis: Willa Cather in Pittsburgh, 1896–1906* (Pittsburgh: The Historical Society of Western Pennsylvania, 1982) 4–5.

15. Lucius Beebe and Charles Clegg, *Rio Grande: Mainline of the Rockies* (Berkeley: Howell-North, 1962) 198.

16. *The Cliff Dwellers of Southwestern Colorado,* promotional brochure, the Denver and Rio Grande Railroad [1897], State Historical Society of Colorado, Denver, N. pag.

17. Jackson Thode, foreword, in *Health, Wealth and Pleasure in Colorado and New Mexico* (1881; Santa Fe: Museum of New Mexico Press, 1980) ii.

18. Virginia Donaghe McClurg, *Two Annual Addresses: Pueblo, 1903; Denver, 1904,* Mesa Verde Research Center, Mesa Verde National Park, Colorado, N. pag.

19. Elizabeth Shepley Sergeant, *Willa Cather: A Memoir* (1953; Lincoln: U of Nebraska P, 1967) 165.

20. Another book about the Southwest that Cather seems to have read is *Rocky Mountain Flowers,* by Frederic E. and Edith S. Clements (1914). At least, she said she wished she had written it (see *WCP* 47; Bennett, *World,* 246; and Sergeant, 165). A highly technical catalog of scientific data about regional plants, this book seems an unlikely object for the authorship desires of a romanticist. It does contain some beautiful illustrations, but it seems less concerned with beauty and more with science. Some of the plants growing in Cather's Blue Mesa are listed here, but others are not. Thus, the influence of this book upon "Tom Outland's Story" seems negligible. This is not to say that Cather was unconcerned about the botanical authenticity of her story, however. Every plant she mentions has been found either in New Mexico or Colorado. For more on Cather's concern with botanical accuracy, see Bennett, *World,* 141.

21. Irv Diamond, letter to the author, 8 and 9 Mar. 1991.

22. Olof W. Arrhenius, *Stones Speak and Waters Sing: The Life and Works of Gustaf Nordenskiold,* ed. Robert H. Lister and Florence C. Lister (Colorado: Mesa Verde National Park and Mesa Verde Museum Association, [1984]) 4–5 ff.

23. Willa Cather, "Mesa Verde Wonderland Is Easy to Reach," *Denver Times* 31 Jan. 1916: 7. Subsequent citations will appear in the text, with the abbreviation "MV" substituting for the full title. Incidentally, now there are three American editions of Nordenskiold's book. Two of them are listed by Rosowski and Slote (92): Antiquities of the New World Series, Vol. 12, AMS Press; and the Beautiful Rio Grande Classic edition, which is the one used here. Finally, the Mesa Verde Museum Association recently published a paperback edition of the original 1893 English version.

24. Beverly Cunningham, letter to the author, 15 Feb. 1989.

25. Duane A. Smith, letter to the author, 14 May 1987.

26. Herbert L. Cowing, letter to Frank McNitt, 13 Mar. 1953, Frank McNitt Collection, New Mexico State Records Center and Archives, Santa Fe.

27. Richard Wetherill, letter to Gustaf Nordenskiold, 21 Dec. 1893, Mesa Verde Research Center, Mesa Verde National Park.

28. Rosowski and Slote, 87.

29. Rosowski and Slote, 87.

30. Quoted in Rosowski and Slote, 87.

31. Willa Cather, *The Professor's House* (New York: Alfred A. Knopf, 1925) 198. Subsequent citations will appear in the text, with the abbreviation *PH* substituting for the full title.

32. Gustaf Nordenskiold, *The Cliff Dwellers of the Mesa Verde,* trans. D. Lloyd Morgan (1893; Glorieta, New Mexico: The Rio Grande Press, 1979) 73–74.

33. Nordenskiold, 12. Actually, it was Wetherill alone who discovered Spruce Tree House after he and Mason separated to look for other ruins. Then the next day he and Mason together happened upon Square Tower House (see Frank McNitt, *Richard Wetherill: Anasazi,* rev. ed. [Albuquerque: U of New Mexico P, 1966] 25).

34. Later in the story, Roddy Blake finds "four other villages, smaller than the first" (*PH* 204).

35. Nordenskiold, 30. In an article for a scholarly journal, Nordenskiold describes the access to the upper floor of a dwelling in Spruce Tree House: "no ladder seems to have been used, several stones projecting from the wall providing instead the necessary foothold" *(Letters of Gustaf Nordenskiold,* ed. Irving L. Diamond and Daniel M. Olson, trans. Daniel M. Olson, (Mesa Verde National Park: The Mesa Verde Museum Association, 1991) 71.

36. Nordenskiold, *The Cliff Dwellers,* 96, 20, 19, and 39.

37. Nordenskiold, *The Cliff Dwellers,* 39.

38. Nordenskiold, *The Cliff Dwellers,* 54.

39. Nordenskiold, *The Cliff Dwellers,* 52.

40. Nordenskiold, *The Cliff Dwellers,* 16.

41. Nordenskiold, *The Cliff Dwellers,* 108.

42. Edward Oxford, "George Eastman: The Man Who Wrought the Kodak," *American History Illustrated* (Sept. 1988): 16 ff.

43. Arrhenius, 25–26.

44. Nordenskiold, *The Cliff Dwellers,* 21, n. 1. See also Benjamin Alfred Wetherill, *The Wetherills of the Mesa Verde: Autobiography of Ben-*

jamin Alfred Wetherill, ed. Maurine S. Fletcher (1977; Lincoln: U of Nebraska P, 1987) 119.

45. Nordenskiold, *The Cliff Dwellers,* 49.

46. Nordenskiold, *The Cliff Dwellers,* 56.

47. Nordenskiold, *The Cliff Dwellers,* 59.

48. Thomas Rickner, letter to the Secretary of the Interior, 13 Feb. 1915, Mesa Verde National Park Library, Vault.

49. Duane A. Smith, *Mesa Verde National Park: Shadows of the Centuries* (Lawrence: U of Kansas P, 1988) 211.

50. Twice "the author" of the brochure alludes to other publications of his: "the descriptions of the Hopi Kiva rites elsewhere published by the author" (12) and "my report on Spruce Tree House" (22). Fewkes published several studies of Hopi rituals, and his 1909 report on Spruce Tree House is listed in the brochure's bibliography. The anonymous author also mentions in passing that he has "exhumed the skeleton of an adult" from a particular room. Fewkes was the first professional archaeologist to do extensive work at Mesa Verde, and he was still at work when Cather and Lewis were there.

51. One other indication that Cather had read this brochure is that in her 1916 essay she calls Nordenskiold "Baron," as the brochure does, although mistakenly. Of course, it is possible that she picked up the title in conversation with someone (her Wetherill contacts would have called him Gustaf), but seeing it in print in an official publication would more likely incline her to use it herself.

52. *The Prehistoric Cliff Dwellings: Mesa Verde National Park, Southwestern Colorado* (Washington: GPO, 1915) 8.

53. *Prehistoric Cliff Dwellings,* 23.

54. *Prehistoric Cliff Dwellings,* 9.

55. *Prehistoric Cliff Dwellings,* 3.

56. *Prehistoric Cliff Dwellings,* 2, 5, 10.

57. Nordenskiold, *The Cliff Dwellers,* 61–62.

58. *Prehistoric Cliff Dwellings,* 1–2, 5, 18.

59. *Prehistoric Cliff Dwellings,* 24.

60. *Prehistoric Cliff Dwellings,* 10. This astronomical theory is still current among modern scientists. See "Anasazis May Have Had Stars in Their Eyes," *Albuquerque Journal* 10 Jul. 1990: E1.

61. Nordenskiold, *The Cliff Dwellers,* 56. According to Irv Diamond, Nordenskiold and Fewkes probably never met. Nordenskiold did write to Fewkes after the publication of *Cliff Dwellers of the Mesa Verde,* saying he hoped to see him at the Americanists Conference in Stockholm in 1894; but Fewkes's name does not appear in the published proceedings (letter to the author, 8 and 9 Mar. 1991).

62. Jesse W. Fewkes, "Ancient Remains in Colorado: The Mesa Verde National Park, Landmark of a Lost Race," *Scientific American* 122 (29 May 1920): 609.

63. Jesse W. Fewkes, "A Prehistoric Observatory," *Literary Digest* 75 (11 Nov. 1922): 27.

64. Jesse W. Fewkes, "Cremation in Cliff-Dwellings," *Records of the Past* 9 (May–June 1910): 155.

65. Janet Robertson, letter to the author, 26 Sept. 1987.

66. March, 598.

67. D. Smith, *Mesa Verde,* 41.

68. Janet Robertson, letter to the author, 4 Mar. 1989.

69. Wetherill, 192.

70. D. Smith, *Mesa Verde,* 41.

71. D. Smith, *Mesa Verde,* 42 ff.

72. Arthur Chapman, "Mesa Verde Relics Are Preserved by Women," *The Denver Times* 29 June 1915: 1.

73. McClurg, N. pag.

74. J. H. Gore, *Report of the Director of the Organization of International Congresses,* in *Report of the Commissioner-General for the United States to the International Universal Exposition, Paris, 1900,* 6 vols. (Washington: GPO, 1901) 6: 41, 42, 354.

75. Gore, 31, 33, 37. Another connection between Cather and McClurg is little more than a curiosity, but it bears noting. One of the pieces written about McClurg appeared in the July [1902] issue of *Woman's Home Companion,* a magazine that during the twenties and thirties published several of Cather's short stories and whose editor, Frederick Collins, was one of the reorganizers of *McClure's* in 1910.

76. James Woodress, letter to the author, 16 Jan. 1989.

77. Robert Grant, "People Who Did Not Go to the Fair," *The Cosmopolitan* 16 (Dec. 1893): 161.

78. Willa Cather, *The Kingdom of Art: Willa Cather's First Principles and Critical Statements, 1893–1896,* ed. Bernice Slote (Lincoln: U of Nebraska P, 1966): 196. Subsequent citations of Willa Cather's words from this book will appear in the text, with the abbreviation *KA* substituting for the full title.

79. For these World's Fair allusions I am indebted to John March (letter to the author, 27 Jan. 1989). The three stories are "The Count of Crow's Nest" (1896), "A Death in the Desert" (1905), and "The Bohemian Girl" (1912); for the precise references see pp. 449, 199, and 5 respectively in *Willa Cather's Collected Short Fiction, 1892–1912,* rev. ed., ed. Virginia Faulkner (Lincoln: U of Nebraska P, 1970). Subsequent citations will appear in the text, with the abbreviation *CSF* substituting for the full title.

80. *The Wonders of the World's Fair,* souvenir ed. (Buffalo: Barnes, Hengerer & Co., [1894]) 111.

81. Smith, *Mesa Verde,* 36.

82. Ricardo Torres-Reyes, *An Administrative History of Mesa Verde National Park* (Washington: United States Department of the Interior, National Park Service, 1970) 379.

83. McNitt, *Richard Wetherill,* 56–57. Eleven years later Richard and his youngest brother Win took a better organized presentation to St. Louis for that World's Fair (McNitt, *Richard Wetherill,* 214–15). For Cather, this was another missed opportunity to meet the man who would inspire her story.

84. Alessandro Pezzati, letter to the author, 28 June 1989.

85. Floyd W. Sharrock, "The Hazzard Collection," ts., 1962, the University Museum Archives, University of Pennsylvania, Philadelphia, 15.

86. Sergeant, 204.

87. Harvey Leake, letter to the author, 3 Apr. 1989.

88. Frances Gillmor and Louisa Wade Wetherill, *Traders to the Navajos: The Story of the Wetherills of Kayenta* (Boston: Houghton Mifflin Company, 1934) 103.

89. Leake.

90. Gillmor and Wetherill, 191.

91. Gillmor and Wetherill, 107.

92. McNitt, *Richard Wetherill,* 210.

93. Gillmor and Wetherill, 192.

94. Often the parties themselves included famous people. Perhaps the most notable was Theodore Roosevelt, who came there in the summer of 1913, a year after Cather's trip to Arizona, and hired John Wetherill to take him and his party to Rainbow Bridge (Gillmor and Wetherill 193–94), a recently discovered phenomenon about forty miles northwest of Kayenta, just across the Utah border. Not long afterward, Roosevelt wrote for *Outlook* magazine a characteristically exuberant account of his adventure, heaping praise upon John and Louisa Wetherill.

95. Willa Cather, *One of Ours* (1922; New York: Vintage Books, 1971) 103. Subsequent citations will appear in the text, with the abbreviation *OO* substituting for the full title.

96. Sergeant, 122–23.

97. Sergeant, 124.

98. Belinda Kaye, letter to the author, 21 Jan. 1988.

99. Woodress, *A Literary Life,* 259. See also David Stouck, "Cather's *Archbishop* and Travel Writing," *Western American Literature* 17.1 (Spring 1982): 4.

100. Sergeant, 164–65, 207–08. One obvious exception is Tony Luhan.

101. Butcher, "Purpose," 9.

102. Stuart Sherman, *Critical Woodcuts* (New York: Charles Scribner's Sons, 1926) 32.

Chapter 2

1. *Mesa Verde* (Washington: GPO, 1986) N. pag.

2. *Prehistoric Cliff Dwellings,* [i].

3. Sergeant, 132.

4. Jack E. Smith, Chief Archaeologist at Mesa Verde National Park, has identified the ruin (letter to the author, 16 Mar. 1989).

5. For the information from this post card to Sergeant, I am indebted to James Woodress.

6. Sergeant, 132.

7. Lewis, 93–94.

8. Lewis, 101.

9. Philip Gerber, *Willa Cather* (Boston: Twayne Publishers, 1975) 63.

10. *The Cliff Dwellers of Southwestern Colorado*. Perhaps it was diction

such as this that inspired *Harper's Weekly* to praise "the literary excellence" of the D&RG's advertising matter (see Beebe and Clegg, 198).

11. *Prehistoric Cliff Dwellings* N. pag.

12. See the map in Robert A. LeMassena, *Rio Grande to the Pacific!* (Denver: Sundance Limited, 1974) 350.

13. Beebe and Clegg, 194.

14. Lewis erroneously reports that she and Cather rode the narrow gauge all the way from Denver when in fact the track between Denver and Antonito had been standard gauge for years (Robert G. Athearn, *Rebel of the Rockies: A History of the Denver and Rio Grande Western Railroad* [New Haven: Yale UP, 1962] 166 ff.). Between Alamosa and Antonito the track was three-rail, to accommodate both standard and narrow gauges, and thereafter it was narrow gauge only (Gilbert A. Lathrop, *Rio Grande Glory Days* [San Marino, California: Golden West Books, 1976] map on inside front cover). The narrow gauge ended in Santa Fe.

15. Leander F. Hayes, untitled ts. about travels through the Four Corners region, late 1893 through early 1894, in the possession of Walter Goff, Mancos, Colorado, N. pag.

16. Henry McCabe, *Cowboys, Indians and Homesteaders* (Henry and Lena McCabe: Deseret Press, 1975) 168.

17. It was contortions of track just such as this that gave rise to narrow-gauge folklore. Some of the curves were said to be so tight that locomotives had to be hinged in the middle to negotiate them; others so sharp that "the conductor, in the caboose, could borrow the engineer's chewing-tobacco plug on one curve and return it on the next. . ." (Athearn, 316). Less picturesque but more realistic, one early passenger who took the circle tour reported his amazement at passing the same house three times only to gain "a few rods in running 3 miles" (Hayes).

18. Willa Cather was not the only distinguished visitor to stay in the Mancos area longer than planned. In a letter to his father, Gustaf Nordenskiold wrote, "It was my intention to spend about one week in Mancos Cañon. That week has now gone by, and I have decided to extend my stay to one or two months" (*Letters,* 29).

19. See Fern Ellis, *Come Back to My Valley: Historical Remembrances of Mancos, Colorado* (Cortez: Cortez Printers, 1976) 13–17.

20. Bennett, *World,* 43.

21. Fern Ellis, letter to the author, 4 May 1989.

22. Woodress, *Literary Life,* 102.

23. Ellis, *Valley,* 62.

24. Woodress, *Literary Life,* 281. Lewis notes that when Willa Cather was working in Pittsburgh, she suffered "perpetual homesickness" for Red Cloud (43).

25. D. Smith, *Mesa Verde,* 36–39.

26. Ellis, *Valley,* 72 ff.

27. Rosowski and Slote, 86.

28. See Bennett, *World,* 94, and Woodress, *Literary Life,* 46, for lists of these transformations.

29. Thomas Rickner, *Report for 1915,* Mesa Verde National Park Library, Vault.

30. *Prehistoric Cliff Dwellings,* [i].

31. D. Smith, *Mesa Verde,* 48–49; Bader, letter to the author, 10 Dec. 1987.

32. *Mancos Times-Tribune* 5 Aug. 1898: 4.

33. D. Smith, *Mesa Verde,* 73.

34. D. Smith, *Mesa Verde,* 76–77.

35. Richard Wright, letter to the Secretary of the Interior, 17 May 1911, bound volume of correspondence, 1911–1913, Mesa Verde National Park Library, Vault.

36. *Trip to the Cliff Dwellers,* report for the Denver and Rio Grande Railroad Co., 15 Oct. 1906, Mesa Verde Research Center, Mesa Verde National Park, Colorado, 1–2.

37. *Charles B. Kelly: Mancos, Colorado,* advertising circular, 1909, State Historical Society of Colorado, Denver.

38. Thomas Rickner, correspondence, Mesa Verde National Park Library, Vault.

39. D. Smith, *Mesa Verde,* 93. Kelly's permit fee, incidentally, was $2.50 per month per vehicle (T. Rickner, correspondence).

40. *Prehistoric Cliff Dwellings* N. pag.

41. Jean Bader, letter to the author, 26 Feb. 1989.

42. Bader, letter to the author, 26 Feb. 1989.

43. Ellis, *Valley,* 84.

44. Woodress, *Literary Life*, 8–9.

45. The closest I have come to a record of their visit is this tantalizing item from a special insert in the *Denver Times*, dateline Mancos, 26 August: "At the hotel in Mancos the other day two young women were debating whether they should go on with their scheduled trip or return to the Mesa Verde Park. They had overstayed their scheduled time as it was. They had planned to go to Santa Fe and other points, but were almost on the point of abandoning pleasure seeking elsewhere and returning to the cliff dwellings" (Arthur Chapman, "Mesa Verde National Park Lures Many," N. pag.). Maybe these "two young women" are Cather and Lewis, maybe not. At any rate, they also escaped notice at a hotel in Taos a few days later.

46. Lewis, 94–95.

47. D. Smith, *Mesa Verde*, 39.

48. Martha Wetherill Stewart to John March, 23 May 1950, Willa Cather Historical Center, Red Cloud, Nebraska.

49. "Mancos Best Trading Point," *Mancos Times-Tribune* 9 Jul. 1915: 1.

50. Frank McNitt to Herbert L. Cowing, 12 Mar. 1953, Frank McNitt Collection, New Mexico State Records Center and Archives, Santa Fe.

51. Carol Ann Wetherill, letter to the author, 31 Mar. 1987. During the summer of 1915, Wetherill says, John and his wife Louisa were at Kayenta, Arizona; Al and Mary were in Gallup, New Mexico; Win was either at Black Mountain or Covered Water, Arizona; and Charlie and Anna Wetherill Mason were on the Rio Grande. Clayton, on the other hand, was "back and forth" between the Rio Grande drainage and the Mancos area regularly and served, in fact, as the favorite guide of Mesa Verde archaeologist Jesse Walter Fewkes in the summers of 1914 and 1915.

52. Willa Cather was not the only famous author Clayton met. On more than one occasion he guided parties for Zane Gray. When one of his friends asked Clayton what he thought of Gray, Clayton responded: "I don't like him. . . . He made me look like such a damn fool. I had to wear a beaded hat band, fringed leggings and carry two guns when I didn't need any. I charged him $13.00 a day extra because he made me look like such a damn fool" (Ruth Jocelyn Wattles to Frank McNitt, 25 Oct. 1964, Frank McNitt Collection, New Mexico State Records Center and Archives).

53. Considering her fondness for the cottonwood (*WCP* 40 and 145; Bennett, *World,* 145), Willa Cather must have appreciated the name of the Wetherills' ranch.

54. McNitt, *Richard Wetherill,* 179–180.

55. C. A. Wetherill, letter to the author, 14 Apr. 1987.

56. C. A. Wetherill, letter to the author, 25 Feb. 1989.

57. See David Harrell, " 'We contacted Smithsonian': The Wetherills at Mesa Verde," *New Mexico Historical Review* 62.3 (Jul. 1987): 233–34.

58. McNitt, *Richard Wetherill,* 36–37.

59. *Mancos Times-Tribune* 24 June 1898: 4.

60. B. A. Wetherill, 116.

61. Quoted in McNitt, *Richard Wetherill,* 37.

62. B. A. Wetherill, 104.

63. Marietta Wetherill, interview with Lou Blachly, Tape 440 Pioneers Foundation, University of New Mexico Zimmerman Library (15 July 1953), transcription by Mary Blumenthal, 9.

64. Arthur H. Seigfried, "Al Wetherill of the Mesa Verde," *True West* (Sept.–Oct. 1965): 24.

65. Don Watson, *Cliff Dwellings of the Mesa Verde* (Colorado: Mesa Verde Museum Association, n. d.) 12; and Don Watson, *Indians of the Mesa Verde* (Colorado: Mesa Verde National Park and Mesa Verde Museum Association, 1961) 27.

66. B. K. Wetherill, letter to William Henry Holmes, 11 Feb. 1890, Record Unit 189, Smithsonian Institution Archives, Washington, D. C.

67. Seigfried, 25.

68. The Wetherills may also have suggested the nationality of Cather's foreign buyer of artifacts. Jesse Nusbaum, superintendent at Mesa Verde during the twenties, thirties, and forties, quotes John Wetherill as saying that part of one of their collections "was purchased by a German [unnamed] who sent it to a museum in Berlin" (Jesse Nusbaum to Don Watson, 8 Dec. 1948, Mesa Verde Research Center, Mesa Verde National Park, Colorado).

69. McNitt, *Richard Wetherill,* 27.

70. Duane A. Smith, letter to the author, 14 May 1987. With a few minor changes, Mason's manuscript was published in *The Denver Post,* 1 July 1917. It was reprinted in McNitt, *Richard Wetherill* 323–29.

71. On this point, Mason says, "it appeared as though the inhabitants had left everything they possessed right where they had used it last" (see C. C. Mason, "The Story of the Discovery and Early Exploration of the Cliff Houses at the Mesa Verde," 1918 [date of acquisition], State Historical Society of Colorado, Denver, 10.

72. Mason, 10.

73. Nordenskiold, *The Cliff Dwellers,* 45 and 170.

74. McNitt, *Richard Wetherill,* 106.

75. Mason, 4–5.

76. Although Cather considered the novel itself "very successful" (*KA* 209), full of the charms "of mystery and awful age, of reckless daring and of careless love" (*KA* 268), she called the dramatization "as awful as the people who play it" (*KA* 268).

77. H. Rider Haggard, *She,* in *Three Adventure Novels* (1887; New York: Dover Publications, 1951) 173, 114, and 219. At the end of the novel, a fiery ritual transforms She into a "hideous little monkey frame" (222) that looks her age, which is 2,200 years. Depending upon how much of the book they had read at the time, the Wetherills' name for the mummy they found was either highly ironic or simply descriptive.

78. Bennett, *World,* 32.

79. Cather may have learned about other real-life prototypes for the violent death of Mother Eve. In a letter to Gustaf Nordenskiold, Richard Wetherill tells about some finds made in Grand Gulch, Utah: "We have back bones with stone spear points still sticking in them and several breast bones shot through with arrows and some broken heads and arms" (quoted in Arrhenius, 82). Clayton Wetherill was not a member of this exploring party, but John and Al were (McNitt, *Richard Wetherill,* 63).

80. Readers familiar with the Rio Grande Press edition of Gustaf Nordenskiold's *Cliff Dwellers* might be tempted to identify as the prototype of Mother Eve the mummy of a female given another Biblical name, Esther, whose photograph is one of several added to this recent edition by the National Park Service. Such a connection is impossible, however, because Esther was not discovered until the late 1930s, at a site near Durango (D. A. Smith, letter to the author, 5 Sept. 1989; J. E. Smith, letter to the author, 7 Sept. 1989).

81. Lewis, 93.

82. C. A. Wetherill, letter to the author, 31 Mar. 1987.

83. Lewis, 98.

84. "Two Noted Women Get Lost All Night in Mesa Verde Wilds," *Denver Times* 25 Aug. 1915: 1.

85. Willa Cather, post card to Elizabeth Shepley Sergeant, 20 Aug. 1915, the Pierpont Morgan Library, New York, New York.

86. The card bears a Mancos postmark because there was no post office at the park until 1924 (Smith, *Mesa Verde,* 113). Mail did pass between the town and the park, though, compliments of C. B. Kelly (J. E. Rickner, letter to the author, 20 Apr. 1988).

87. Willa Cather, post card to Elizabeth Shepley Sergeant, 31 Aug. 1915, the Pierpont Morgan Library, New York, New York.

88. Sergeant, 142. Sergeant's phrase "tiny station" is probably too kind. Until the fall of 1915, when a new depot was constructed, a box car had been used as the station at Taos Junction (David Myrick, *New Mexico's Railroads: An Historical Survey* [Golden, Colorado: The Colorado Railroad Museum, 1970] 103).

89. Sergeant, 142. Known locally as Long John Dunn, this man was one of the most colorful characters in the history of Taos. A gambler and adventurer wanted by Texas authorities, Dunn had been operating the stage line in the Taos area since the early 1900s (John A. Gjevre, *Chili Line: The Narrow Rail Trail to Santa Fe* [1969; Española, New Mexico: Las Trampas Press, 1984] 26). He was well known not only for his ruggedness and self-assurance, but also his sense of humor, which he often employed when passengers expressed their apprehension over the precipitous route that his stage took between Taos Junction and Taos. Once, he says, "a big, fat feller leaned out and looked down several hundred feet to the bottom of the rocky gorge, and asked, 'Say, driver, does a stage fall off this road very often?' 'No, only once,' I answered. The heavy man shut up the rest of the trip" (Max Evans, *Long John Dunn of Taos* [Los Angeles: Westernlore Press, 1962] 135). Cather probably saw Dunn again because he stayed in business until 1930, and Mabel Dodge Lujan often called on him "to entertain her friends" with his "direct, salty, nasal-whanging tales" (Evans 142–43).

90. José I. Naranjo, interview at Española, New Mexico, 11 Feb. 1989.

91. Lewis, 99.

92. James Woodress, letter to the author, 27 Oct. 1988.

93. Lewis, 94.

94. Such a reading of Lewis's memoir is well advised. Several recent investigations have shown that, as a source of factual information, Lewis is at best inconsistent (see Marilyn Arnold, "Foreword," in *Willa Cather Living* [1953; Athens: Ohio UP, 1989] vii–xxviii]; Mildred Bennett, "At the Feet of Willa Cather: A Personal Account of Edith Lewis as Protector," *Willa Cather Pioneer Memorial Newsletter* (Fall 1989): 19–22; David Harrell, "Edith Lewis's Tall Tales of the Southwest," *Willa Cather Pioneer Memorial Newsletter* (Fall 1989): 15–19; James Woodress, "Cather Biography Redivivus," Third National Seminar on Willa Cather, Hastings, Nebraska, 14 June 1987; and Patricia Lee Yongue, "Edith Lewis Living," *Willa Cather Pioneer Memorial Newsletter* (Fall 1989): 12–15). Therefore, it would seem prudent to accept only what can be corroborated and at least to question what contradicts other evidence. When he reviewed the trio of Willa Cather books published in 1953, Cather's friend Witter Bynner astutely characterized Lewis's memoir as having "the meagre simplicity of a one–fingered melody heard from a determined child" ("A Willa Cather Triptych," *New Mexico Quarterly* 23 [Autumn 1953]: N. pag.).

Chapter 3

1. Duane A. Smith, "A Love Affair that Almost Wasn't . . . Durango and Mesa Verde National Park," *Mesa Verde Occasional Papers* 1.2 (Oct. 1981): 7; D. Smith, *Mesa Verde,* 88 and 91; Torres-Reyes, 39–40.

2. T. Rickner, correspondence.

3. *Prehistoric Cliff Dwellings,* 29.

4. Lewis, 94.

5. Lewis, 94.

6. Here is further evidence that Cather had read Gustaf Nordenskiold's *Cliff Dwellers of the Mesa Verde.* At the beginning of the book Nordenskiold describes the conditions of his trip: "At the time of my arrival, there was no railway to the west from Durango, though one was in course of construction. I made the journey from Durango to Mancos, a distance of 45 kilom., with a buggy and pair" (1).

7. Jean Kelly Bader, interview at Mancos, Colorado, 22 June 1986.

8. Bennett, *World,* 27 and 150.

9. "The Studebaker Four," *Mancos Times-Tribune* 25 June 1915: 5.

10. *Prehistoric Cliff Dwellings,* 5.

11. Jack E. Smith, interview at Mesa Verde National Park, Colorado, 4 Aug. 1987.

12. D. Smith, *Mesa Verde,* 93.

13. According to Bernice Slote, Cather "could write some places and not others." For some reason, tents seem to have been especially congenial. Cather set up "her own tent" in the meadow near the Shattuck Inn in Jaffrey, New Hampshire; she strung "a canvas over the upper porch" at her home in Red Cloud; and in 1920 "she put up a tent near Hyeres on the Mediterranean and worked there for six weeks" (Slote, "Introduction," xxv).

14. T. Rickner, correspondence. Incidentally, Superintendent Rickner was one of the prime movers behind that first automobile road up the Mesa Verde, the one that Lewis says did not exist. The year the road opened, Rickner bought a Model T, but he seems to have shared Cather's dislike for automobiles. The car "didn't last long," his son says. "It never understood 'whoa' and 'get up'" (J. E. Rickner, letter to the author, 24 Sept. 1987). If Cather met Thomas Rickner, it may have been in Mancos rather than at the park because Rickner had followed the practice of his predecessors in maintaining the park headquarters in town, in the First National Bank Building (Duane A. Smith, letter to the author, 4 Dec. 1987).

15. D. Smith, *Mesa Verde,* 96.

16. Fred T. Jeep, letter to the author, 11 Nov. 1988.

17. T. Rickner, correspondence.

18. Quoted in Torres-Reyes, 67.

19. Woodress, *Literary Life,* 8.

20. Bennett, *World,* 37.

21. Lewis, 95.

22. Torres-Reyes, 191.

23. "New Cliff Ruin Found on Park," *Mancos Times-Tribune* 18 June 1915: 1.

24. Lewis, 95. The identity of "Tower House" is something of a mystery. One would guess that it is Square Tower House, which had been

named but not excavated by 1915, except that this ruin is located on the east wall of Navajo Canyon, opposite the direction in which Cather and Lewis were taken. It could be, though, as Jack Smith suggests, that this is the ruin the guide had in mind and he was simply so inexperienced that he went down the wrong canyon looking for it (letter to the author, 16 Mar. 1989).

25. "Walking Club Arrives," *Mancos Times-Tribune* 20 Aug. 1915: 1. A week later the members of this club declared that they "had never been treated better nor had a more pleasant and profitable stay anywhere than here" *(Mancos Times-Tribune* 27 Aug. 1915: 1).

26. Torres-Reyes, 56.

27. Lewis, 95–96.

28. Ellis, *Valley,* 161.

29. J. E. Rickner, letter to the author, 24 Sept. 1987.

30. *Mancos Times-Tribune* 22 May 1915: 3.

31. J. E. Rickner, letter to the author, 24 Sept. 1987.

32. Fred T. Jeep, telephone interview, 16 Oct. 1988.

33. A more likely source of Tom Outland's invention, though connected only tangentially with Mesa Verde, is Samuel Pierpont Langley, the Secretary of the Smithsonian with whom B. K. Wetherill corresponded. Meredith Machen seems to have been the first to suggest this possibility (see "Home as Motivation and Metaphor in the Works of Willa Cather," diss., U of New Mexico, 1979, 264, n. 70).

Like Orville and Wilbur Wright, Langley was a pioneer in aviation who conducted a series of experiments with flying machines around the turn of the century. One of his publications, *Experiments in Aerodynamics,* laid to rest the scientific dispute over the probability of flight by demonstrating that the problem could eventually be solved (Webster Prentiss True, *The Smithsonian Institution,* Vol. I of The Smithsonian Series [New York: Smithsonian Institution Series, 1944] 289). Cather seems not to have known Langley personally, but she was familiar with his work. According to Edith Lewis, Cather had known a friend of Langley's when she was living in Pittsburgh, and she "had always found Langley's story moving and fascinating." (One of his machines crashed ingloriously into a river, occasioning what Lewis describes as "a storm of ridicule and failure.") Then in 1924, when Cather and Orville Wright were given honorary degrees by the University of Michigan, Cather and Wright discussed Langley. Lewis says, "I think even the slight stimulus of this meeting contributed in a sense to the story she was then doing [*The Professor's House*]—it somehow heightened and coloured her mood" (137). In commenting upon this account, Cather's niece Helen Cather Southwick suggests that what heightened and colored Cather's mood may have been "memories of her days in Washington and the Smithsonian" (letter to the author, 29 Apr. 1987).

Finally, it is unlikely that Wright would have had anything good to say about Langley. In 1914 the Smithsonian contracted with Glen H. Curtiss to attempt a flight with the Langley machine of 1903 (Curtiss had lost a court battle with the Wrights and been declared an infringer on their patent). After the success of this 1914 experiment, the Smithsonian proclaimed in five separate publications that Langley's machine, not the Wright brothers', was the first "heavier-than-air machine capable of maintaining sustained human flight." Orville Wright was so incensed by this ploy that he sent the original Kitty Hawk plane to England. Only after a published retraction and apology by a later Smithsonian official was the plane returned to the United States (C. G. Abbot, "The 1914 Tests of the Langley 'Aerodrome,'" *Smithsonian Miscellaneous Collections* 103.8 [Washington: Smithsonian Institution, 1942: 1–8]. Incidentally, it was *McClure's* that presented to readers "the first magazine accounts of the Wright brothers' flight. . . ." (Woodress, *Literary Life,* 185).

34. Lewis, 96–97.

35. Lewis, 141.

36. Slote, *Kingdom of Art,* 97–98.

37. Lewis, 97.

38. James C. Work, "Discovering Willa Cather's Rock," *Magazine of the Midlands,* Sunday supplement to the *Omaha World-Herald* 14 June 1987: 30.

39. Work, "Willa Cather's Rock," 30.

40. James C. Work, letter to the author, 28 Jan. 1987.

41. Lewis, 97.

42. Lewis's characterization of their two rescuers as "splendid men—kind, chivalrous, resourceful, and full of high spirits and encouragement" (98)—is probably accurate. Jack Rickner remembers Clint Scharf as a

buddy with whom he explored the ruins (letter to the author, 20 Apr. 1988), and Walter Goff calls him a "jack-of-all-trades—nice to associate with," who was always out digging (interview at Mancos, Colorado, 3 Aug. 1987). Information about the other rescuer, Audrey Grey Pearl, has so far been elusive, however. No one in the Mancos area whom I have contacted has ever heard of him. Two men with similar names who worked at the park during this time are G. R. Graybeal and Pearl Shey (T. Rickner, correspondence; J. E. Rickner, letter to the author, 26 Aug. 1988). Perhaps, as the *New York Times* story says, several men participated in the rescue and Lewis confused and condensed their names.

43. This is probably the same spot described by a member of an earlier party who was dismayed at the sight of "two more great rocks which now appeared to check our further progress completely, but, there is an opening on our side under one of them, [sic] looking under, away up at the other side we can see day light. Tis perhaps 30 to 40 feet through. By getting down on our hands and knees, and crawling, entering where we are we can get out up there, tis our only chance. So down we go. . . ." (L. F. Hayes N. pag.). Traversing such terrain would leave almost anyone "tired and stiff" (cf. Lewis, 99).

44. Lewis, 98.

45. J. E. Smith, interview at Mesa Verde National Park, 3 Apr. 1986.

46. The name Swallows Nest, incidentally, is only one of many instances of avian imagery that observers of cliff dwellings often use. For instance, William Henry Jackson, one of the earliest explorers of Mesa Verde, mentions seeing "a number of little nest-like habitations" ("Ancient Ruins in Southwestern Colorado," in *Hayden Survey, 1874–1876: Mesa Verde and the Four Corners,* ed. Jack L. Benham [1876; Ouray, Colorado: Bear Creek Publishing Co., 1981] 375). Moreover, Cather herself had already employed this imagery in *The Song of the Lark* with the phrase a "timid, nest-building folk, like the swallows" (*SL* 375). It appears again in the passage above in the words "nestling" and "perched," and also later in the story when Tom Outland says that the town "hung like a bird's nest in the cliff" (*PH* 213) and when he gives the name Eagle's Nest to the high arch where he and Blake find the mummy that Henry christens Mother Eve (*PH* 214).

47. William Howarth, "The Country of Willa Cather," *National Geographic Magazine* 162.1 (Jul. 1982): 88.

48. Lewis, 99.

49. "Lost in Colorado Canyon," *New York Times* 26 Aug. 1915: 20.

50. Lewis, 98.

51. Alden C. Hayes, letter to the author, 6 May 1987.

52. "Visit Park This Fall," *Mancos-Times Tribune* 10 Sept. 1915: 1.

53. Torres-Reyes, 189; A. C. Hayes. Smithsonian historian Webster True says, "many hundreds of tourists met him [Fewkes] and heard the informal talks on the ruins" (123).

54. D. Smith, *Mesa Verde*, 71.

55. J. E. Rickner, letter to the author, 26 Aug. 1988.

56. D. Smith, *Mesa Verde*, 93.

57. Susan J. Rosowski, "Willa Cather's Chosen Family: Fictional Formations and Transformations," in *Willa Cather: Family, Community, and History*, ed. John J. Murphy (Provo: BYU Humanities Publications Center, 1990): 74. James Maxfield defines the familial roles a little differently: in this "all-male version of the traditional nuclear family," Roddy is the father, Henry the mother, and Tom the son (79–80).

58. J. E. Rickner, letter to the author, 20 Apr. 1988.

Chapter 4

1. Sergeant 203. Similarly, Cather said that *A Lost Lady* had been in her mind as a "beautiful ghost" for twenty years before she wrote it (Woodress, *Literary Life*, 341).

2. Bennett, *World*, 43.

3. Bernice Slote, "Willa Cather and Her First Book," in *April Twilights (1903)*, ed. Bernice Slote (1903; Lincoln: U of Nebraska P, 1962): xxix.

4. Even earlier than "The Treasure of Far Island" Cather has characters dreaming of discovering ancient ruins. In "Eric Hermanson's Soul" (1900), Margaret refers to the dream that she and her brother Wyllis had of "going to discover the ruins of Troy together some day" (*CSF* 364).

5. Slote, "Her First Book," xxxviii.

6. Willa Cather, "Dedicatory," in *April Twilights (1903)*, 3.

7. Slote, "Her First Book," xxxiv.

8. Sullivan, 26.

9. Bernice Slote, "Willa Cather," in *Sixteen Modern American Authors* (Durham: Duke UP, 1974): 49. See also Arthur Hobson Quinn, *American Fiction: An Historical and Critical Survey* (New York: D. Appleton-Century Company, 1936): 684–85.

10. Gerber, *Willa Cather,* 121. J. M. Ferguson, Jr., also comments generally and briefly on the connection between "The Enchanted Bluff" and "Tom Outland's Story" (61–62), as does Cynthia Chaliff (63).

11. Mildred R. Bennett, "Introduction," in *Willa Cather's Collected Short Fiction,* rev. ed., ed. Virginia Faulkner (Lincoln: U of Nebraska P, 1970): xxxiv.

12. Willa Cather, *Alexander's Bridge* (1912; New York: Bantam Books, 1962) 94. Subsequent citations will appear in the text, with the abbreviation *AB* substituting for the full title.

13. Willa Cather, to M[rs.] George Sibel [sic], 12 May 1912, letter 68, Willa Cather Historical Center, Red Cloud, Nebraska. For this citation, I am indebted to Chapel Petty-Schmitt.

14. Woodress, *Literary Life,* 255 and 265.

15. Willa Cather, *The Song of the Lark* (1915; Boston: Houghton Mifflin, 1983) 368. Subsequent citations will appear in the text, with the abbreviation *SL* substituting for the full title.

16. Quoted in Bennett, *World,* 92.

17. Bennett, *World,* 24–25.

18. Mason, 2.

19. Mason, 2.

20. David Harrell, "Who Discovered Cliff Palace?" The Wetherill Symposium, Mesa Verde National Park, 18 Dec. 1988.

21. McNitt, *Richard Wetherill,* 29.

22. Hugh Hetherington calls Cather to task for accepting the Wetherill legend without question. However, he adds that perhaps "she knew it as legend and valued it as such; perhaps she had in mind also Frink or some other lone cowboy who had chanced upon the ruins even earlier" (*"The Professor's House* and the Discovery of Mesa Verde," ts., Mesa Verde Research Center, Mesa Verde National Park, Colorado: N. pag.).

23. It is also interesting to note that in this letter the Richard Wetherill

of the 1916 essay has become Dick Wetherell. Cather is not the only one to misspell his last name, but he was never known to anyone as Dick. Gary Topping, like others familiar with the Cather-Wetherill connection, finds this change quite curious (letter to the author, 6 May 1987). There is probably little to be made of it except to see it as an additional illustration that what always mattered for Cather was the idea of an historical event, not its details.

24. John J. Murphy, "The Mesa Verde Story and Cather's 'Tom Outland's Story,' " *Notes on Modern American Literature* 5.2 (Spring: 1981): N. pag.

25. Cather made a similar assertion about *Death Comes for the Archbishop*, but she qualified it by introducing it with the phrase "In the main" and by adding that she also incorporated some of her own experiences and some of her father's (*WCOW* 12).

26. Rosowski and Slote, 91.

27. D. Smith, *Mesa Verde* 9–10; Jack E. Smith, *Mesas, Cliffs and Canyons: The University of Colorado Survey of Mesa Verde National Park, 1971–1977* (Colorado: Mesa Verde Museum Association, 1987) 5.

28. Rosemary Nusbaum, *Tierra Dulce: Reminiscences from the Jesse Nusbaum Papers* (Santa Fe: The Sunstone Press, 1980) 77.

29. Rosowski and Slote, 88.

30. Howarth, 88.

31. Elaine Yvonne Smith Hawkins, "Ideals and Imagination in the Novels of Willa Cather," diss., Stanford U, 1984: 20.

32. Barbara Wild, " 'The Thing Not Named' in *The Professor's House*," *Western American Literature* 12.4 (Feb. 1978): 269.

33. Doris Grumbach also sees Tom "in the romantic tradition" of not knowing his exact age and of being orphaned young ("A Study of the Small Room in *The Professor's House*," *Women's Studies* 3 [1984]: 339).

34. John N. Swift, "Memory, Myth and *The Professor's House*," *Western American Literature* 20.4 (Feb. 1986): 304.

35. John Swift has suggested that the name of Mother Eve "whispers in the date of Tom's first sight of the Cliff City: Christmas Eve, a holy day whose name reconciles the figures of sacrificed Son and primal Mother around the miracle of communion" (305).

36. McNitt, *Richard Wetherill*, 27.

37. McNitt, *Richard Wetherill,* 30.

38. Murphy, "Tom Outland's Story," N. pag.

39. McNitt, *Richard Wetherill,* 38.

40. That snow is reported in most of the accounts of the Wetherill-Mason discovery may be a case of history imitating art. Referring to the 1916 newspaper story, Mesa Verde historian Duane A. Smith says that Cather's is the earliest reference to snow on the day of discovery that he has ever found. Thus, he suspects that this particular detail, which has reappeared in virtually all of the subsequent historical accounts, may have originated in Cather's fiction, not in fact (letter to the author, 14 May 1987).

41. Woodress, *Literary Life,* 282.

42. Woodress, *Literary Life,* 323.

43. Lewis, 137.

44. In the course of her feminist examination of Willa Cather's life, Sharon O'Brien offers a credible explanation of why Cather often expressed herself through male characters: "Cather . . . detach[ed] the artist's creative power and vocation from socially defined notions of masculinity and femininity; having done so, she was able to create artist-figures—both male and female—who combine 'masculine' and 'feminine' powers" *(Willa Cather: The Emerging Voice* [New York: Oxford UP, 1987] 425). Hermione Lee, another feminist critic, makes a similar point: "Virginia Woolf's well-known ideal of an artist with an androgynous, 'man-womanly' mind . . . finds its best illustration, in an American context, in Willa Cather's writing" *(Willa Cather: Double Lives* [New York: Pantheon Books, 1989] 10).

45. Willa Cather, *O Pioneers!* (1913; Boston: Houghton Mifflin Company, 1967) 307.

46. James Woodress, *Willa Cather: Her Life and Art* (1970; Lincoln: U of Nebraska P, 1975) 211. Similarly, Hugh Hetherington calls Tom Outland Cather's "dream son" *("The Professor's House"* N. pag.).

47. Rosowski, *Voyage,* 132–33.

Chapter 5

1. For examples, see Comeau, 223; Edel, "A Cave of One's Own," 204; Murphy, "The Mesa Verde Story," N. pag.; Randall, *Landscape,* 205 and

212; Stouck, *Imagination,* 104; and Sullivan, 31. Moreover, the same problem has plagued *Death Comes for the Archbishop,* which many readers have unfortunately accepted as historically accurate. See chapter 8, n59.

2. Slote, "First Book," xxxx.

3. Frank McNitt says that the Spaniards named the river "out of respect for their lame or crippled horses" (*Richard Wetherill,* 12), but Maurine S. Fletcher cites two other possibilities: Ira S. Freeman says the name resulted from an accident that crippled one of the Spanish explorers, and Herbert Eugene Bolton somewhat warily attributes the name to local stories of Indians whose hands had been cut off (*The Wetherills of the Mesa Verde: Autobiography of Benjamin Alfred Wetherill* [1977; Lincoln-Bison: U of Nebraska P, 1987] 48, n2).

4. For a good discussion of Cather's meaningful use of names, see Mildred R. Bennett, "How Willa Cather Chose Her Names," *Names* 10 (Mar. 1962): 29.

5. Blake is a good one to make this point, incidentally, because he is one of the characters most conspicuously associated with money, especially the physical coins and bills, yet the character least affected by it. When Outland first meets him, Blake has taken the jackpot from a begrudging group of railroad men. Despite the large sum involved—"sixteen hundred dollars . . . in banknotes and gold"—Blake's attitude is fairly casual. He does collect his winnings, putting the bills in his hatband, the gold in his pockets, and the rest in "his big red neckerchief," but he seems unconcerned about them. When Outland asks what he will do with the money, Blake replies, "Lose it, to-morrow night. I'm no hog for money." As if to prove the point, Blake falls asleep without undressing so that "the gold ran out of his pockets and rolled over the bare floor in the dark" (*PH* 181–82). The next morning he is ready to share with Outland: "I'll go halvers. Easy come, easy go" (*PH* 184). As the rest of the novel affirms, Blake is the only character who believes that, or lives by it.

6. Sister Peter Damian Charles, "*The Professor's House*: An Abode of Love and Death," *Colby Library Quarterly* 8.2 (June 1968): 76–77.

7. Slote, *Kingdom of Art,* 88.

8. Nordenskiold, *The Cliff Dwellers,* 3.

9. McNitt, *Richard Wetherill,* 12.

10. Jackson, 370.

11. McNitt, *Richard Wetherill,* 16.

12. Cowing to McNitt.

13. Gilbert R. Wenger, *The Story of Mesa Verde National Park* (Colorado: Mesa Verde Museum Association, 1980) 11.

14. Wenger, 7.

15. This moment anticipates another Christmas eve revelation, the reverential unpacking and displaying of the creche in *Shadows on the Rock* ([1931; New York: Vintage Books, 1971] 102 ff.).

16. *Prehistoric Cliff Dwellings,* 15.

17. Jackson, 373, 375, and 376.

18. Jack E. Smith, "Introduction," in Jesse L. Nusbaum, *The 1926 Re-Excavation of Step House Cave, Mesa Verde National Park,* Mesa Verde Research Series, Paper No. 1 (Colorado: Mesa Verde Museum Association, 1981): v.

19. Nordenskiold, *The Cliff Dwellers,* 15.

20. Nordenskiold, *The Cliff Dwellers,* 19.

21. Smith, *Mesa Verde,* 29.

22. B. A. Wetherill, 216.

23. Lillian E. Prudden, *Biographical Sketches and Letters of T. Mitchell Prudden, M. D.* (New Haven: Yale UP, 1927) 130.

24. Jack E. Smith, "Pioneering Archaeology in Mesa Verde: The Nusbaum Years," *Mesa Verde Occasional Papers* 1.2 (Oct. 1981): 19.

25. Cather also kindly has them deduce the presence of domesticated turkeys from feathers rather than from Nordenskiold's evidence, "[h]uge layers of excrement," sometimes as much as two or three hundred cubic meters, "which must have taken a long time to collect" (*The Cliff Dwellers* 95).

26. Nordenskiold, *The Cliff Dwellers,* 53.

27. Wenger, 41.

28. J. E. Smith, letter to the author, 16 Mar. 1989.

29. Lewis, 95.

30. T. Rickner, correspondence.

31. "National Parks and Monuments," *El Palacio* 14.6 (15 Mar. 1923): 90.

32. Palmer Henderson, "The Cliff Dwellers," *The Literary Northwest* 3.2 (May 1893): 82.

33. B. A. Wetherill, 203.
34. Nordenskiold, *The Cliff Dwellers,* 14.
35. Nordenskiold, *Letters,* 35.
36. J. E. Smith, letter to the author, 16 Mar. 1989.
37. Nordenskiold, *The Cliff Dwellers,* 51.
38. G. Retzius, "Human Remains Collected by M. Gustaf Nordenskiold in the Cliff Dwellings of the Mesa Verde," in Nordenskiold, *The Cliff Dwellers of the Mesa Verde,* v.
39. Retzius, ix.
40. Retzius, x.
41. Wenger, 33.
42. See Retzius, x, and Wenger, 33.
43. Charlie Mason, and presumably the Wetherills as well, advanced the siege theory: "The final tragedy of the cliff dweller probably occurred at Cliff Palace. There is scarcely room to doubt that the place withstood an extended siege" (Mason 9–10). The most recent theory of abandonment that I have heard attributes the departure of the cliff dwellers to crop failures caused by the depletion of the phosphate content in the fields. At least by the time the Spanish explorers arrived, however, pueblo Indians had learned that the fields could be restored to productivity by a yearly transfer of soil (phosphate-rich) from their habitations (Gustaf Arrhenius, "Why Was Mesa Verde Abandoned: Evidence of Soil Exhaustion," The Wetherill Symposium, Mesa Verde National Park, 18 Dec. 1988).
44. The opulence of late nineteenth-century Pullman Palace Cars was legendary, almost oppressive. One traveler described it this way: "The sleeping cars are fitted with oiled walnut, carved and gilded . . . and stained plate glass, metal trappings heavily silver-plated, seats cushioned with thick plushes, washstands of marble and walnut, damask curtains and massive mirrors in frames of gilded walnut. The floors are carpeted in the most beautiful and costly Brussels, the roof beautifully frescoed in mosaics of gold, of emerald green, crimson, sky-blue, violet, drab and black" (Beebe and Clegg, 194–95). To imagine Tom Outland in such a setting is to picture an uncomfortable incongruity all the way to Washington.
45. Cather's use of titles is confusing. The chief official at the Smithsonian Institution has always been called the secretary, not the director.

46. It is possible, though not really demonstrable, that Cather based this secretary on William Henry Holmes, the staff archaeologist at the Smithsonian who answered one of B. K. Wetherill's letters. Although he makes no mention of escorting royalty, Holmes devotes much of his reply to his own experience in and familiarity with ancient ruins in the Southwest, without giving much credence to the discoveries and work of the Wetherills. In his dealings with amateurs, Holmes seems to have been more open-minded than most of his colleagues (Curtis M. Hinsley, *Savages and Scientists: The Smithsonian Institution and the Development of American Anthropology, 1846–1910* [Washington: Smithsonian Institution P, 1981] 107), but this is probably not the opinion the Wetherills formed of him.

47. See Gore, 12–13 and 23 especially.

48. Charles D. Walcott, *Report of the U. S. National Museum, 1898* (Washington: GPO, 1900): 76–77.

49. Otis T. Mason, "Progress of Anthropology in 1889," in *Annual Report of the Smithsonian Institution, 1889,* ed. S. P. Langley (Washington: GPO, 1890): 595–96.

50. For more details on the work of the Smithsonian and the interests and attitudes of its officials, see Harrell, " 'We contacted Smithsonian,' " 242 ff.

51. Gerber, *Willa Cather,* 116.

52. Nordenskiold, *The Cliff Dwellers,* 23.

53. Irv Diamond, letter to author, 8 and 9 Mar. 1991.

54. Nordenskiold, *Letters,* 45.

55. Nordenskiold, *Letters,* 45 ff. See Lister and Lister, "The Legacy of Gustaf Nordenskiold," in *Stones Speaks and Waters Sing,* 31–32.

56. Lister and Lister, 32.

57. "He Is Under Arrest," *Rocky Mountain News* 19 Sept. 1891: N. pag. In a letter to his father dated 16 Sept., Nordenskiold sourly alludes to another similar story about him, calling it "[a]n ignorant newspaper article containing expressions such as 'vandalism,' 'robbery,' and 'must be stopped at once' " (*Letters,* 52). By 23 Oct. Nordenskiold's sense of humor had returned so that he could write his cousin about his "interesting collection of newspaper clippings, wherein Mr. Nordinjskod or Kortinskid or worse is accused of 'carrying away the ruins from the Mancos Cañon,' etc., and saying that 'he ought to be lynched.' " Nordenskiold also

confides to his cousin, "I have gotten my hair cut quite short, so that the value of my scalp will be more problematic" (*Letters,* 63).

58. Lister and Lister, 33.

59. In a letter to his father on 19 Sept., Nordenskiold sarcastically remarks, "Americans would rather that cowboys, miners, etc., dig amongst their antiquities, than foreigners" (*Letters,* 53).

60. See his *Letters.* It is a rare letter in this collection that does not include some reference to Nordenskiold's need for money or his prospect of earning money.

61. Hetherington, N. pag.

62. Carol Ann Wetherill, telephone interview, 28 Mar. 1987; Tom Wetherill, letter to the author, 13 Jul. 1987.

63. Prudden, 133.

64. Swift, 305.

65. Woodress, *Literary Life,* 372.

66. This passage illuminates an interesting parallel between Roddy Blake and Ray Kennedy in *The Song of the Lark.* Both Kennedy and Blake are facilitators, patrons, who make personal sacrifices to enrich the lives of other people who have gifts or abilities that they themselves lack but nevertheless appreciate. The things Ray Kennedy admired "had always been away out of his reach: a college education, a gentleman's manner, an Englishman's accent—things over his head" (*SL* 186). For Thea Kronborg, however, such trappings of refinement are possible because of her talent, if only she had the means to start her career in the right way. Ray Kennedy's life insurance policy gives her the means. Likewise, Roddy Blake had always wanted Tom Outland to receive a good education. "He said if I once knew Latin, I wouldn't have to work with my back all my life like a burro. He had great respect for education" (*PH* 188), respect from a distance, like Kennedy's. It was for this end that Blake worked for Fechtig. "You're not going to be a day-labourer like me," he tells Outland (*PH* 243). These similarities notwithstanding, the circumstances of each man's sacrifice are different, of course, as are the results. Ray Kennedy's dream is fulfilled, Roddy Blake's is shattered. Tom Outland does receive his education, but it is at the expense of the friendship rather than the bank account, thus adding another dimension to Outland's obsession. In this sense, even for Tom Outland everything "come[s] to money in the

end," money earned through the best of intentions but money that Outland refuses because of extraordinary scruples.

67. Cynthia Chaliff sees in Henry's "symbolic death" a preparation for "the discovery that in this Eden, too, there was a Fall (70).

68. Another point in Roddy's favor is his repeated insistence upon the innocence of Alfred Dreyfus, the French soldier accused of selling military secrets to the Germans. "It was a point he would never pass up," Outland says (*PH* 243). Although sometimes overlooked by critics, this historical allusion seems intended to suggest Blake's innocence by associating his case with that of another accused man who was ultimately exonerated (like the Wetherills, incidentally). As Paul Comeau has noted, Blake's reference to Dreyfus "undercuts the disdainful tone of Outland's accusations. . . ." (224). Furthermore, if Cather admired the courage of Émile Zola, Dreyfus's most famous champion, for "taking on the French establishment" (Woodress, *Literary Life,* 143), she must also have admired the similar actions of Anatole France, the same author whose novel *Le mannequin d'osier* and whose character M. Bergeret account for some of the components of *The Professor's House.* France joined the Dreyfusards around the time that *Le mannequin* was published (Comeau 219), and he died in 1924, when Cather was writing *The Professor's House.* According to one recent study, the "mild and skeptical Anatole France astonished everyone by the passion with which he fought for the release of an innocent man" (Robert Wernick, "The officer who was no gentlemen," *Smithsonian* 20.5 [Aug. 1989]: 127). Perhaps France's passion is reflected in Roddy Blake.

69. Cecil L. Moffitt, "Anti-Intellectualism as Theme in Willa Cather's *The Professor's House,*" *Research Studies* 37 (Sept. 1969): 239.

70. Moffitt, 239.

Chapter 6

1. James Fenimore Cooper, "Preface to the Leather-Stocking Tales," in *Anthology of American Literature,* 2 Vols., ed. George McMichael, et al. (New York: Macmillan Publishing Co., Inc., 1980) 624.

2. Nathaniel Hawthorne, *The House of the Seven Gables* (1851; New York: W. W. Norton & Company, 1967) 1.

3. Slote, *Kingdom of Art,* 59.

4. Bruce E. Miller, for instance, has identified "the struggle to realize an ideal" as one of the tenets of Cather's humanism ("The Testing of Willa Cather's Humanism: *A Lost Lady* and Other Cather Novels," *Kansas Quarterly* 5 [Fall 1973]: 43). A recent work that comments at length upon Cather's technique of idealization, with references to earlier studies, is Smith Hawkins, "Ideals and Imagination in the Novels of Willa Cather."

5. Maxfield, 79.

6. Although many people have commented upon the artistic aspects of the Blue Mesa and Tom Outland's life there, no one else, as far as I have been able to determine, has equated the mesa with Cather's Kingdom of Art. Richard Giannone comes close, however, when he calls it "the kingdom of the soul" (*Music in Willa Cather's Fiction* [Lincoln: U of Nebraska P, 1968] 152). Ironically, Bernice Slote sees *The Professor's House* as one of three books (*A Lost Lady* and *My Mortal Enemy* are the other two) in which "the 1893–1896 material virtually disappears from view" (*Kingdom of Art,* 110).

7. Esther Lanigan Stineman, *Mary Austin: Song of a Maverick* (New Haven: Yale UP, 1989) 208–09.

8. Slote, *Kingdom of Art,* 31.

9. Slote, *Kingdom of Art,* 82.

10. Slote, *Kingdom of Art,* 5.

11. Matt. 13.44–46. All Biblical citations are taken from the King James Version.

12. Matt. 19.24.

13. Matt. 20.16.

14. Matt. 13.22

15. Matt. 19.14.

16. On the one hand, Clive Hart accepts Father Duchene's explanation as Cather's means of introducing sin and violence into Tom Outland's "Arcadian retreat" ("*The Professor's House:* A Shapely Story," *Modern Language Review* 67 [April 1972]: 271–81). On the other hand, Jean Schwind rejects it, seeing it as a chauvinist "frame-up" that denies "the realities of mesa life" ("Pictorial Art," 93 ff.). Schwind has also noted the qualifying terms in Duchene's commentary ("This Is a Frame-Up: Mother

Eve in *The Professor's House,*" The Santa Fe Conference on Willa Cather, 11 Aug. 1989).

17. Doane, "Defense," 300.

18. *Prehistoric Cliff Dwellings,* 3.

19. Nordenskiold, *The Cliff Dwellers,* 138 ff.

20. Slote, *Kingdom of Art,* 42.

21. Gen. 2:21–23.

22. There is an interesting autobiographical correspondence between this interpretation and a point made by Sharon O'Brien: because she dared "to claim·novel-writing as her vocation, Cather [thought she] merited punishment for her overreaching desire" *(Voice* 384).

23. Gen. 3.5.

24. John Milton, *Paradise Lost,* XII 648–49.

25. Cather may have based this part of Father Duchene's role upon Father Ghislain Haelterman, "that fine Belgian priest" (Lewis, 100) whom she and Edith Lewis visited in Española, New Mexico, in 1916. He too served as a military chaplain in WWI *(La Iglesia de Santa Cruz de la Cañada, 1733–1983* [Santa Cruz, NM: Santa Cruz Parish, 1983] 42).

26. Slote, *Kingdom of Art,* 59.

27. Smith Hawkins, 75; Brown and Edel, 241. Without doubt, these parallels with Keats's ode are deliberate. Surely Cather read the poem either on her own or in school, and she taught it to her students in Pittsburgh (Byrne and Snyder, 60). For a musical connection between Cather's Cliff City and Keats's ode, see Joseph X. Brennen, "Music and Willa Cather," *The University Review* 31.4 (June 1965): 260.

28. Moffitt, 239.

29. Ernest Becker, *The Denial of Death* (1973; New York: The Free Press, 1975) 5.

30. Bernice Slote and Lucia Woods, *Willa Cather: A Pictorial Memoir* (Lincoln: U of Nebraska P, 1973) 108.

31. Cather echoes Outland's sentiment herself when, writing about *Death Comes for the Archbishop,* she laments the practice of New Mexican priests replacing the "old homely images and decorations" in the churches with "conventional, factory-made church furnishings from New York. It is a great pity. All Catholics will be sorry about it, I think, when it is too late, when all those old paintings and images and carved doors that have

so much feeling and individuality are gone—sold to some collector in New York or Chicago, where they mean nothing" (*WCOW* 6).

32. In the 1890s Willa Cather believed that the American public, as well as its artists, had a long way to go. Noting how frequently American audiences imported foreign artists, she was troubled that a country with the ability to buy art from other nations may not be as eager as it should to support its own artists (Slote, *Kingdom of Art,* 194). A related concern (though just as much a celebration of revenge) was that European artists were paid more in America than in Europe even though they did not perform as well: "American audiences are for the most part snobbish and stupid and vulgar; they deserve to be 'worked' and cheated as much as they have been and more" (Cather, *KA* 197).

33. Henry Seidel Canby, [Review of *The Professor's House*], in *Critical Essays on Willa Cather,* ed. John J. Murphy (Boston: G. K. Hall & Co., 1984): 200.

34. Sharon O'Brien, "Becoming Noncanonical: The Case Against Willa Cather," *American Quarterly* 40.1 (Spring 1988): 118. Patricia Lee Yongue has pointed out that "the descriptions of the Colorado landscape [in *The Professor's House*] specifically evoke the edenic image of America associated with American landscape painting" ("Dutch Genre Painting," 158).

35. Slote, *Kingdom of Art,* 31. For a discussion of how Cather's position in the American literary canon has shifted according to the tenor of the times, see O'Brien, "Becoming Noncanonical."

36. Butcher, "Purpose," 9.

37. Becker, 12.

38. Slote, *Kingdom of Art,* 56.

39. Moffitt, 238. Likewise, James Maxfield calls Tom Outland "the most idealized character in the novel" (84), and Glen Love contends that Outland is a western hero whose life "is more stereotypically heroic than even Hollywood would dare to venture. . . . [W]ho, in bald summary, would believe it?" ("Willa Cather's Code Hero: Tom Outland as Shane," *Heritage of the Great Plains* 14 [Winter 1981]: 3).

40. Maxwell Geismar, *The Last of the Provincials* (Boston: Houghton Mifflin Company, 1947) 185.

41. Slote, *Kingdom of Art,* 49.

42. Slote, *Kingdom of Art,* 98.

43. Woodress, *Literary Life,* 304.

44. Willa Cather, *Not Under Forty* (1936; Lincoln: U of Nebraska P, 1988) 144–45. Subsequent citations will appear in the text, with the abbreviation *NUF* substituting for the full title.

45. Philip Gerber says that "Tom Outland's Story" "exists as an illustration" of St. Peter's belief that art and religion are the same thing (*Willa Cather,* 115).

46. Glen E. Lich, "Tom Outland: A Central Problem," *Southwestern American Literature* 8.1 (Fall 1982): 43.

47. Rosowski, *Voyage,* 133.

48. Bloom, "Poetics," 117.

49. Giannone, *Music,* 160.

50. Woodress, *Literary Life,* 331 and 385.

51. Henry David Thoreau, *Walden and Civil Disobedience,* ed. Owen Thomas (W. W. Norton & Company, Inc., 1966) 61.

52. Henry David Thoreau, *A Week on the Concord and Merrimack Rivers* (Boston: Houghton, Osgood and Company, 1880) 364. In the passage preceding this couplet, Thoreau speaks of the life as art as "a poem not printed on paper" (363). Although the idea is different, the words are strangely suggestive of Cather's concept of "the inexplicable presence of the thing not named" in "The Novel Demeuble" (*WCOW* 41).

53. Becker, 173.

54. Slote, *Kingdom of Art,* 46.

55. Thoreau, *Walden,* 213.

56. Machen, "Home," 263, n. 68.

57. This refrain from Job 1:14–19 is the epigraph to the epilogue of *Moby-Dick.*

58. Rosowski, *Voyage,* 133.

59. Sergeant, 217.

60. John J. Murphy, "Willa Cather: The Widening Gyre," in *Five Essays on Willa Cather: The Merrimack Symposium,* ed. John J. Murphy (North Andover: Merrimack College, 1974): 70.

61. These actions are reminiscent of Douglass Burnham's wistful recollection in "The Treasure of Far Island": "We were artists in those days,

creating for the day only; making epics sung once and then forgotten, building empires that set with the sun" (*CSF* 280).

62. In another sense, however, Outland's failure as an artist could be likened to that of *Hamlet,* which, according to Cather, is "greater than success. Whoso loseth his life shall find it. . . . Their kingdoms were not of this world, their lives did not save this world, but their memories have. They gave the world the ideals by which we live, for which we die" (Cather, *KA* 308).

63. Schroeter, 371.

64. Yet another example is Henri Bergson, a biologist, psychologist, and philosopher who won the Nobel Prize for Literature in 1927. Willa Cather knew and respected his work.

65. Cooper, 623.

66. Slote, *Kingdom of Art,* 81, 66, and 79. In his autobiography, Yehudi Menuhin, a young friend of Cather's during her last years, says that, "representing America and presenting us with the values of Europe, Aunt Willa possessed the unity in diversity which underlay all my life" (*Unfinished Journey* [New York: Alfred A. Knopf, 1976] 131).

67. Bloom, "Poetics," 105.

68. Stouck, *Imagination,* 107.

69. Some striking parallels exist between Tom Outland and an American poet living in France at the time of the war, Alan Seeger. Born in 1888, the year that Richard Wetherill and Charlie Mason discovered Cliff Palace, Seeger joined the French Foreign Legion in 1914, the same year as Outland; he was killed in 1916, the same year as Outland; and at the time of his death he was twenty-eight years old, approximately the same age as Outland. Beyond these circumstantial similarities, Alan Seeger, like Tom Outland, "was, by choice, something of the odd man out. He was a dreamer, remote from the others, invariably courteous while permitting no one to become too friendly" (Geoffrey Bocca, *La Legion! The French Foreign Legion and the Men Who Made It Glorious* [New York: Thomas Y. Crowell Company, 1964] 47–48). He was also "a poet who sacrificed his life for an ideal" (James Wellard, *The French Foreign Legion* [Boston: Little, Brown and Company, 1974] 81). It is quite possible that Cather had heard of Seeger or his work. The best known of the swarm of Americans who joined the Legion in 1914, he wrote war poems, war articles for the

New York Sun, a long diary, and long letters to his family (Bocca, 48). Probably his best known war poem is "I Have a Rendezvous with Death," which was first published in the *New Republic* early in 1916. *Poems by Alan Seeger* was published in December 1916 and *Letters and Diary of Alan Seeger* in May 1917. Both were widely read (Irving Werstein, *Sound No Trumpet: The Life and Death of Alan Seeger* [New York: Thomas Y. Crowell, 1967] 124 and 130). Interestingly, John Murphy has applied the idea of a rendezvous with death to the condition of Godfrey St. Peter, though without connecting Seeger with Tom Outland ("The Widening Gyre," 71). Finally, like Cather herself, Seeger was a Francophile. In one of his letters home, he writes, "I never took arms out of hatred against Germany or the Germans, but purely out of love for France" (quoted in Bocca, 48).

70. Fray Garces, whose diary Outland and St. Peter follow, is probably based upon Fray Francisco Garcés, a Spanish missionary who kept a detailed daily record of his travels in Arizona and California from October 1775 to September 1776. Much of his journey, like that of Cather's Fray Garces, was along the Rio Colorado. See Fray Francisco Garcés, *A Record of Travels in Arizona and California, 1775–1776,* ed. and trans. John Galvin (San Francisco: John Howell-Books, 1967). Another possible source for Cather's missionary, this one connected with the history of Mesa Verde, is Fray Silvestre Escalante, a member of an expedition that camped on the Mancos River in August 1776 and who noted in his journal the presence of small ruins in the Dolores River Valley (see Smith, *Mesa Verde,* 8).

71. Wasserman, 238. Jean Schwind believes that Lillian dislikes Tom because he became romantically involved with both St. Peter daughters at the same time ("Frame-Up" N. pag.).

72. A few second-person references, undoubtedly to Professor St. Peter, serve as subtle reminders that "Tom Outland's Story" is a first-person oral narrative originally told one-on-one: "I wish I could tell you what I saw there" (*PH* 201); "Hook, you remember, had done all our hauling for us" (*PH* 237); "You must take my word for it"; and "In the spring, just a year after I quarrelled with Roddy, I landed here and walked into your garden, and the rest you know" (*PH* 253).

73. Slote, *Kingdom of Art,* 91.

74. Matt. 25.34. Thea Kronborg receives an artistic inheritance also,

one that "she herself had laid up . . . , the fullness of the faith she had kept before she knew its name or meaning" (*SL* 571).

Chapter 7

1. Matt. 16.18–19. At least six other readers of *The Professor's House* have already noted this scriptural background to the Professor's name but with different emphases. James C. Work says, "Godfrey (Peace of God) St. Peter . . . has a name which echoes that of the St. Peter in Matthew XVI.18, the name which Jesus puns upon by saying 'upon this rock I will build my church'" ("Cather's Confounded Conundrums in *The Professor's House*," *Western American Literature* 18.4 [Feb. 1984]: 304); Barbara Wild suggests that Cather uses the play on names to establish the friendship between Tom Outland and Godfrey St. Peter, which becomes a model for other male friendships in other works (273); Meredith Machen says that Godfrey St. Peter "is the rock on which, or rather, into which, Tom Outland's story is built" ("Home" 236); Susan Rosowski sees in the Professor's name "images that are both larger than and detached from life, for they are names of heroic intermediaries: the worldly gatekeeper to knowledge; the saintly gatekeeper to salvation" ("The Pattern of Willa Cather's Novels," *Western American Literature* 15.4 [Feb. 1981]: 257); John Randall compares Godfrey St. Peter to "the original St. Peter who holds the keys to the kingdom of heaven much as his namesake holds the key to history" (*Landscape* 209); and, closest to my interpretation, Rhoda Orme-Johnson says, "Just as St. Peter was the disciple of Jesus, so Godfrey St. Peter is Tom's, particularly in the sense of publishing Tom's excavation journal. . . ." ("The Meaning of Names in Willa Cather's Novel *The Professor's House*, ts [Maharishi International U, 1987] 3).

2. Godfrey St. Peter and Tom Outland have also been interpreted as father and son. Smith Hawkins says, "Tom Outland had been both a son and—in the way of sons and fathers—a younger version of himself" (181).

3. Bloom, "Poetics," 101.

4. Anyone who has struggled to decipher Cather's handwriting might recognize another autobiographical parallel between the author and her character.

5. Randall, *Landscape,* 211.

6. Murphy, "The Widening Gyre," 70.

7. Rosowski, *Voyage Perilous,* 141. Loretta Wasserman calls "Tom Outland's Story" the Professor's "reminiscence, told in Tom's words" (235).

8. Richard Giannone, "Willa Cather and the Human Voice," in *Five Essays on Willa Cather: the Merrimack Symposium,* ed. John J. Murphy (North Andover, MA: Merrimack College, 1974) 36.

9. Slote, *Kingdom of Art,* 77.

10. One of Cather's students from the Pittsburgh days recalled that Cather herself had beautiful hands (Byrne 60).

11. Lewis, 174.

12. Woodress, *Literary Life,* 27.

13. Woodress, *Literary Life,* 30.

14. Rosowski, *Voyage,* 137.

15. Rosowski, *Voyage,* 137–38.

16. Rosowski, *Voyage,* 134.

17. Becker, 84.

18. Maxfield, 73. St. Peter's inaction at this point also contrasts with his Biblical namesake, who throughout his life was known as a man of action.

19. Leon Edel, *Willa Cather: The Paradox of Success* (Washington: The Library of Congress, 1960) 9.

20. For a good summary of St. Peter's depressed state of mind that answers Edel's objections, see Maxfield, 73.

21. Nathaniel Hawthorne, "Wakefield," in *The Celestial Railroad and Other Stories* (New York: The New American Library, 1963): 70 and 72.

22. Lich, 42.

23. Yongue, "Godfrey St. Peter," 18.

24. Sergeant, 194.

25. Maxfield, 78.

26. Tillie Olsen, *Silences* (New York: Delacorte Press/Seymour Lawrence, 1978) 8 ff.

27. Michael A. Klug, "Willa Cather: Between Red Cloud and Byzantium," *Canadian Review of American Studies* 12.3 (Winter 1981): 298.

28. Sherman, 48.

29. Slote, *Kingdom of Art,* 35.

30. Stouck, *Imagination,* 99.

31. Kubitschek, 18.

32. Shelton, 12.

33. Sergeant, 215.

34. Critics have seen St. Peter letting go of a great many things: Tom Outland (Grumbach, 343); "romanticism and idealism" (Bohlke, "Delacroix," 37); "the will to power through love, the instinct to possess and dominate" (Stouck, *Imagination,* 103); "the will to fight for his separateness" (Arnold, "Structure," 177); "something precious—the lover" (Rosowski, *Voyage,* 138); his "solitary original self as well as the secondary self" (Murphy, "The Widening Gyre," 71); "the better part of himself" (Ferguson, 63); "his youth and his passion, the strength to pursue the ideals that make life worth living" (Jamie Ambrose, *Willa Cather: Writing at the Frontier* [Oxford: Berg Publishers Limited, 1988] 113); "his past life" (Fritz Oehlschlaeger, *Indisponibilité* and the Anxiety of Authorship in *The Professor's House, American Literature* 62.1 [March 1990]:86); "his will to live" (Giannone, *Music,* 166); and "the delusion that he wants to die" (Maxfield, 85).

35. Charles, 72.

36. Robert Frost, *The Poetry of Robert Frost,* ed. Edward Connery Latham (New York: Holt, Rinehart and Winston, 1969) 197–99.

37. By contrast, Andor Harsanyi had foretold a different sort of peace for Thea Kronborg: "when you find your way to that gift and to that woman [you were meant to be] you will be at peace" (*SL* 265). Thea is also more fortunate in her experience of letting go: "Thea seemed to be taking very little through the wood with her. The personality of which she was so tired seemed to let go of her. The high, sparkling air drank it up like blotting-paper" (*SL* 368). Finally, despite all its conflicts and dilemmas, Thea's life is simpler than the Professor's: with few exceptions, the forces within and around her contribute to the development of her artistic self so that, unlike St. Peter, Thea is pulled essentially in only one direction.

38. Quinn, 690.

39. Giannone, *Music,* 167.

40. Gleason, 291.

41. Moffitt, 235.

42. Maxfield, 78.

43. Murphy, "The Widening Gyre," 72.

44. Glen A. Love, "*The Professor's House:* Cather, Hemingway, and the Chastening of American Prose Style," *Western American Literature* 24.4 (Feb. 1990): 305.

Chapter 8

1. Brown and Edel, 238.
2. Woodress, *Literary Life,* 368–69.
3. Helen Cather Southwick, "Willa Cather's Early Career: Origins of a Legend," *The Western Pennsylvania Historical Magazine* 65.2 (April 1982): 97.
4. Woodress, *Literary Life,* 369.
5. Woodress, *Literary Life,* 291.
6. Woodress, *Literary Life,* 203–04.
7. Butcher, "Purpose," 9. Doubtless many readers will disagree with Cather's assessment, citing ironic aspects in earlier books as well. Moreover, it is certainly possible that Cather used the word "first" not in its literal sense but as a means of emphasizing her point.
8. Wayne C. Booth, *A Rhetoric of Irony* (Chicago: U of Chicago P, 1974) 61.
9. Woodress, *Literary Life,* 371–72.
10. Margaret Doane, "Bishop Latour and Professor St. Peter: Cather's Esthetic Intellectuals," *Arizona Quarterly* 41.4 (Spring 1985): 61.
11. Giannone, *Music,* 166.
12. Woodress, *Literary Life,* 372.
13. Stouck, *Imagination,* 107.
14. Maxfield, 84.
15. Lich, 42.
16. Leo Vincent Jacks, "Willa Cather and the Southwest," *New Mexico Quarterly* 27 (Spring–Summer 1957): 86.
17. Patricia Lee Yongue, "*The Professor's House* and Rip Van Winkle," *Western American Literature* 18.4 (Feb. 1984): 293. Likewise, John Randall has called Outland's pride an "insidious danger" (*Landscape* 223).
18. Walter Licht, *Working for the Railroad: The Organization of Work in the Nineteenth Century* (Princeton: Princeton UP, 1983) 220.
19. For a historical account of the role of the call boy, see Stewart

Holbrook, *The Story of American Railroads* (New York: Crown Publishers, 1947) 266.

20. Holbrook, 266; Licht, 220. A case in point is H. E. Bryon, who began his career as a call boy when he was sixteen (Outland's approximate age, incidentally) and ended it as president of the Chicago, Milwaukee & St. Paul Railway (Slason Thompson, *A Short History of America's Railways* [New York: D. Appleton & Company, 1922] 421).

21. Butcher, "Purpose," 9.

22. Loretta Wasserman finds the Professor's nickname appropriate too, but for a different reason: "The temptation St. Peter is caught in is the one Faust resists—the temptation to stop time, to rest in the past" (238).

23. Merrill Maguire Skaggs, *After the World Broke in Two* (Charlottesville: UP of Virginia, 1990) 76.

24. Rosowski, *Voyage*, 131–32. Elsewhere, Rosowski says, "St. Peter's belief that 'nothing about the vulgar success of Outland's idea could possibly matter to Crane beyond gratifying his pride as a teacher and friend' . . . is grossly insensitive at best" ("Patterns" 259).

25. Maxfield, 83. St. Peter's exclusivity may be another of the novel's autobiographical elements. One of the teachers who followed Cather at Allegheny High School in Pittsburgh "recalled critical and bitter feelings still existing among the faculty members because of Cather's devotion to the brilliant students and her intolerance of those who did not learn quickly" (Byrne, 62).

26. Lionel Trilling, "Willa Cather," in *Willa Cather and Her Critics,* ed. James Schroeter (Ithaca: Cornell UP, 1967): 152.

27. Kubitschek, 19.

28. Grumbach, 335.

29. Maxfield, 75.

30. Woodress, *Literary Life,* 375.

31. Thomas F. Strychacz, "The Ambiguities of Escape in Willa Cather's *The Professor's House,*" *Studies in American Fiction* 14.1 (Spring 1986): 56.

32. Hart, 277–78.

33. Schwind, "Frame-Up," N. pag.

34. The word adventurers also emphasizes the less honorable of the multiple motives that brought the Spaniards into North America. In the

twenties, as sometimes even now, settlement and religious conversion were often overlooked. A case in point is James Maxfield's oversimplified reference to "the militaristic Spanish adventurers" (75). If, as Patricia Lee Yongue believes, Cather knew Adolf Bandelier's *The Gilded Man,* the irony in St. Peter's title may indeed be deliberate. At one point Bandelier protests specifically against the misleading and inaccurate label "Spanish adventurers" ("Search and Research: Willa Cather in Quest of History," *Southwestern American Literature* 5 [1976]: 39, n. 17).

35. Stouck, *Imagination,* 106.

36. Brown and Edel, 242.

37. Stouck, *Imagination,* 102.

38. Kubitschek, 15.

39. Slote, "Introduction," xxiv.

40. Oehlschlaeger, 82.

41. Moseley, 8–9.

42. Bette S. Weidman, "Willa Cather's Art in Historical Perspective: Reconsidering *Death Comes for the Archbishop,*" in *Padre Martinez: New Perspectives from Taos,* ed. E. A. Mares (Taos: Millicent Rogers Museum, 1988): 53.

43. Booth, ix.

44. Willa Cather, *The World and the Parish: Willa Cather's Articles and Reviews, 1893–1902,* 2 vols, ed. William M. Curtin (Lincoln: U of Nebraska P, 1970) 49.

45. Woodress, *Literary Life,* 93. It seems entirely appropriate that *Vanity Fair* magazine once listed Cather, along with Dreiser, Wharton, Cabell, and Anderson, among "American Novelists Who Have Set Art above Popularity" (Cleveland Amory and Frederic Bradlee, eds., *Vanity Fair: Selections from America's Most Memorable Magazine: A Cavalcade of the 1920s and 1930s* [New York: The Viking P, 1960] 58).

46. James Woodress, "A Dutiful Daughter: Willa Cather and Her Parents," in *Willa Cather: Family, Community, and History (The BYU Symposium),* ed. John J. Murphy (Provo: BYU Humanities Publications Center, 1990) 23 and 30.

47. Rosowski, *Voyage,* 132.

48. Judith Fryer, *Felicitous Space: The Imaginative Structures of Edith Wharton and Willa Cather* (Chapel Hill: U of North Carolina P, 1986) 306.

49. Murphy, "The Widening Gyre," 70.

50. Woodress, *Literary Life,* 451–52.

51. Woodress, *Literary Life,* 379.

52. For an extended discussion of the meanings behind the name "Berengaria," see Alice Bell, "The Professor's Marriage," in *Willa Cather: Family, Community, and History (The BYU Symposium),* ed. John J. Murphy (Provo: BYU Humanities Publications Center, 1990) 121. See also Orme-Johnson, 10.

53. Woodress, *Literary Life,* 93.

54. Bennett, *World,* 35.

55. Bynner, 333.

56. Woodress, *Literary Life,* 366–67. Even so, Elizabeth Moorhead quotes Cather as saying, "I am always glad to hear a good word for *The Professor's House*" (*These Two Were Here: Louise Homer and Willa Cather* [Pittsburgh: U of Pittsburgh P, 1950] 60).

57. According to Bernice Slote, Cather knew Housman's "To an Athlete, Dying Young" as early as 1898 and found it to express a sentiment that appealed to her ("First Book" xiii and xxiv). In addition, Sergeant notes that Cather created only three young heroes—Paul, Claude Wheeler, and Tom Outland—and all three die young (182).

58. Fanny Butcher, "The Literary Spotlight," *Chicago Sunday Tribune* 4 May 1947: 4.

59. Fanny Butcher, *Many Lives—One Love* (New York: Harper & Row, Publishers, 1972) 354.

60. A further autobiographical case could be made in that Cather seems to suffer her own "diminution of ardor" (*PH* 13) after *The Professor's House.* Of the five novels that follow it—all of them certainly interesting and evocative in one way or another—*Death Comes for the Archbishop* is the only one that would surely have secured a lasting place solely on its own merits. The others receive the attention they do more because Cather wrote them than because they justify careful scrutiny in and of themselves; and the place secured by *Archbishop* would be due not to its overall quality but to the excellence of so many of its scenes. As David Stouck suggests, the book is best approached either as a Saint's legend (*Imagination* 129 ff.) or as travel writing ("Cather's *Archbishop*" 3–12). However, the first approach is undermined by the emphasis upon

Father Latour's temporal nature, along with the fact that his veneration is accomplished partly at the expense of the villification of Padre Martinez; and the numerous historical errors in general undermine the second approach. For discussions of some of the historical problems with *Archbishop*, see David Lavender, "The Tyranny of Facts," in *Old Southwest, New Southwest: Essays on a Region and Its Literature,* ed. Judy N. Lensink (Tucson: Tucson Public Library, 1987): 62–73; E. A. Mares, "The Many Faces of Padre Antonio José Martinez: A Historiographic Essay," in *Padre Martinez: New Perspectives from Taos,* ed. E. A. Mares (Taos, New Mexico: Millicent Rogers Museum, 1988) 18–47; Jerome J. Martinez y Alira [sic], "The Apotheosis of Bishop Lamy/Local Faith Perspectives," *Willa Cather Pioneer Memorial Newsletter* 35.3 (Fall 1991): 19–22; Patricia Clark Smith, "Achaeans, Americanos, Prelates and Monsters: Willa Cather's *Death Comes for the Archbishop,*" in *Padre Martinez* 101–24; Ralph H. Vigil, "Willa Cather and Historical Reality," *New Mexico Historical Review* 50.2 (April 1975): 123–34; Ted J. Warner, *"Death Comes for the Archbishop:* A Novel Way of Making History," in *Willa Cather: Family, Community, and History (The BYU Symposium),* ed. John J. Murphy (Provo: BYU Humanities Publications Center, 1990) 265–273; and Weidman, 48–70.

61. Bloom, "Poetics," 118.

62. Booth, 36.

63. Randall, *Landscape,* 225.

64. Chaliff, 70.

65. Klug, 298.

66. Miller, 45. Merrill M. Skaggs agrees: "Cather does not end any novel . . . without some hope" (83).

Chapter 9

1. Slote, *Kingdom of Art,* 67. In addition, Susan Rosowski cites one of Cather's letters to Dorothy Canfield Fisher as evidence that Cather "turned to dreams as stays against loss and change" (*Voyage,* 141).

2. Bennett, *World,* 29.

3. Lich, 42.

4. Hart, 275.

5. Stouck, *Imagination,* 104. Likewise, Cynthia Chaliff calls Cliff City "the core of the core" (69).

6. Maxfield, 79.

7. Sergeant, 120 and 230.

8. Cather's Professor Sherman would hasten to point out that the actual tally is twenty-five out of twenty-eight.

9. Hinz, 74.

10. For a detailed account of the differences between Tom Outland's language and Professor St. Peter's language, see Lee 252–58.

11. Wasserman, 238.

12. Smith Hawkins, 89.

13. Long before *The Professor's House,* Cather had used the technique of the story told and retold (in "The Namesake," for example), but the merging of personalities and the blending of times are much more pronounced here.

14. This implicit theme is made explicit in "The Treasure of Far Island": "The island is known chiefly to the children who dwell in that region, and generation after generation of them have claimed it. . . ." (*CSF* 265).

15. Stephen Tennant, "The Room Beyond," in *Willa Cather on Writing,* ed. Stephen Tennant (1949; Lincoln-Bison: U of Nebraska P, 1988): v.

16. Wasserman, 229.

17. Lee, 244.

18. Rosowski and Slote, 88–89.

19. Smith Hawkins, 38.

20. Thirty-six years after *The Professor's House* was published, Ernest Hemingway chose the other recourse open to the artist, consciously lifting his hand against himself once the Kingdom of Art had eluded him. "If he saw the bright day outside," Carlos Baker says, "it did not deter him" (*Ernest Hemingway: A Life Story* [New York: Charles Scribner's Sons, 1969] 563); and the maxim that corresponded to Cather's—*"il faut (d'abord) durer"*—was succeeded by another: *"il faut (apres tout) mourir"* (Baker 564). Writers and readers alike might debate which alternative is the proper solution to this frequent artistic dilemma. Although she certainly would have sympathized with Hemingway's anguish, Cather would side

with St. Peter. Despite his clumsy and vacillating method, St. Peter does chose to live, to bear, a choice that Cather reaffirmed in her last three stories (see Marilyn Arnold, "Cather's Last Three Stories," *Great Plains Quarterly* 4.4 [Fall 1984]: 239).

21. Maxfield, 85.

22. Gleason, 296.

23. One in whom the fire has reignited is Ernest Gaines, author of *The Autobiography of Miss Jane Pittman, A Gathering of Old Men,* and several other books. His connection to Cather is direct and seminal. When he began reading fiction, he was unsatisfied with the way white writers in the South wrote about blacks (a dissatisfaction similar to the one that Cather says moved her to write *O Pioneers!* [*WCP* 37]); therefore, he says, "I chose to read other writers who wrote about peasant life. And I discovered John Steinbeck and Willa Cather. They didn't write about blacks, but I liked the way they wrote about peasants. They gave them a humanity that I didn't find in the Southern writer who wrote about blacks." Gaines now describes his work as a writer as carving figures out of a heavy block of a live oak tree that his people cut for him at his rural Louisiana home. Often the work seems too great a burden and he feels "cursed, not blessed"; but then he remembers the faces of those who cut the block for him and others "who never had my chance. . . . And I would pick up the hammer and the chisel or one of the knives and go back to work." Like Cather, Gaines believes in the artistic legacy. "Twenty-five years later, it is I who have begun to search faces for that one to whom I can pass the tools. I'm not through with the block yet, but at the same time, I'm looking" ("Bloodline in Ink," *CEA Critic* 51.2–3 [Winter–Spring 1989]: 6, 10–12).

24. David Stouck, *"The Professor's House* and the Issues of History," in *Willa Cather: Family, Community, and History* (*The BYU Symposium,* ed. John J. Murphy (Provo: BYU Humanities Publications Center, 1990) 202–03.

25. T. S. Eliot, "Tradition and the Individual Talent," in *American Literature: The Makers and the Making,* 2 Vols., ed. Cleanth Brooks et al. (New York: St. Martin's Press, 1973) 2830.

26. Butcher, "Purpose," 9.

27. Lewis, 126.

28. Slote, "Her First Book," xxxviii.

29. Sergeant, 116.

30. Hermione Lee has recently reached a similar conclusion though from a different direction and with a different focus. Speaking briefly of the novel "as a writer's disguised autobiography," she says that "Tom Outland's Story" itself "mimics the act of authoring [and] . . . could stand on its own as a metaphor for the writer's process of finding, losing and recreating experience" (230). Then later, speaking again of the novel as a whole, Lee calls *The Professor's House* "an epitome of all Cather's writing, in which she divides herself between two writers: Tom as the instinctual explorer and the Professor as the conscious reviser" (255). She fails, however, to see much of a connection between the two writer figures: "Only at the end, and with difficulty, are the two parts made to cohere" (230).

31. Such a reading of *The Professor's House* is especially significant in light of an observation by Linda Huf: "Unlike men, women have only rarely written artist novels; that is, autobiographical novels depicting their struggles to become creative artists. . . ." (*A Portrait of the Artist as a Young Woman: The Writer as Heroine in American Literature* [New York: Frederick Ungar Publishing, 1983] 1). *The Song of the Lark* has always been cited as Cather's contribution to this effort, although Loretta Wasserman reads *My Antonia* also as a story about "the development of the artist" (231). Now *The Professor's House* could be included, too. As Hermione Lee says, "Cather has written a writer's autobiography" (258). Similarly, Fritz Oehlschlaeger reads *The Professor's House* "as an intense drama of the woman writer's anxiety of authorship, her struggling with male definitions of herself and of her art" (77). One need not be a feminist critic or apply feminist themes, however, to see *The Professor's House* as a metaphor for the art of composition.

❋ Bibliography

Primary References

Alexander's Bridge. 1912. New York: Bantam Books, 1962.

April Twilights. 1903. Lincoln: U of Nebraska P, 1962.

The Kingdom of Art: Willa Cather's First Principles and Critical Statements, 1893–1896. Ed. Bernice Slote. Lincoln: U of Nebraska P, 1966.

Letter to M[rs.] George Sibel [sic], 12 May 1912. Letter 68. Willa Cather Historical Center, Red Cloud, Nebraska.

"Mesa Verde Wonderland Is Easy to Reach." *Denver Times* (31 Jan. 1916): 7.

Not Under Forty. 1936. Lincoln: Bison-U of Nebraska P, 1988.

O Pioneers! 1913. Boston: Houghton Mifflin Company, 1976.

One of Ours. 1922. New York: Vintage Books, 1971.

Post cards to Elizabeth Shepley Sergeant. 20 and 31 August 1915. The Pierpont Morgan Library, New York, New York.

The Professor's House. New York: Alfred A. Knopf, 1925.

Shadows on the Rock. 1931. New York: Vintage Books, 1971.

The Song of the Lark. 1915. Boston: Houghton Mifflin Company, 1983.

Willa Cather in Person: Interviews, Speeches, and Letters. Ed. L. Brent Bohlke. Lincoln: U of Nebraska P, 1986.

Willa Cather on Writing. Ed. Stephen Tennant. 1920. Lincoln: Bison-U of Nebraska P, 1988.

Willa Cather's Collected Short Fiction. Rev. ed. Ed. Virginia Faulkner. Lincoln: U of Nebraska P, 1970.

The World and the Parish: Willa Cather's Articles and Reviews, 1893–1902. 2 vols. Ed. William M. Curtin. Lincoln: U of Nebraska P, 1970.

Secondary References

BOOKS

Ambrose, Jamie. *Willa Cather: Writing at the Frontier.* Oxford: Berg Publishers Limited, 1988.

Amory, Cleveland, and Frederic Bradlee, Eds. *Vanity Fair: Selections from America's Most Memorable Magazine: A Cavalcade of the 1920s and 1930s.* New York: The Viking Press, 1960.

Arrhenius, Olof W. *Stones Speak and Waters Sing: The Life and Works of Gustaf Nordenskiold.* Ed. Robert H. Lister and Florence C. Lister. Colorado: Mesa Verde National Park and Mesa Verde Museum Association, Inc., [1984].

Athearn, Robert G. *Rebel of the Rockies: A History of the Denver and Rio Grande Western Railroad.* New Haven: Yale UP, 1962.

Baker, Carlos. *Ernest Hemingway: A Life Story.* New York: Charles Scribner's Sons, 1969.

Becker, Ernest. *The Denial of Death.* 1973. New York: The Free Press, 1975.

Beebe, Lucius, and Charles Clegg. *Rio Grande: Mainline of the Rockies.* Berkeley: Howell-North, 1962.

Bennett, Mildred R. *The World of Willa Cather.* 1951. New ed. Lincoln: Bison-U of Nebraska P, 1961.

Bocca, Geoffrey. *La Legion! The French Foreign Legion and the Men Who Made It Glorious.* New York: Thomas Y. Crowell Company, 1964.

Bohlke, L. Brent, Ed. *Willa Cather in Person: Interviews, Speeches, and Letters.* Lincoln: U of Nebraska P, 1986.

Book of Genesis. King James Version.

Book of Job. KJV.

Book of Matthew. KJV.

Booth, Wayne C. *A Rhetoric of Irony.* Chicago: The U of Chicago P, 1974.

Brown, E. K., and Leon Edel. *Willa Cather: A Critical Biography.* 1953. Lincoln: Bison-U of Nebraska P, 1987.

Butcher, Fanny. *Many Lives—One Love.* New York: Harper & Row, 1972.

Byrne, Kathleen D., and Richard C. Snyder. *Chrysalis: Willa Cather in*

Pittsburgh, 1896–1906. Pittsburgh: Historical Society of Western Pennsylvania, 1981.

Clements, Frederic E., and Edith S. Clements. *Rocky Mountain Flowers.* 1914. New York: Hafner Publishing Company, 1963.

Ellis, Fern D. *Come Back to My Valley: Historical Remembrances of Mancos, Colorado.* Cortez: Cortez Printers, 1976.

Evans, Max. *Long John Dunn of Taos.* Los Angeles: Westernlore Press, 1962.

Fletcher, Maurine S., Ed. *The Wetherills of the Mesa Verde: Autobiography of Benjamin Alfred Wetherill.* 1977. Lincoln: Bison-U of Nebraska P, 1987.

Frost, Robert. *The Poetry of Robert Frost.* Ed. Edward Connery Lathan. New York: Holt, Rinehart and Winston, 1969.

Fryer, Judith. *Felicitous Space: The Imaginative Structures of Edith Wharton and Willa Cather.* Chapel Hill: The U of North Carolina P, 1986.

Garcés, Fray Francisco. *A Record of Travels in Arizona and California, 1775–1776.* Ed. and Trans. John Galvin. San Francisco: John Howell-Books, 1967.

Geismar, Maxwell. *The Last of the Provincials.* Boston: Houghton Mifflin Company, 1947.

Gerber, Philip. *Willa Cather.* Boston: Twayne Publishers, 1975.

Giannone, Richard. *Music in Willa Cather's Fiction.* Lincoln: U of Nebraska P, 1968.

Gillmor, Frances, and Louisa Wade Wetherill. *Traders to the Navajos: The Story of the Wetherills of Kayenta.* Boston: Houghton Mifflin Company, 1934.

Gjevre, John A. *Chili Line: The Narrow Rail Trail to Santa Fe.* 1969. Española, New Mexico: Las Trampas Press, 1984.

Gore, J. H. *Report of the Director of the Organization of International Congresses.* Washington: GPO, 1901. Vol. 6 of *Report of the Commissioner-General for the United States to the International Universal Exposition, Paris, 1900.* 6 vols.

Haggard, H. Rider. *She.* 1887. In *Three Adventure Novels.* New York: Dover Publications, 1951.

Hawthorne, Nathaniel. *The House of the Seven Gables.* 1851. New York: W. W. Norton & Company, 1967.

Hinsley, Curtis M. *Savages and Scientists: The Smithsonian Institution and the Development of American Anthropology, 1846–1910.* Washington: Smithsonian Institution Press, 1981.

Holbrook, Stewart. *The Story of American Railroads.* New York: Crown Publishers, 1947.

Huf, Linda. *A Portrait of the Artist as a Young Woman: The Writer as Heroine in American Literature.* New York: Frederick Ungar Publishing, 1983.

La Iglesia de Santa Cruz de la Cañada, 1733–1983. Santa Cruz, New Mexico: Santa Cruz Parish, 1983.

Lathrop, Gilbert A. *Rio Grande Glory Days.* San Marino, California: Golden West Books, 1976.

LeMassena, Robert A. *Rio Grande to the Pacific!* Denver: Sundance Limited, 1974.

Lee, Hermione. *Willa Cather: Double Lives.* New York: Pantheon Books, 1989.

Lewis, Edith. *Willa Cather Living: A Personal Record.* 1953. Lincoln: Bison-U of Nebraska P, 1976.

Licht, Walter. *Working for the Railroad: The Organization of Work in the Nineteenth Century.* Princeton: Princeton UP, 1983.

McCabe, Henry. *Cowboys, Indians and Homesteaders.* Henry and Lena McCabe: Deseret Press, 1975.

McNitt, Frank. *Richard Wetherill: Anasazi.* Rev. ed. Albuquerque: U of New Mexico P, 1966.

Menuhin, Yehudi. *Unfinished Journey.* New York: Alfred A. Knopf, 1976.

Milton, John. *Paradise Lost.* Ed. Scott Elledge. New York: W. W. Norton, 1975.

Moorhead, Elizabeth. *These Two Were Here: Louise Homer and Willa Cather.* Pittsburgh: U of Pittsburgh P, 1950.

Myrick, David F. *New Mexico's Railroads: An Historical Survey.* Golden, Colorado: The Colorado Railroad Museum, 1970.

Nordenskiold, Gustaf. *The Cliff Dwellers of the Mesa Verde.* Trans. D. Lloyd Morgan. 1893. Glorieta, New Mexico: The Rio Grande Press, 1979.

———. *Letters of Gustaf Nordenskiold.* Ed. Irving L. Diamond and

Daniel M. Olson. Trans. Daniel M. Olson. Mesa Verde National Park: Mesa Verde Museum Association, 1991.

Nusbaum, Rosemary. *Tierra Dulce: Reminiscences from the Jesse Nusbaum Papers.* Santa Fe: The Sunstone Press, 1980.

O'Brien, Sharon. *Willa Cather: The Emerging Voice.* New York: Oxford UP, 1987.

Olsen, Tillie. *Silences.* New York: Delacorte Press/Seymour Lawrence, 1978.

Overton, Richard C. *Burlington Route: A History of the Burlington Lines.* New York: Alfred A. Knopf, 1965.

Prudden, Lillian. *Biographical Sketches and Letters of T. Mitchell Prudden, M. D.* New Haven: Yale UP, 1927.

Quinn, Arthur Hobson. *American Fiction: An Historical and Critical Survey.* New York: D. Appleton-Century Company, 1936.

Randall, John H., III. *The Landscape and the Looking Glass.* Boston: Houghton Mifflin Company, 1960.

Rosowski, Susan J. *The Voyage Perilous: Willa Cather's Romanticism.* Lincoln: U of Nebraska P, 1986.

Sergeant, Elizabeth Shepley. *Willa Cather: A Memoir.* 1953. Lincoln: Bison-U of Nebraska P, 1967.

Sherman, Stuart. *Critical Woodcuts.* New York: Charles Scribner's Sons, 1926.

Skaggs, Merrill Maguire. *After the World Broke in Two: The Later Novels of Willa Cather.* Charlottesville: UP of Virginia, 1990.

Slote, Bernice, Ed. *The Kingdom of Art: Willa Cather's First Principles and Critical Statements, 1893–1896.* Lincoln: U of Nebraska P, 1966.

Slote, Bernice, and Lucia Woods. *Willa Cather: A Pictorial Memoir.* Lincoln: U of Nebraska P, 1973.

Smith, Duane A. *Mesa Verde National Park: Shadows of the Centuries.* Lawrence: U of Kansas P, 1988.

Smith, Jack E. *Mesas, Cliffs and Canyons: The University of Colorado Survey of Mesa Verde National Park, 1971–1977.* Colorado: Mesa Verde Museum Association, 1987.

Stegner, Wallace. *The Sound of Mountain Water.* Garden City, New York: Doubleday & Company, 1969.

Stineman, Esther Lanigan. *Mary Austin: Song of a Maverick.* New Haven: Yale UP, 1989.

Stouck, David. *Willa Cather's Imagination*. Lincoln: U of Nebraska P, 1975.

Thompson, Slason. *A Short History of America's Railways*. New York: D. Appleton & Company, 1922.

Thoreau, Henry D. *Walden and Civil Disobedience*. Ed. Owen Thomas. W. W. Norton & Company, 1966.

————. *A Week on the Concord and Merrimack Rivers*. Boston: Houghton, Osgood and Company, 1880.

Torres-Reyes, Ricardo. *Mesa Verde National Park: An Administrative History, 1906–1970*. Washington: United States Department of the Interior, National Park Service, 1970.

True, Webster Prentiss. *The Smithsonian Institution*. Vol. I of The Smithsonian Series. New York: Smithsonian Institution Series, 1944.

Walcott, Charles D. *Report of the U. S. National Museum, 1898*. Washington: GPO, 1900.

Watson, Don. *Cliff Dwellings of the Mesa Verde*. Colorado: Mesa Verde Museum Association, n. d.

————. *Indians of the Mesa Verde*. Colorado: Mesa Verde National Park and Mesa Verde Museum Association, 1961.

Wellard, James. *The French Foreign Legion*. Boston: Little, Brown and Company, 1974.

Wenger, Gilbert R. *The Story of Mesa Verde National Park*. Colorado: Mesa Verde Museum Association, 1980.

Werstein, Irving. *Sound No Trumpet: The Life and Death of Alan Seeger*. New York: Thomas Y. Crowell, 1967.

Wetherill, Benjamin Alfred. *The Wetherills of the Mesa Verde: Autobiography of Benjamin Alfred Wetherill*. Ed. Maurine S. Fletcher. 1977. Lincoln: Bison-U of Nebraska P, 1987.

Woodress, James. *Willa Cather: Her Life and Art*. 1970. Lincoln: Bison-U of Nebraska P, 1975.

————. *Willa Cather: A Literary Life*. Lincoln: U of Nebraska P, 1987.

ARTICLES

Abbot, C. G. "The 1914 Tests of the Langley 'Aerodrome.'" In *Smithsonian Miscellaneous Collections*. Vol. 103. Washington: Smithsonian Institution, 1942: 1–8.

"Anasazis May Have Had Stars in Their Eyes." *Albuquerque Journal* 10 Jul. 1990: E1.

Arnold, Marilyn. "Cather's Last Three Stories." *Great Plains Quarterly* 4.4 (Fall 1984): 238–44.

———. "Foreword." In *Willa Cather Living.* 1953. Athens: Ohio UP, 1989: vii–xxviii.

———. "The Function of Structure in Cather's *The Professor's House.*" *Colby Library Quarterly* 11 (Sept. 1975): 169–78.

Baker, Bruce P., III. "*The Professor's House:* An Early Source." *Willa Cather Pioneer Memorial Newsletter* 24 (Summer 1985): 13–14.

Bell, Alice. "The Professor's Marriage." In *Willa Cather: Family, Community, and History (The BYU Symposium).* Ed. John J. Murphy. Provo: BYU Humanities Publications Center, 1990: 117–123.

Benham, Jack L. "Publishers' Preface and Introduction." In *Mesa Verde and the Four Corners.* Ouray, Colorado: Bear Creek Publishing, 1981: N. pag.

Bennett, Mildred R. "At the Feet of Willa Cather: A Personal Account of Edith Lewis as Protector." *Willa Cather Pioneer Memorial Newsletter* (Fall 1989): 19–22.

———. "How Willa Cather Chose Her Names." *Names* 10 (March 1962): 29–37.

———. "Introduction." In *Willa Cather's Collected Short Fiction.* Rev. ed. Ed. Virginia Faulkner. Lincoln: U of Nebraska P, 1970: xiii–xli.

Bloom, Edward A., and Lillian D. Bloom. "The Genesis of *Death Comes for the Archbishop.*" *American Literature* 26 (Jan. 1955): 479–506.

Bloom, Lillian D. "The Poetics of Willa Cather." In *Five Essays on Willa Cather: The Merrimack Symposium.* North Andover, Massachusetts: Merrimack College, 1974: 97–119.

Bohlke, L. Brent. "Godfrey St. Peter and Eugene Delacroix: A Portrait of the Artist in *The Professor's House.*" *Western American Literature.* 17.1 (Spring 1982): 21–38.

Brennen, Joseph X. "Music and Willa Cather." *The University Review* 31.4 (June 1965): 257–64.

Butcher, Fanny. "The Literary Spotlight." *Chicago Sunday Tribune* 4 May 1947: 4.

———. "Willa Cather Tells Purpose of New Novel." *Chicago Daily Tribune* 12 Sept. 1925: 9.

Bynner, Witter. "A Willa Cather Triptych." *New Mexico Quarterly* 23 (Autumn 1953): 330–38.

Chaliff, Cynthia. "The Art of Willa Cather's Craft." *Papers in Language and Literature* 14.1 (Winter 1978): 61–73.

Chapman, Arthur. "Mesa Verde National Park Lures Many." *Denver Times* 26 Aug. 1915: N. pag.

———. "Mesa Verde Relics Are Preserved by Women." *The Denver Times* 29 June 1915: 1 ff.

Charles, Sister Peter Damian. "*The Professor's House*: An Abode of Love and Death." *Colby Library Quarterly* 8.2 (June 1968): 70–82.

Comeau, Paul. "*The Professor's House* and Anatole France." In *Critical Essays on Willa Cather.* Ed. John J. Murphy. Boston: G. K. Hall, 1984.

Cooper, James Fenimore. "Preface to the Leather-Stocking Tales." In *Anthology of American Literature.* 2 Vols. Ed. George McMichael. New York: Macmillan Publishing, 1980: 622–24.

Doane, Margaret. "Bishop Latour and Professor St. Peter: Cather's Esthetic Intellectuals." *Arizona Quarterly* 41.4 (Spring 1985): 61–70.

———. "In Defense of Lillian St. Peter: Men's Perceptions of Women in *The Professor's House.*" *Western American Literature* 18.4 (Feb. 1984): 299–302.

Edel, Leon. "A Cave of One's Own." In *Critical Essays on Willa Cather.* Ed. John J. Murphy. Boston: G. K. Hall & Co., 1984: 200–17.

Eliot. T. S. "Tradition and the Individual Talent." In *American Literature: The Makers and the Making.* 2 Vols. Ed. Cleanth Brooks et al. New York: St. Martin's Press, 1973: 2829–2834.

Ferguson, J. M., Jr. " 'Vague Outlines': Willa Cather's Enchanted Bluffs." *Western Review: A Journal of the Humanities* 7 (Spring 1970): 61–64.

Fewkes, Jesse W. "Ancient Remains in Colorado: The Mesa Verde National Park, Landmark of a Lost Race." *Scientific American* 122 (29 May 1920): 598 ff.

———. "Cremation in Cliff-dwellings." *Records of the Past* 9 (May–June 1910): 154–56.

———. "A Prehistoric Observatory." *Literary Digest* 75 (11 Nov. 1922): 27.

Gaines, Ernest J. "Bloodline in Ink." *CEA Critic* 51.2–3 (Winter–Spring 1989): 2–12.

Gerber, Philip L. "Willa Cather and the Big Red Rock." *College English* 19 (Jan. 1958): 152–57.

Giannone, Richard. "Willa Cather and the Human Voice." In *Five Essays on Willa Cather: The Merrimack Symposium*. Ed. John J. Murphy. North Andover, Massachusetts: Merrimack College, 1974: 21–49.

Gleason, John B. "The 'Case' of Willa Cather." *Western American Literature* 20.4 (Feb. 1986): 275–99.

Grant, Robert. "People Who Did Not Go to the Fair." *The Cosmopolitan*. 16 (Dec. 1893): 158–64.

Grumbach, Doris. "A Study of the Small Room in *The Professor's House*." *Women's Studies* 3 (1984): 327–45.

Harrell, David. "Edith Lewis's Tall Tales of the Southwest." *Willa Cather Pioneer Memorial Newsletter* (Fall 1989): 15–19.

———. " 'We contacted Smithsonian': The Wetherills at Mesa Verde." *New Mexico Historical Review* 62.3 (Jul. 1987): 229–48.

Hart, Clive. "*The Professor's House*: A Shapely Story." *Modern Language Review* 67 (April 1972): 271–81.

Hawthorne, Nathaniel. "Wakefield." In *The Celestial Railroad and Other Stories*. New York: The New American Library, 1963: 67–75.

"He Is Under Arrest." *Rocky Mountain News* 19 Sept. 1891: N. pag.

Henderson, Palmer. "The Cliff Dwellers." *The Literary Northwest*. 3.2 (May 1893): 79–86.

Hinz, Joseph P. "A Lost Lady and *The Professor's House*." *Virginia Quarterly Review* 29 (Winter 1953): 70–85.

Holmes, Willian Henry. "Report on the Ancient Ruins of Southwestern Colorado, Examined During the Summers of 1875 and 1876." 1878. Reprint. *Hayden Survey, 1874–1876: Mesa Verde and the Four Corners*. Ed. Jack L. Benham. Ouray, Colorado: Bear Creek Publishing, 1981: 383–408.

Howarth, William. "The Country of Willa Cather." *National Geographic Magazine* 162.1 (Jul. 1982): 71–93.

Jacks, Leo Vincent. "Willa Cather and the Southwest." *New Mexico Quarterly* 27 (Spring–Summer 1957): 83–87.

Jackson, William Henry. "Ancient Ruins in Southwestern Colorado."

Hayden Survey, 1874–1876: Mesa Verde and the Four Corners. Ed. Jack L. Benham. 1876. Ouray, Colorado: Bear Creek Publishing, 1981: 369–81.

Klug, Michael A. "Willa Cather: Between Red Cloud and Byzantium." *Canadian Review of American Studies* 12.3 (Winter 1981): 287–99.

Kubitschek, Missy Dehn. "St. Peter and the World All Before Him." *Western American Literature* 17.1 (May 1982): 13–20.

Lavender, David. "The Tyranny of Facts." In *Old Southwest, New Southwest: Essays on a Region and Its Literature.* Ed. Judy N. Lensink. Tucson: Tucson Public Library, 1987: 62–73.

Lich, Glen E. "Tom Outland: A Central Problem." *Southwestern American Literature* 8.1 (Fall 1982): 42–48.

Lister, Robert H., and Florence C. Lister. "The Legacy of Gustaf Nordenskiold." In *Stones Speak and Waters Sing.* Ed. Robert H. Lister and Florence C. Lister. Colorado: Mesa Verde Museum Association, [1984]: 69–86.

"Lost in Colorado Canyon." *New York Times* 26 Aug. 1915: 20.

Love, Glen A. *"The Professor's House:* Cather, Hemingway, and the Chastening of American Prose Style." *Western American Literature* 24.4 (Feb. 1990): 295–311.

———. "Willa Cather's Code Hero: Tom Outland as Shane." *Heritage of the Great Plains* 14 (Winter 1981): 3–12.

Machen, Meredith R. "Carlyle's Presence in *The Professor's House.*" *Western American Literature* 14.4 (Winter 1980): 273–86.

"Mancos Best Trading Point." *Mancos Times-Tribune* 9 Jul. 1915: 1.

Mancos Times-Tribune. 24 June 1898: 4; 5 Aug. 1898: 4; 22 May 1915: 3; 27 Aug. 1915: 1.

Mares. E. A. "The Many Faces of Padre Antonio José Martinez: A Historiographic Essay." In *Padre Martinez: New Perspectives from Taos.* Ed. E. A. Mares. Taos, New Mexico: Millicent Rogers Museum, 1988: 18–47.

Martinez et Alira [sic], Jerome J. "The Apotheosis of Bishop Lamy/Local Faith Perspectives." *Willa Cather Pioneer Memorial Newsletter* 35.3 (Fall 1991): 19–22.

Mason, Otis T. "Progress of Anthropology in 1889." In *Annual Report of* the Smithsonian Institution, 1889. Ed. S. P. Langley. Washington: GPO, 1890: 595–96.

Maxfield, James F. "Strategies of Self-Deception in Willa Cather's *The Professor's House.*" *Studies in the Novel* 16.1 (Spring 1984): 72–86.

Miller, Bruce E. "The Testing of Willa Cather's Humanism: *A Lost Lady* and Other Cather Novels." *Kansas Quarterly* 5 (Fall 1973): 43–50.

Moffitt, Cecil L. "Anti-Intellectualism as Theme in Willa Cather's *The Professor's House.*" *Research Studies* 37 (Sept. 1969): 235–41.

Murphy, John J. "The Mesa Verde Story and Cather's 'Tom Outland's Story.'" *Notes on Modern American Literature* 5.2 (Spring 1981): N. pag.

———. "Willa Cather: The Widening Gyre." In *Five Essays on Willa Cather: The Merrimack Symposium.* Ed. John J. Murphy. North Andover: Merrimack College, 1974: 51–74.

"National Parks & Monuments." *El Palacio* 14.6 (15 Mar. 1923): 89–90.

"New Cliff Ruin Found on Park." *Mancos Times-Tribune* 18 June 1915: 1.

O'Brien, Sharon. "Becoming Noncanonical: The Case Against Willa Cather." *American Quarterly* 40.1 (Spring 1988): 110–26.

Oehlschlaeger, Fritz. "Indisponibilité and the Anxiety of Authorship in *The Professor's House.*" *American Literature* 62.1 (Mar. 1990): 74–86.

Oxford, Edward. "George Eastman: The Man Who Wrought the Kodak." *American History Illustrated* (Sept. 1988): 16–27, 46–47.

Retzius, G. "Human Remains Collected by M. Gustaf Nordenskiold in the Cliff Dwellings of the Mesa Verde." In *The Cliff Dwellers of the Mesa Verde.* By Gustaf Nordenskiold. 1893. Reprint. Glorieta, New Mexico: The Rio Grande Press, 1979: i–xi ff.

Rosowski, Susan J. "The Pattern of Willa Cather's Novels." *Western American Literature* 15.4 (Feb. 1981): 243–63.

———. "Willa Cather's Chosen Family: Fictional Formations and Transformations." In *Willa Cather: Family, Community, and History.* Ed. John J. Murphy. Provo: BYU Humanities Publications Center, 1990: 67–78.

Rosowski, Susan J., and Bernice Slote. "Willa Cather's 1916 Mesa Verde Essay: The Genesis of *The Professor's House.*" *Prairie Schooner* 58.4 (Winter 1984): 81–92.

Salo, Alice Bell. "*The Professor's House* and le mannequin d'osier: A Note on Willa Cather's Narrative Technique." *Studies in American Fiction* 8 (Autumn 1980): 229–31.

Schroeter, James. "Willa Cather and *The Professor's House.*" In *Willa Cather and Her Critics.* Ed. James Schroeter. Ithaca: Cornell UP, 1967: 363–81.

Seigfried, Arthur H. "Al Wetherill of the Mesa Verde." *True West* (Sept.–Oct. 1965): 22–25 ff.

Shelton, Frank W. "The Image of the Rock and the Family in the Novels of Willa Cather." *Markham Review* 6 (Fall 1976): 9–14.

Slote, Bernice. "Introduction." *Uncle Valentine and Other Stories: Willa Cather's Uncollected Short Fiction, 1915–1929.* 1973. Lincoln: Bison-U of Nebraska P, 1986: ix–xxx.

————. "Willa Cather." In *Sixteen Modern American Authors.* Durham: Duke UP, 1974: 29–73.

————. "Willa Cather and Her First Book." In *April Twilights (1903).* 1903. Ed. Bernice Slote. Lincoln: U of Nebraska P, 1962: v–xxxxv.

Smith, Duane A. "A Love Affair that Almost Wasn't . . . Durango and Mesa Verde National Park." *Mesa Verde Occasional Papers* 1.2 (Oct. 1981): 1–7.

Smith, Jack E. "Introduction." *The 1926 Re-Excavation of Step House Cave, Mesa Verde National Park.* By Jesse L. Nusbaum. Mesa Verde Research Series, No. 1. Colorado: Mesa Verde Museum Association, 1981: v–vii.

————. "Pioneering Archaeology in Mesa Verde: The Nusbaum Years." *Mesa Verde Occasional Papers* 1.2 (Oct. 1981): 9–23.

Smith, Patricia Clark. "Achaeans, Americanos, Prelates and Monsters: Willa Cather's *Death Comes for the Archbishop.*" In *Padre Martinez: New Perspectives from Taos.* Ed. E. A. Mares. Taos, New Mexico: Millicent Rogers Museum, 1988: 101–24.

Southwick, Helen Cather. "Willa Cather's Early Career: Origins of a Legend." *The Western Pennsylvania Historical Magazine* 65.2 (April 1982): 85–98.

Steen, Charlie. "Introduction." In *The Cliff Dwellers of the Mesa Verde.* 1893. Glorieta, New Mexico: The Rio Grande Press, 1979: 17–29.

Stouck, David. "Cather's *Archbishop* and Travel Writing." *Western American Literature* 17.1 (Spring 1982): 3–12.

————. "*The Professor's House* and the Issues of History." In *Willa Cather: Family, Community, and History (The BYU Symposium)*. Ed. John J. Murphy. Provo: BYU Humanities Publications Center, 1990: 201–11.

Strychacz, Thomas F. "The Ambiguities of Escape in Willa Cather's *The Professor's House*." *Studies in American Fiction* 14.1 (Spring 1986): 49–61.

"The Studebaker Four." *Mancos Times-Tribune* 25 June 1915: 5.

Sullivan, Patrick. "Willa Cather's Southwest." *Western American Literature* 7 (Spring 1972): 25–38.

Swift, John N. "Memory, Myth and *The Professor's House*." *Western American Literature* 20.4 (Feb. 1986): 301–14.

Tennant, Stephen. "The Room Beyond." In *Willa Cather on Writing*. Ed. Stephen Tennant. 1949. Lincoln: Bison-U of Nebraska P, 1988: v–xxiv.

Thode, Jackson. "Foreword." In *Health, Wealth and Pleasure in Colorado and New Mexico*. 1881. A Centennial Edition. Santa Fe: Museum of New Mexico P, 1980: N. pag.

Trilling, Lionel. "Willa Cather." In *Willa Cather and Her Critics*. Ed. James Schroeter. Ithaca: Cornell UP, 1967: 148–55.

"Two Noted Women Get Lost All Night in Mesa Verde Wilds." *Denver Times* 25 Aug. 1915: 1.

Vigil, Ralph H. "Willa Cather and Historical Reality." *New Mexico Historical Review* 50.2 (Apr. 1975): 123–34.

"Visit Park This Fall." *Mancos-Times Tribune* 10 Sept. 1915: 1.

"Walking Club Arrives." *Mancos Times-Tribune* 20 Aug. 1915: 1.

Warner, Ted J. "*Death Comes for the Archbishop*: A Novel Way of Making History." In *Willa Cather: Family, Community, and History (The BYU Symposium)*. Ed. John J. Murphy. Provo: BYU Humanities Publications Center, 1990: 265–73.

Wasserman, Loretta. "The Music of Time: Henri Bergson and Willa Cather." *American Literature* 57.2 (May 1985): 226–39.

Weidman, S. Bette. "Willa Cather's Art in Historical Perspective: Reconsidering *Death Comes for the Archbishop*. In *Padre Martinez: New Perspectives from Taos*. Ed. E. A. Mares. Taos, New Mexico: Millicent Rogers Museum, 1988: 48–70.

Wernick, Robert. "The officer who was no gentleman." *Smithsonian* 20.5 (Aug. 1989): 114–28.

Wild, Barbara. " 'The Thing Not Named' in *The Professor's House.*" *Western American Literature* 12.4 (Feb. 1978): 263–74.

Woodress, James. "A Dutiful Daughter: Willa Cather and Her Parents." In *Willa Cather: Family, Community, and History (The BYU Symposium).* Ed. John J. Murphy. Provo: BYU Humanities Publications Center, 1990: 19–31.

———. "The Uses of Biography: The Case of Willa Cather." *Great Plains Quarterly* 2.4 (Fall 1982): 195–203.

Work, James C. "Cather's Confounded Conundrums in *The Professor's House.*" *Western American Literature* 18.4 (Feb. 1984): 303–12.

———. "Discovering Willa Cather's Rock." *Magazine of the Midlands,* Sunday supplement to the *Omaha World-Herald* 14 June 1987: 4–5 ff.

Yongue, Patricia Lee. "Edith Lewis Living." *Willa Cather Pioneer Memorial Newsletter* (Fall 1989): 12–15.

———. "*The Professor's House* and 'Rip Van Winkle.' " *Western American Literature* 18.4 (Feb. 1984): 281–97.

———. "Search and Research: Willa Cather in Quest of History." *Southwestern American Literature* 5 (1976): 27–39.

———. "Willa Cather's *The Professor's House* and Dutch Genre Painting." *Renascence* 31 (Spring 1979): 155–67.

REVIEWS

Canby, Henry Seidel. [Review of *The Professor's House*]. In *Critical Essays on Willa Cather.* Ed. John J. Murphy. Boston: G. K. Hall & Co., 1984: 198–200.

Krutch, Joseph Wood. "Second Best." In *Willa Cather and Her Critics.* Ed. James Schroeter. Ithaca: Cornell UP, 1967: 54–56.

BIBLIOGRAPHIES

Arnold, Marilyn. *Willa Cather: A Reference Guide.* New York: G. K. Hall, 1986.

Crane, Joan. *Willa Cather: A Bibliography.* Lincoln: U of Nebraska P, 1982.

Franke, Paul R. *Bibliography for Mesa Verde National Park.* Colorado: Mesa Verde National Park, n. d.

Lathrop, JoAnna. *Willa Cather: A Checklist of Her Published Writing.* Lincoln: U of Nebraska P, 1975.

Miller, Mamie Ruth Tanquist. *An Author, Title, and Subject Check List of Smithsonian Institution Publications Relating to Anthropology.* Albuquerque: U of New Mexico P, 1946.

O'Connor, Margaret Anne. "A Guide to the Letters of Willa Cather." *Resources for American Literary Study* 4 (Autumn 1974): 145–72.

DISSERTATIONS

Machen, Meredith. "Home as Motivation and Metaphor in the Works of Willa Cather." U of New Mexico, 1979.

Petty-Schmitt, Chapel. "Patterns in Willa Cather's Fiction." U of New Mexico, 1989.

Schwind, Jean. "Pictorial Art in Willa Cather's Fiction." U of Minnesota, 1983.

Smith Hawkins, Elaine Yvonne. "Ideals and Imagination in the Novels of Willa Cather." Stanford U, 1984.

BULLETINS, BROCHURES, AND PAMPHLETS

Charles B. Kelly: Mancos, Colorado. Advertising circular. 1909. State Historical Society of Colorado, Denver.

The Cliff Dwellers of Southwestern Colorado. Promotional brochure. The Denver and Rio Grande Railroad. [1897]. State Historical Society of Colorado, Denver.

Edel, Leon. *Willa Cather: The Paradox of Success.* The Library of Congress, 1960.

McClurg, Virginia Donaghe. *Two Annual Addresses: Pueblo, 1903; Denver, 1904.* Mesa Verde Research Center, Mesa Verde National Park, Colorado.

Mesa Verde. Washington: GPO, 1986.

The Prehistoric Cliff Dwellings: Mesa Verde National Park, Southwestern Colorado. Washington: GPO, 1915.

Rickner, Thomas. *Report for 1915.* Mesa Verde National Park Library, Vault.

Trip to the Cliff Dwellers. Report for the Denver and Rio Grande Railroad Co. 15 Oct. 1906. Mesa Verde Research Center, Mesa Verde National Park, Colorado.

The Wonders of the World's Fair. Souvenir Ed. Buffalo: Barnes, Hengerer & Co., [1894].

TYPESCRIPTS

Hayes, Leander F. Untitled ts. about travels through the Four Corners region, late 1893 through early 1894. Ts. in possession of Walter Goff, Mancos, Colorado.

[Hetherington, Hugh W.]. *"The Professor's House* and the Discovery of Mesa Verde." Mesa Verde Research Center, Mesa Verde National Park, Colorado.

March, John. *Handbook to Willa Cather.* Ts. in possession of John March, Lawton, Oklahoma; currently being edited for publication by Marilyn Arnold at Brigham Young U, Provo, Utah.

Mason, C. C. "The Story of the Discovery and Early Exploration of the Cliff Houses at the Mesa Verde." 1918 [date of acquisition]. State Historical Society of Colorado, Denver. (This story was first printed in *The Denver Post* [1 Jul. 1917], p. 6; it was reprinted in McNitt, *Richard Wetherill* 323–29).

Mierendorf, Constance. "The Turquoise and Silver Bracelet: An Indian Perspective on *The Professor's House.*" Minneapolis Community College, 1988.

Orme-Johnson, Rhoda. "The Meaning of Names in Willa Cather's Novel *The Professor's House.*" Maharishi International U, 1987.

Sharrock, Floyd W. "The Hazzard Collection." The U Museum Archives. U of Pennsylvania, Philadelphia, 1962.

Wetherill, Marietta. Interview with Lou Blachly. Tape 440, Pioneers Foundation, U of New Mexico Zimmerman Library (15 July 1953). Trans. Mary Blumenthal. (For these interviews and Mabel Wright's unfinished biography of Marietta Wetherill, see Albert E. Ward and Jerold G. Widdison, *Marietta Palmer Wetherill: Reminiscences of a Southwestern Pioneer* [Albuquerque: Center for Anthropological Studies, forthcoming]).

Yongue, Patricia Lee. "Godfrey St. Peter: Willa Cather's Cliff Dweller." U of Houston, 1987.

CORRESPONDENCE

Bader, Jean Kelly. To the author. 10 Dec. 1987.

Cowing, Herbert L. To Frank McNitt. 13 Mar. 1953. Frank McNitt Collection: New Mexico State Records Center and Archives, Santa Fe.

Cunningham, Beverly. To the author. 15 Feb. 1989.

Diamond, Irving. To the author. 8 and 9 Mar. 1991.

Ellis, Fern. To the author. 4 May 1989.

Hayes, Alden C. To the author. 6 May 1987.

Jeep, Fred T. To the author. 11 Nov. 1988.

Kaye, Belinda. To the author. 21 Jan. 1988.

Leake, Harvey. To the author. 3 Apr. 1989.

March, John. To the author. 27 Jan. 1989.

McNitt, Frank. To Herbert L. Cowing. 12 Mar. 1953. Frank McNitt Collection, New Mexico State Records Center and Archives, Santa Fe.

Nusbaum, Jesse. To Don Watson. 8 Dec. 1948. Mesa Verde Research Center, Mesa Verde National Park, Colorado.

Pezzati, Alessandro. To the author. 28 June 1989.

Rickner, J. E. To the author. 24 Sept. 1987, 20 Apr. 1988, 26 Aug. 1988.

Rickner, Thomas. Correspondence. Mesa Verde National Park Library, Vault.

———. To the Secretary of the Interior. 13 Feb. 1915. Mesa Verde National Park Library, Vault.

Robertson, Janet. To the author. 26 Sept. 1987 and 4 Mar. 1989.

Smith, Duane A. To the author. 14 May 1987 and 5 Sept. 1989.

Smith, Jack E. To the author. 16 Mar. 1989 and 7 Sept. 1989.

Southwick, Helen Cather. To the author. 29 Apr. 1987.

Stewart, Martha Wetherill. To John March. 23 May 1950. Willa Cather Historical Center, Red Cloud, Nebraska.

Stouck, David. To the author. 31 Jan. 1989.

Topping, Gary. To the author. 6 May 1987.

Wattles, Ruth Jocelyn. To Frank McNitt. 25 Oct. 1964. Frank McNitt Collection, New Mexico State Records Center and Archives, Santa Fe.

Wetherill, B. K. To William Henry Holmes. 11 Feb. 1890. Record Unit 189, Smithsonian Institution Archives, Washington, D. C.

Wetherill, Carol Ann. To the author. 31 Mar. 1987, 14 Apr. 1987, and 25 Feb. 1989.

Wetherill, Richard. To Gustaf Nordenskiold. 21 Dec. 1893. Mesa Verde Research Center, Mesa Verde National Park, Colorado.

Wetherill, Tom. To the author. 13 Jul. 1987.

Woodress, James. To the author. 27 Oct. 1988 and 16 Jan. 1989.

Work, James C. To the author. 28 Jan. 1987.

Wright, Richard. To the Secretary of the Interior. 17 and 24 May 1911. Bound volume of correspondence, 1911–1913. Mesa Verde National Park Library, Vault.

INTERVIEWS

Bader, Jean Kelly. At Mancos, Colorado. 22 June 1986.

Goff, Walter D. At Mancos, Colorado. 3 Aug. 1987.

Jeep, Fred. T. Telephone interview. 16 Oct. 1988.

Naranjo, José I. At Española, New Mexico. 11 Feb. 1989.

Smith, Jack E. At Mesa Verde National Park, Colorado. 4 Aug. 1987.

Wetherill, Carol Ann. Telephone interview. 28 Mar. 1987.

PRESENTATIONS

Arrhenius, Gustaf. "Why Was Mesa Verde Abandoned: Evidence of Soil Exhaustion." The Wetherill Symposium, Mesa Verde National Park. 18 Dec. 1988.

Harrell, David. "Who Discovered Cliff Palace?" The Wetherill Symposium, Mesa Verde National Park. 18 Dec. 1988.

Miritello, Mary. "The 'design of life' in Willa Cather's *The Professor's House*." Fourth National Seminar on Willa Cather, Santa Fe, New Mexico. 21 June 1990.

Schwind, Jean. "This Is a Frame-Up: Mother Eve in *The Professor's House*." The Santa Fe Conference on Willa Cather. 11 Aug. 1989.

Woodress, James. "Cather Biography Redivivus." Third National Seminar on Willa Cather, Hastings, Nebraska. 14 June 1987.

❊ Index